PROGRAMMING ON PURPOSE

Essays on Software Design

P.J. Plauger

P T R Prentice Hall
Englewood Cliffs, New Jersey 07632

Editorial/production supervision: *Brendan M. Stewart*
Buyer: *Mary Elizabeth McCartney*
Acquisitions editor: *Paul Becker*

 Published by PTR Prentice Hall, Inc.
A Simon & Schuster Company
Englewood Cliffs, New Jersey 07632

The publisher offers discounts on this book when ordered
in bulk quantities. For more information, contact:

Corporate Sales Department
PTR Prentice Hall
113 Sylvan Avenue
Englewood Cliffs, New Jersey 07632

Phone: 201-592-2863
Fax: 201-592-2249

Printed in the United States of America
10 9 8 7 6 5 4 3 2 1

ISBN 0-13-721374-3

Prentice-Hall International (UK) Limited, *London*
Prentice-Hall of Australia Pty. Limited, *Sydney*
Prentice-Hall Canada Inc., *Toronto*
Prentice-Hall Hispanoamericana, S.A., *Mexico*
Prentice Hall of India Private Limited, *New Delhi*
Prentice-Hall of Japan, Inc., *Tokyo*
Simon & Schuster Asia Pte. Ltd., *Singapore*
Editora Prentice-Hall do Brasil, Ltda., *Rio de Janeiro*

In memory of John von Neumann,
who taught us
that a few elegant concepts
recursively applied
can change the world

PERMISSIONS

The essays in this book originally appeared as installments
of the monthly column "Programming on Purpose" by P.J. Plauger
in the magazine *Computer Language*, published by Miller Freeman Inc.
All are reprinted by permission of the author.

TRADEMARKS

Compaq SLT/386s-20 is a trademark of Compaq Computer Corporation.
Corel Draw is a trademark of Corel Systems.
IBM PC and System/370 are trademarks of IBM Corporation.
Macintosh is a trademark of Apple Computer.
MS-DOS and Windows are trademarks of Microsoft Corporation.
UNIX is a trademark of AT&T Bell Laboratories.
Ventura Publisher is a trademark of Ventura Software Inc.

TYPOGRAPHY

This book was typeset in Palatino, Avant Garde,
Bitstream Cloister Black, and Courier bold by the author
using a Compaq SLT/386s-20 computer running
Ventura Publisher 4.0.1 and Corel Draw 2.01L
under Microsoft Windows 3.1.

Table of Contents

Preface

$\mathfrak{I}$ began a journey in July, 1986, that continues to this day. That month marks the first installment of my column "Programming on Purpose" in the magazine *Computer Language*. Many years and many issues later, I find myself still writing those monthly columns. And, *mirabile dictu*, I have yet to miss an issue.

Do something every month for six or more years and material accumulates. I have been asked repeatedly by readers to make some of that accumulated material more widely available. For many years my excuse was that I was too busy to do so. I was president of my own software company, Whitesmiths, Ltd. Then I sold the company to become a full-time writer. Packaging these essays has at last risen to the top of the queue.

This particular collection concerns itself with software design. That's been a preoccupation of mine for decades. (Indeed, my original motivation in writing a monthly column was to exercise material I had accumulated on software design methods. As a book project, it repeatedly took a back seat to running the company.) Brian Kernighan and I wrote our first two books on the subject — *The Elements of Programming Style* and *Software Tools*. I even preached the gospel for several years as a Vice President at Yourdon inc. For many years, Yourdon inc. was an incubator for innovators of software design methods.

This particular offering is much more cohesive than a collection of essays might imply. Because they were originally intended as chapters in a textbook, the essays are highly interrelated. (I provided cross references and a unified bibliography at the end of the book.) As a principal textbook in design methods, this book lacks exercises and thorough coverage of fringe topics. But as a source book for design approaches, I think it is uniquely catholic in scope.

Thus, this collection is suitable for supplemental reading in an intermediate or advanced course on software design methods or software engineering. For "remedial software engineering," it can be quite useful. The independent reader can use it to gain a broader knowledge of the sometimes Balkanized field of design methods.

I follow each essay with a brief Afterword. That gives me the opportunity to fill in historical context where necessary. It also lets me excuse away the worst naivetes. I chose to present these notes as Afterwords rather than

Forewords so as not to bias the reader up front. Mostly, the essays speak for themselves.

Other collections from "Programming on Purpose" deal with other themes. Besides program design, I have written essays on (among other things): programming technology, software standards development, the business of software, and the people who love and write computer software. Some essays are humorous, some are deadly serious. A few are gems, but I like to think that all are worth reading. If you enjoy what you find here, please consider the other collections as well.

The magazine business sees considerable turnover of editorial staff. Miller Freeman, the publisher of *Computer Language*, is no exception. I have thus enjoyed the services of many editors over the years. All have worked hard to rescue my prose from its more florid excursions. They have nevertheless permitted me to retain a certain colloquial illiteracy that I find comfortable. I thank all the people at Miller Freeman who, over the years, have helped make these essays more readable. You should too.

Two people in particular deserve oak-leaf clusters. Regina Starr Ridley, now a publisher at Miller Freeman, was one of my earliest editors. And Nicole Freeman, now a managing editor there, has cheerfully haunted my career in many editorial guises. I am happy to acknowledge their continuing assistance in making "Programming on Purpose" better. I am also happy to count both as good friends.

Having given credit where it is due, I must issue a warning. I re-edited these essays from the original machine readable. I certainly strove to recapture the spirit of *Computer Language* edits, but I make no pretense at following them to the letter. If any have lost ground as a result, you can blame me.

P.J. Plauger
Concord, Massachusetts

1 Which Tool is Best?

If you had to build a wooden table, which tool would you use? A saw gets you off to a good start, but it's lousy for shaping round legs and for driving screws. It also leaves much to be desired when it comes to finishing the surface and applying paint. With a lathe, you can do a great job of turning those legs. But I leave it to your comic imagination to envision how you would use it on the other jobs. And if those images don't brighten your day, replay the scenes with, in turn: a hammer, a screw driver, and a pair of pliers. The best compromise might be the proverbial Swiss Army Knife, which is equally poor at all operations.

It is ridiculous, of course, to even think of building something as elaborate as a table with just one tool. Try to convince a practicing carpenter to do so and you'll be dismissed as daft. Yet this is exactly what goes on in the programming profession every day. A handful of tool sellers keep trying to convince us that there is one right tool for developing software.

Speaking as someone who spent years selling programming development methods (read: Snake Oil Miracle Cure) with the best of them, I can tell you that life ain't that simple. I have since done ten years' penance for my sins, by writing hundreds of thousands of lines of commercial software. Most of that has been for my company, Whitesmiths, Ltd. More recently, I've watched others write still more. The experience has been humbling.

What we have learned collectively is that there are many good techniques for building software, but no one is "best." No one technique is even *adequate* when taken alone. We follow all the rules of *The Elements of Programming Style* (**K&P74, K&P78**), and then some. We write structured code, nearly all the time, and practice top-down design as much as possible. We use the latest program-development software as described in *Software Tools* (**K&P76, K&P81**), and then some. In short, we practice what I've preached for years. But that isn't enough.

There is the apocryphal story of the famous mathematician giving a lecture. He fills board after board with abstruse formulae, his audience slaving furiously to keep up with his leaps of logic. A few less hardy souls cringe when, for the sixth time, he begins a sentence with, "It is obvious that ..." But this time he hesitates. He repeats the dread phrase and hesitates again. Then he walks out of the room! Ten minutes later, just as the audience is getting restless, he returns. He picks up the chalk, says, "It *is* obvious." And continues with his lecture.

That's how we found that top-down design works much of the time. Once you have composed a program, it is easy to look at it and see how you *should* have arrived at it by the orderly process of stepwise refinement from a global statement of purpose. Getting there from a standing start is a different matter entirely. For a test tube sized problem, you can almost always succeed. For a problem whose "shape" is familiar, you just build a structure of similar shape and you have a good chance of getting to the bottom without going astray. But for something big enough (by the standards of your experience) and new enough (ditto), you can get just as lost starting at the top as you can at the bottom.

To put it crassly, top-down design is a great way to *redesign* a program you already know how to write.

Does that make it wrong to teach top-down design to programmers? Not at all. As you acquire experience, you get better and better at making good programs top down. And if you can succeed by stepwise refinement, you almost always get a better product than with the undisciplined approach most programmers adopted in the past. It wasn't even that programmers coded bottom up instead, for bottom-up design is a perfectly good discipline that also has its arena of applicability. No, most programmers of my acquaintance *just started writing code,* following no discipline whatsoever. And that is a technique that works well only for people with *lots* of experience.

I have a brother-in-law who is a skilled cartoonist. He can start in the upper left corner of a sheet of paper and elaborate a brilliant drawing. All the proportions are right and everything is in proper perspective. Us mortals must follow the usual art-school rules (see back of match cover for advertisement), block out the shapes, then fill in the detail. Ken Thompson, the originator of the UNIX operating system, has a similar skill with programming. He can write a chunk of code *in assembly language* that is half again more complex than you or I would tackle in C or Pascal, and get it right on the first draft. People like him give top-down design a bad name.

It is more fair to say that top-down design has not been practiced nearly enough, by every day programmers, unless it's really pushed. Now it has been oversold, in some circles, to the point that people feel obliged to use it even when it is not the best technique.

I had to write my third C compiler before I began to see how to design the whole thing from the top down. Don't misunderstand — great chunks of parsing code and symbol table management were designed top down from the outset. But then I'd done that sort of thing for various assemblers and editors in the past. The compiler as a whole did not make sense until I figured out that it had *at least three "tops."* And that insight I got from applying data-flow analysis, which is nominally a tool of structured analysis. (See **deM79**.)

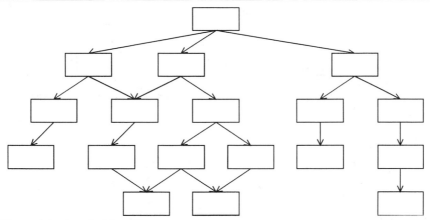

Figure 1.1 *A typical (small) structure chart.*

very method for designing software that's worth its salt comes with some way to document your design. For top-down design, the ultimate goal is to produce a *structure chart* or, as IBM commercialized it, a *HIPO Chart*. HIPO stands for Hierarchy with Input, Process, and Output.

What it is is an upside down tree (root at the top) of boxes. Each box is a subroutine and all its subordinates in the tree are the subroutines that it calls. You can even document the passing of arguments up and down the tree by drawing little arrows with names on them, beside the bigger arrows connecting the boxes. (See Figure 1.1.) A structure chart reflects the fundamental belief of top-down design that you design a program by decomposing it into successively less abstract subroutines. When you get down to subroutines that do atomic operations, such as **READ** and **WRITE** statements or simple calculations, you are done.

There are some fundamentalist sects in top-down design. Those who take the acronym HIPO seriously insist that every box should have *exactly* three subordinates, one to get Input, one to do the Process, and one to emit the Output. (See Figure 1.2.) This Procrustean attitude reminds me of Frederic the Great's reputed approach to organizing the Prussian Army, which can be overstated as three principles:

1. Any officer who has fewer than seven subordinates hasn't delegated enough responsibility. Get rid of him.
2. Any officer who has more than seven subordinates can't keep track of them all. Get rid of him.
3. Any officer who can't guess the first two rules doesn't know how to organize an army. Get rid of him.

The result is obvious.

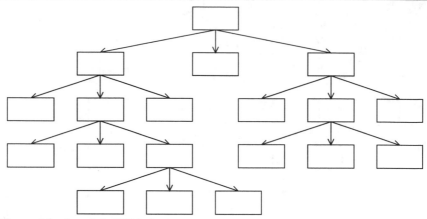

Figure 1.2 *A purist's HIPO chart.*

nother fundamentalist sect has it that each of the lower level boxes is called by only one superior, at the next level up. (See Figure 1.3.) This is the pure "stepwise refinement" approach that shuns any attempt to identify common subroutines and use them to advantage. In sooth, such attempts are akin to library building, which is one of the principal activities in bottom-up design.

In bottom-up design, the approach is to try to guess all of the low level routines you are going to need, then stockpile them. Build enough of them and you can see how to write fancier routines that call on the ones you wrote earlier. If you guess right, eventually you will be able to write a main routine that calls on your library of lower-level routines to do all the hard stuff. You have reached the top.

In real life, you do both top-down and bottom-up design on any non-trivial program. You practice stepwise refinement for a spell, until you start

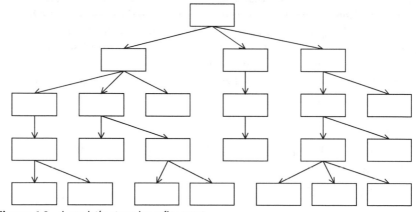

Figure 1.3 *A purist's stepwise refinement.*

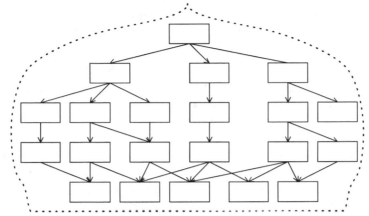

Figure 1.4 *A mosque-shaped structure chart.*

to notice that different parts of the program need to call upon the environment in similar ways. You then begin to compromise among various needs
for, say, opening files or allocating chunks of memory, until you end up with
a dozen or so *primitives* that perform all interactions with the environment.
These dozen-odd primitives form the bottom level of a structure chart that
may fan out to several times as many functions part way down.

So instead of ending up with a pyramid-shaped structure chart, as the
stepwise-refinement purists would have it, you get a "mosque." (See Figure
1.4.) Like the turrets in Arabian architecture, your chart flares out from a
point at the top, then necks back in at the bottom. Larry Constantine was
the first person I know to describe mosque-shaped structure charts, and the
forces that bring them into existence. (See **Y&C89** for some practical techniques for building programs.)

In summary, you judge a design method by the documentation it produces. For top-down design, you look at structure charts. The more
dogmatic you are about applying a design method, the fewer real-life
problems you are going to solve. I have never seen a real-life structure chart,
for a program of significant size, that follows the HIPO "rule of three" or
the stepwise refinement "fan-out-only rule." People who are best at doing
what they call top-down design have a wealth of experience to draw upon.
Part of this wealth is skill in one or more other design techniques, which
they apply almost subconsciously.

With that as a preamble, I can now tell you where top-down design *really*
falls down.

I drew a structure chart of the first C compiler I wrote. It was a clean,
well organized program (as compilers go), but the structure chart was a
mess. Why? Because of a little design choice I made. It was one that no
COBOL programmer ever had to make, a design choice that is almost not

a choice at all for any writer of modern compilers. I made heavy use of recursion. Consider the simple grammar for an arithmetic expression:

```
expr := term | expr BINOP term
term := NUMBER | UNOP term | ( expr )
```

This defines an expression as either a term or (recursively) an expression followed by a binary operator (**BINOP**) and a term. A term is some **NUMBER**, or a unary operator (**UNOP**) followed (recursively) by a term, or a parenthesized expression.

The last item brings the recursion full circle. You can (and should) express this as two functions:

- **get_expr** — which obtains an expression, by calling itself and **get_term**
- **get_term** — which obtains a term, by calling itself and **get_expr**

The structure chart consists of two boxes, *each of which points at the other.* (See Figure 1.5.) You write **get_expr** as the higher-level function, because the rest of your program will always be looking for expressions, never terms. But this little loop back creates a tangle unanticipated by the developers of structure charts. There were few widely used recursive languages in those days.

Now imagine a C compiler with a much more elaborate subtree of functions for computing expressions. It has a few back loops in its structure chart, including at least one back to the top. That compiler also has a fairly complex subtree of functions for parsing types. These types are also recursively defined, so the structure chart for that part also has one or more backloops. And now for the fun part: C uses expressions in defining types, such as the values of enumeration constants, the size of bit fields, and the size of arrays. C also uses types in defining expressions, for writing type cast operators!

The structure chart for the whole works looks like the New York City subway system. (No figure attempted.)

One of the strong selling points for structured programming is that it makes for more readable flow charts. You use a flow chart to document the control flow *within* a routine much as you use a structure chart to document the control flow *among* separate routines. Unstructured routines were rightly accused of resembling a bowl of spaghetti, because their flow charts sprawled seemingly at random. Tracing one strand was an exercise in despair.

If a document doesn't help you control complexity by partitioning it into manageable chunks, it is not pulling its weight. It also makes you suspect the utility of the design strategy that leads to a document you find hard to understand. In this example, I see failure at two extremes. The simple grammar has a structure chart that is trivial, and captures almost none of

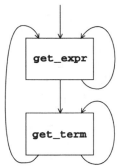

Figure 1.5 *Structure chart for the expression parser.*

the complexity of the problem. The original grammar was best at doing that. And the complex C compiler has a structure chart which is as tangled as many an unstructured program. Perhaps structure charts are not appropriate for documenting certain programs.

I have picked on top-down design at length because it is best entrenched as the Right Way to do things. If you have your own favorite design method, I can assure you that there are practical situations where it breaks down as well. Do you believe in data-structured design, as taught by Jean Dominique Warnier and/or Ken Orr(**War78, Orr77**)? Try it on a sort module and see how far you get. Do you believe that data-flow design, mentioned earlier, is best? See how much it helps you write a fast Fourier transform.

It is only natural that, when you discover a technique that helps you solve an interesting class of problems, you focus on the arena where you get successes, to the exclusion of others. It is also only natural for someone selling books or training on a given design method to play down its limitations. But neither of these tendencies is an excuse for misapplying a technique where it is useless at best and harmful at worst. As a colleague of mine likes to say, to a five-year-old with a hammer, everything looks like a nail.

My goal in writing this premiere essay is to convince you that no one tool is best for developing computer programs. My goal in coming essays is to introduce you to the many tools that I have added to my carpenter's bench over the years. For each I will show where you can use it, how it works, and how you know when you are done with it. I will also show you where it is not at its best, or where you should not use it at all.

I have chosen the title "Programming on Purpose" for two reasons. First, I want to contrast the methods described here with the programming by accident that happens altogether too often. And second, I intend to address my remarks to the serious, goal-oriented programmer. If you haven't got a clear purpose in writing code, then you are "hacking" in the worst sense of that word. I personally have little interest in that pastime.

In the near quarter century since I started programming for a living, I have seen the profession change dramatically. What was once regarded as a black art became in time an art form that many could master. It is now changing from an art to a craft, a trade that can be mastered by almost anyone with the proper patience and motivation. (The term "craft" also has overtones of producing something useful, not merely decorative.) Only parts of computer programming have become an engineering discipline, and fewer parts still have matured to a science. Like any earnest craftsman, I borrow freely from engineering and science where they help get a job done. I make no pretense at being either a software engineer or a computer scientist.

Several years ago, I gave a series of ACM lectures in New York City under the title, "Methods of System Design." Despite the dry title, the lectures were well received (or so it appeared to me). These essays draw upon that material, plus the experience I have acquired since then. I hope you find them useful. □

Afterword: This, obviously, was my premiere column. My fear as I was writing it was that I was out of touch with the business of software-design methodologies. All my references were old! It took a bit of hurried reading for me to learn that those old references were still current. Few books were published on the business of software design in the early 1980s. (The trade has since picked up, but still not to the level of the late 1970s.)

I find this essay to be a good overview of software-design methods. It also gives a succinct statement of intent for the columns that follow.

2 Writing Predicates

METHOD: Inside-out design.

DESCRIPTION: Inside-out design focuses on the actual expression of a module. It is invariably the last stage in the process of capturing an algorithm in executable code. The name suggests that you are working from the middle of a program (the processing of data) out to the edges (the input/output interface).

Since all programs deal with conditional logic, or predicates, the principal technology of inside-out design is aimed at getting predicates correct, readable, and efficient (in that order). Completeness checks, de Morgan's Rules, decision tables, and Karnaugh maps all serve this end.

DOCUMENTATION: Decision tables best capture the logic of a complex predicate, at a level that permits of multiple implementations and that serves as a more readable rendition of a given implementation.

LIMITATIONS: Inside-out design involves you in the full complexity of a program at the most detailed level. To apply it before a program has been reduced, by other methods, to a set of functionally cohesive modules is to invite confusion and disaster.

A predicate is that Boolean expression you write following a **WHILE** or **IF** to determine which statement gets executed next. Whatever discipline you use to elaborate the structure of your program, in the end you must get all the predicates right to have a working product. There's lots of technology you can bring to bear on getting predicates right, but I have never seen it put in one place before. This essay is my attempt at summarizing most of the techniques I see good programmers use every day in writing and debugging control-flow logic.

The preamble to this essay is the first in a series of *manual pages* covering various aspects of designing computer software. It may seem rather ponderous for a topic so mundane as expressing **WHILE** and **IF** statements correctly, but I believe that it contains several important reminders, particularly on the topic of limitations. In the company of its siblings, appearing in subsequent essays, it should appear somewhat less pompous.

To begin with a concrete example, consider the classic algorithm for computing the greatest common divisor, or GCD, of two integers. It has been a favorite of computer textbook writers for years, because it is elegant and compact. Or at least it can be. The basic idea is to divide the smaller integer into the larger and keep the remainder. If the remainder is zero, the divisor is the GCD. Otherwise, you replace the dividend with the divisor and the divisor with the remainder, then loop. Eventually, you must converge to the proper answer. All you should have to worry about at the outset is dividing by zero.

So you might write, in pseudo code:

```
gcd(m, n)
    m := abs(m)
    n := abs(n)
    IF (m <= n)
        temp := m
        m := n
        n := temp
    IF (n = 0)
        RETURN (m)
    WHILE (TRUE)
        temp := m REM n
        IF (temp = 0)
            RETURN (n)
        m := n
        n := temp
```

Here **m REM n** is the remainder after dividing **m** by **n**. Some languages offer a **MOD** operator, for "modulus," which is close enough to the remainder operator if you avoid negative values. There are enough interesting variations in how machines divide with negative operands that you should avoid such cases as a matter of habit anyway. If either of the arguments is zero, the GCD is the magnitude of the other operand.

The algorithm is correctly captured in this pseudo code, as far as I can tell. Moreover, it closely parallels the presentation I have seen in several publications. It contains four predicates, **m <= n**, **n = 0**, **TRUE**, and **temp = 0**. Can you find anything to improve on any of them?

If your response is to change **m <= n** to **m < n**, give yourself two points (out of a possible ten). There is no need to exchange the two operands if they are equal, so the code is improved by altering the predicate. If your reason for changing the predicate was just to make the code faster, however, you should take away one point. Readability is at least as important as any efficiency gains to be had by this change. You don't want to suggest to readers that something must be done when the two operands are equal, when that is not truly the case.

You get six points if you observe that the first **IF** is completely unnecessary. Walk through the loop with a case where **m** is less than **n**. The values of **m** and **n** are exchanged on the first iteration. Since the only reason for the first **IF** is to enforce an assertion that doesn't have to be enforced, you should get rid of it.

There are three predicates left. One causes a return if **n** is zero. Another causes a return if **n** is about to become zero. Any time you see almost the same code before the start of a loop and at the bottom of the loop, you should be suspicious. At best, it indicates that the programming language you are using won't let you express the test controlling the loop the way you need to. You may have to perform a computation or obtain some input as part of the test, and you cannot combine this with the test expression proper. At worst, you have written the test controlling the loop incorrectly.

Here, you should assume the worst, because none of the three predicates are at all complicated. Give yourself four points if you revised the loop predicate. Correcting the predicate controlling the **WHILE** makes the others go away:

```
gcd(m, n)
    m := abs(m)
    n := abs(n)
    WHILE (n <> 0)
        temp := m REM n
        m := n
        n := temp
    RETURN (m)
```

The end result is smaller, cleaner, and more elegant. It is probably even more efficient. It eliminates the return from the middle of a loop, which is hard to express in languages such as Pascal.

And it contains none of the original four predicates.

An important lesson to be learned from this example is that a program is not finished just because you have captured the algorithm correctly and readably. It is more cost effective in the long run to spend time revising code when you first write it, while the algorithm is fresh in your mind. Until the code is shorn of all fat, until it has a compelling simplicity, you haven't distilled out the excess complexity. Since the essence of programming is controlling complexity, nothing lowers the cost of debugging and maintaining code so much as eliminating unnecessary logic as early as possible.

With this example in mind, we can now look at a few check lists for reviewing predicates. The simplest predicate is a single Boolean term, like the **TRUE** that controlled the original **WHILE** loop in the example. You must sometimes compute your condition in advance and store it in a Boolean variable. You then write the test as a single term such as **DONE** or **END_OF_FILE**. If the variable **OK** has the answer, you'd think your job is nearly done. But you still have four choices! You can perform the controlled statement:

```
never            always
if OK is false   if OK is true
```

You should consider every one of these possibilities before you choose.

The next simplest predicate you can write performs an arithmetic comparison. Here you have ten possibilities. You can perform the controlled statement:

```
never              always
if equal           if not equal
if less            if greater or equal
if greater         if less or equal
if ordered         if unordered
```

The **unordered/ordered** cases arise mostly with floating-point arithmetic schemes that support one or more NaN (not a number) codes. If you divide by zero, for instance, the result can be represented as a NaN, so you can keep going. But it's hard to say whether a NaN is less than or greater than, say, 5.3. Even if you deal only with conventional wraparound integer arithmetic, you should consider whether any result values represent the **unordered** state. If an integer must be positive, for instance, but has overflowed, then a negative integer may be a NaN in your algorithm.

The classic oversight in choosing which arithmetic comparison to write is to branch the wrong way on equality. In the first GCD example, choosing **m <= n** rather than **m < n** caused a performance bug, but gave the correct result. A similar error in a **WHILE** predicate causes an off-by-one error, which seldom gives acceptable behavior.

Most (unplanned) infinite loops result from a failure to consider the arithmetic branch that "can't happen." A good rule of thumb for **WHILE** predicates is to end the loop at the least excuse. If you write **WHILE (m <> 0)** instead of **WHILE (0 < m)**, your program won't loop should you eventually decrement **m** twice and skip past the zero test.

Programmers often fail to consider the **never/always** cases properly. The GCD example had a predicate **m <= n** which was better written as **never**. It also had a predicate **TRUE (always)** that was better written as **n <> 0**. You might remember to reconsider the **never/always** choice in terms of two precepts:

- If you've gone to the trouble of computing things to test, you should remember to test them.

- Just because there are things to test, that doesn't mean you should test them.

The beauty of these precepts is they appear to be mutually contradictory. Many Truths come packaged this way.

Storing the result of a test in a Boolean variable is something you should avoid as much as possible, by the way. Between the time you store it and test it, opportunities abound for the predicate to get out of phase with reality. Programs with lots of flags are just like programs with lots of **GOTO** statements — it's next to impossible to determine the state of a computation just from the lexical position of the program counter in the program text. Some languages require flags to make up for a lack of expressiveness, so you can't always avoid them. Remember that every flag must be set, tested, and cleared somewhere in your program. The closer together these actions occur, the more likely you will detect any omitted actions or inconsistent states.

One final small point about writing simple predicates: I personally never write the operators **>** or **>=**. Being a mechanistic soul, I have to envision values along the x-axis to determine what a predicate is saying. I can tell at a glance that

```
0 <= c AND c < 256
```

tests whether **c** is within the half-open interval [0, 256), or that

```
x < '0' OR '9' < x
```

tests whether **x** is outside the closed interval ['0', '9']. I make too many mistakes mentally flipping operands about with the other two operators.

Now let's look at complex predicates. There are sixteen ways to combine two predicates, **A** and **B**. No, I'm not going to list them all. Six of them are various ways of ignoring one or both of **A** and **B**. The remaining ten are almost always written using the Boolean operators **NOT**, **AND**, and **OR**. You might try to write out all sixteen ways, after you read the rest of this essay.

It is easy to get tangled up in complex Boolean expressions. I have for years preached the importance of the "telephone test" (**K&P78**) — if you cannot understand a Boolean expression when spoken over a telephone, keep rewriting it until you can. If you can't find a rewriting that makes sense, there is a good chance that the predicate is wrong to begin with.

How do you rewrite predicates? The workhorse transformations are the two identities known as deMorgan's Rules:

```
A AND B = NOT (NOT A OR NOT B)
A OR B = NOT (NOT A AND NOT B)
```

So you can skip processing the digits **0** and **1** by writing

```
IF (NOT (x = '0' OR x = '1'))
```

or

```
IF (x <> '0' AND x <> '1')
```

I prefer the latter version, for readability.

The order in which you evaluate terms of a Boolean expression is often important. It does you no good to write a test such as, "If **i** is a valid subscript and **a[i]** has the value I seek," unless you are sure that the tests are performed in the stated order. The C language has a version of **AND**, written **&&**, and **OR**, written **||**, that guarantee left-to-right evaluation. In

Pascal, you may have to write **THEN IF** for **AND**, or **ELSE IF** for **OR**, to guarantee ordering. You can also use a Boolean variable whose value is accumulated in stages; but see the warning above about using Boolean variables.

The hardest part of writing a complex predicate, however, is making sure you consider all the cases. You should learn to write *decision tables*, when you first code a complex predicate, to be sure you exhaust all combinations of input variables. Your loan-approval program may overlook people under 17 who own their own homes and have an income of greater than $100,000 per year — and you will lose the business of an up-and-coming teenage rock star.

For each input variable, write down all the predicates affected by it. Are there five age groups? Then be sure you know the desired outcome for every combination of other factors in each of the age groups. Don't worry about writing down cases that "can't happen." Just put a big **I**, for "I don't care" in that box, and let your program logic group it with whatever reasonable cases it happens to fall in with. I never fail to be educated about a problem when I write out a complex Boolean expression in decision-table form.

The most orderly way to process decision tables is to reduce all your simple tests to a set of disjoint predicates. Your five age groups reduce to three predicates:

- in groups 0, 1, 2, or 3
- in groups 0, 1, or 4
- in groups 0, 2, or 4

(These are just the three bits of the group number, if you think about it.) If you end up with four predicates, there are sixteen possibilities; if five predicates, then 32; and so on.

You can write such a pure binary decision table as a *Karnaugh map*, which groups terms in such a way that it is easy to identify the simplest Boolean expression that captures the complex decision. Karnaugh maps are used by circuit designers for minimizing the number of **AND** and **OR** gates needed to generate a logic term. They are also useful in writing computer programs. The trick is to order your tests so that adjacent entries in the map always group to advantage.

For a nontrivial example, consider the following problem. The latest all-purpose PC product you are working on is to display the time of day in one corner of the screen. To make it easily visible across the room, you must mimic a seven-bar display, like in all the digital read-outs that abound these days. Instead of merely displaying **12:37**, your program must produce something like:

```
*     *****          *****  *****
*         *    *          *     *
*     *****          *****      *
*         *    *          *     *
*     *****          *****      *
```

our mission, should you decide to accept it, is to write a function that takes as input a decimal digit and produces as output the seven bars that display that digit. The choice of input and output data encoding is open. Try your hand at writing the function before you read on. You can use the following patterns for the ten digits:

```
*****      *  *****  *****  *    *
*    *     *      *      *  *    *
*    *     *  *****  *****  *****
*    *     *  *          *       *
*****      *  *****  *****       *

*****  *****  *****  **A**  *****
*          *      *  B   C  *    *
*****  *****      *  **D**  *****
    *  *    *     *  E   F       *
*****  *****      *  **G**  *****
```

The pattern for digit **8** shows the letter names I chose for each of the seven bars. The input is a four-bit number, which can be represented as four predicates. Each of the bit names gives its numerical weight in the digit.

B8 is on   B4 is on
B2 is on   B1 is on

Table 2.1 shows how you write out the decisions. The funny ordering of values is just that of the Gray code, which changes by only one bit as you increment the value represented. Gray code is used in laying out the tracks on rotational angle sensors, since a small error in pickup alignment doesn't

	NOT B2 AND NOT B1	NOT B2 AND B1	B2 AND B1	B2 AND NOT B1
NOT B8 AND NOT B4	0	1	3	2
NOT B8 AND B4	4	5	7	6
B8 AND B4	12	13	15	14
B8 AND NOT B4	8	9	11	10

Table 2.1 *Karnaugh map showing digit values.*

	NOT B2 AND NOT B1	NOT B2 AND B1	B2 AND B1	B2 AND NOT B1
NOT B8 AND NOT B4	ON	OFF	OFF	ON
NOT B8 AND B4	OFF	OFF	OFF	ON
B8 AND B4	I	I	I	I
B8 AND NOT B4	ON	OFF	I	I

Table 2.2 *Decision table for bar* **e**.

lead to disastrous jumps in numeric value. The read-out doesn't have to handle hexadecimal digits, so values above nine are shaded and will become I-don't-care states for each of the seven bars.

Now look at Table 2.2, which is the decision table for the bar **e**. It is **OFF** for six digits and **ON** for four digits. Yet you can test if it should be **ON** by the predicate:

```
(B2 AND NOT B1) OR
(NOT B4 AND NOT B1)
```

Each term represents a different shaded area of the Karnaugh map. (The map wraps around in both directions, like an early video-game screen.)

For any two adjacent terms, you can ignore one of the basic predicates. For any four in a square or a rectangle, you can ignore two predicates. (Note that in this example, the four corners constitute a handy "square.") For any eight in a rectangle, you can ignore three. And so on. I call the process of covering all cases in the same group "painting the Karnaugh map."

The fun comes in finding the largest possible brush strokes that cover the group you want. I-don't-care cases are invaluable in helping you form larger brush strokes. But even if there are no groupings, you have the satisfaction of knowing that you need to write fully qualified terms to get the right answer. And you are much more likely to write a correct predicate.

You should write the Karnaugh maps for the other six bars, then write the expressions for **ON** as well as **OFF**. The **ON** expression for a given bar may not be the **NOT** of the **OFF** expression for that bar. (Why?) If you are still eager after that, extend the display to handle all sixteen hexadecimal digits. You will have to use lowercase **B** and **D**, and your I-don't-care states go out the window. But the result is interesting.

With just a little practice like this, you can get the hang of writing Karnaugh maps and painting them. Then you will wonder how you ever programmed correctly without them.

You shouldn't assume, however, that every logic problem is best handled by writing a Karnaugh map. Often the best way to capture a decision is to store it in a table, then use the predicates to form an index and look up the answer. Those of you who solved the seven-bar problem this way get high marks. The decimal digit is a natural index, and the bar patterns require just a few bytes of data tables.

Top marks go to people who wrote tables like:

```
char dig2[5][5] = {
    "XXXXX",
    "    X",
    "XXXXX",
    "X    ",
    "XXXXX" };
```

You can tell at a glance whether the table is correct for that digit, because you can see the final output in the data.

As a final footnote, it took me much longer than I had expected to write this essay. One reason was that my company is in the middle of a major development project. The other was that I suffered from the repeated fear that this material was too basic for its audience. (That's you.) I was continually bemused to find, however, that I was applying every one of the principles outlined here in the pursuit of that project. Some of the techniques proved invaluable several times a day in sorting out logic gaffes and crafting small chunks of code. If professional programmers need to be reminded of this stuff on a regular basis, it doesn't hurt to write some of it down. □

Afterword: It was probably a stupid idea to dream up cute names like "inside-out design." Nevertheless, I persisted with these and a dozen more. Those that weren't cute inventions were existing names that I chose to recycle, often with slightly different meaning from the conventional. That practice is probably at least as dangerous as appearing too cutesy.

Still, there's good stuff here. You won't find it in most programming language texts — it's too general. Nor will you find it in most program design texts — it's too low level. It just happens to be the stuff of most pedestrian design decisions you make when writing code.

I wish I could have come up with a more compelling example than the seven-bar display. It illustrates all the necessary points, but it's a straw man. I like to think that most practicing programmers would gravitate quickly to the table-driven approach that I described last.

3 Generating Data

METHOD: Right-to-left design.

DESCRIPTION: Right-to-left design focuses on the structure of the data being generated by a module. It is based on the premise that the structure of a program should closely model that of the generated data. The name derives from the convention of drawing data-flow diagrams from inputs on the left to outputs on the right.

Since most data structures can be effectively composed from primitive forms by concatenation, alternation, and repetition, right-to-left design naturally leads to structured programs (in the traditional sense of the term). Thus, indented pseudo code and Warnier-Orr diagrams (**Orr77, War78**) can be used in conjunction with this discipline.

DOCUMENTATION: Data-structure diagrams best capture the format of a generated file. Procedural representations, such as structured pseudo code or structured flow charts, may capture additional information such as read-ahead logic or running-sum formation.

LIMITATIONS: Right-to-left design is an effective organizing principle only if the structure of the output dominates the problem. If the output is trivial, particularly compared to the calculations involved or the structure of the input data, this approach is not fruitful. If both input and output data structures are nontrivial, you need to apply outside-in design. (See **Essay 9: Marrying Data Structures** and **Essay 10: Divorcing Data Structures**.)

If you cut your teeth on BASIC, assembly language, or even FORTRAN, you tend to forget that data comes in different types. And even Pascal and C programmers have trouble remembering that data has structure as well as type. Once you learn to impose as much structure as possible on the data your program manipulates, many common sources of coding error disappear. And once you learn to reflect that data structure as closely as possible in the structure of your code, many maintenance problems also disappear.

The most aggressive practitioner of this approach that I ever met was A.G. (Sandy) Fraser, at Bell Laboratories. He began each programming task by generating pages of data declarations and accompanying commentary. The comments described what values each data type could assume, the obvious and subtle relationships between different data, and permissible state transitions among data values. By the time Sandy had finished this exercise, all the procedures needed to manipulate the data were easily tacked onto the end of the listing. The code was obvious, barely in need of additional commentary, and easily inherited by more pedestrian programmers like me.

To see how the data structuring approach pays off, let's look at a small example of a data-generating program. The shape of it is likely to be familiar to you, in one guise or another.

The problem is to generate a report showing a batch of transactions involving different customer accounts. Transactions are already sorted by customer account number, so transactions for the same account are grouped and the groups are in proper order. Your program must print one or more pages for each customer. At the top of each page is the customer account number and various column headings. Up to 40 transactions follow, one per line. At the bottom of each page is a page total. If there are more than 40 transactions for one account number, you must print additional pages for that customer. Following the page total at the bottom of each page is either an indication that more pages follow for that account number or a grand total for all pages.

Do you recognize the shape? Here is a program that reads lines of text from its input, one at a time in sequence. It uses that input to generate lines of text to its output, in the same sequence that the input is presented. The program is a classic *filter* that maps input to output in one sequential pass.

If you recognize the shape, then you may also recognize the commonest bugs that you must avoid in crafting the control logic:

- The program must produce no output if there is no input.
- The program must produce no output for a skipped account number.
- The program must always produce an integral number of pages.
- The program must not produce an empty second page if there are exactly 40 transactions for one customer account.
- The program should not terminate early if a numeric input field is ill formed.
- The program should not terminate early if arithmetic overflow occurs in computing the totals.
- The program should indicate on the output any ill-formed fields or totals.

These last three potential bugs are listed as "shoulds" because some programming languages make life difficult for you in these areas. Lapses here are more forgivable.

In the previous essay (**Essay 2: Writing Predicates**), I discussed inside-out design. If we apply that approach here, then the next thing to do is look at all the predicates we will need to express the control flow of the program. Four conditions spring to mind:

```
more_input              new_account
page_full               page_empty
```

The exact expression of these conditions can be deferred until after we express the overall logic. In pseudo code,

```
WHILE (more_input)
   IF (new_account OR page_full)
      <skip to bottom>
      <put footer sums>
      <set page_empty>
   IF (page_empty)
      <put header>
      <initialize sums>
   <put transaction line>
   <accumulate sums>
   <clear page empty>
IF (NOT page_empty)
   <skip to bottom>
   <put footer sums>
```

The next step is to refine each of the terms to make actual executable code. You clearly need an index that can express line numbers between zero and 40. So `page_empty` becomes `i = 0`, `page_full` becomes `i = 40` and `<skip to bottom>` can be written

```
WHILE (NOT page_full)
   <put empty line>
   i := i + 1
```

Refining the other two predicates is messier, because that involves reading input. Aside from the usual worries about handling end-of-file, ill-formed input lines, and possibly even read errors, here you must also perform a classic look ahead. You don't know that you have read all of the transactions for one account number until you have encountered end-of-file or read the first transaction for the next account number that is present. You must look ahead to the next transaction to know how to finish up the output that goes with this one.

We can stuff all these problems into a function that can access the input line buffer, `line_buf`, and the previous account number, `acct_no`. It will read the next line, if present, into `line_buf`, and unpack the account number into `acct_no`. The value of the function is one of the enumerated values:

- **end_of_file** — if the input is exhausted
- **new_account** — if `acct_no` changed value
- **same_account** — if `acct_no` did not change value

If read errors occur, the function will either terminate the program or pass back a laundered value, depending upon the severity of the error.

To prime this machinery, you must initialize **acct_no** to a value that matches no possible input value. (This is always possible, by the way. If all states of **acct_no** are valid account numbers, you just add a second component to the stored account number. The Boolean component **good_acct** is **FALSE** initially, and is made **TRUE** whenever you store a valid account number in **acct_no**. If this smacks of being a first-time switch, well it is, in some ways. But it is a clean one.)

You should now be able to write executable code for the entire program, except for formatting details that have been glossed over. I will leave it as an exercise, since this essay has certain space restrictions. Aside from the input function described above, you will probably feel moved to make a separate module to put out the footer, since that must occur in two places.

Assuming you refine each of these terms properly, you can count on this structure to do the job. Indeed, I have seen programs just like this on fifty-odd occasions over the last quarter century. I have also seen all the bugs mentioned earlier. That wouldn't be so bad, except that often the bugs were introduced during refinement of the predicates. (What does the **read** function return for the very first record? If you answered **new_account**, you have thirty seconds to find the bug.) Worse still, it's easy to add such bugs during maintenance. (The boss just asked that each customer get an even number of pages. Try it!) This is not a robust solution.

The failure here is that we applied inside-out design too early. If you recall, I warned about that danger in the previous essay. (See **Essay 2: Writing Predicates**.) You see, inside-out design helps you get your predicates right, but it doesn't tell you in what order to write them.

In the absence of any other direction, we fell naturally into writing an input-driven program. That is often a good idea, particularly in the presence of look-ahead problems such as we have here. But even as an input-driven program, this one fails to reflect fully the structure of the input. The main loop tells the world that the input consists of **zero or more transactions** but the full structure is

```
zero or more groups, each with
   one or more transactions
```

Does that seem like a small thing to you? I believe Einstein once said something like, "A physical theory of the real world should have no more complexity than the real world, and no less." In the simpler world of programming, that means you had better not write programs with more structure than needed. And you had better not write them with less structure than needed either.

It might be more enlightening to compare different ways of writing loops. Let's say you need a double loop over the indices of a two-dimensional array. In C, you might write something like:

```
for (i = 0;  i < I_MAX; ++i)
    for (j = 0;  j < J_MAX; ++j)
        .....
```

But you could also write it as a single loop:

```
for (i = 0,  j = 0;  j < J_MAX; ++j)
    {
    if (j == J_MAX)
        {
        j = 0;
        if (I_MAX <= ++i)
            break;
        }
    .....
    }
```

You've seen it done. You may even have done it yourself from time to time. Not nearly as readable, is it? Believe it or not, I have even seen the same control written as three loops which disguise the structure:

```
for (i = 0;  i < I_MAX; ++i)
    for (k = 0;  k < J_MAX; ++k)
        for (j = 0;  j < J_MAX; ++j)
            if (j == k)
                .....
```

So there are countless ways to obscure the intent of a program and still do the job, at least until the next poor sucker has to inherit the clever riddles you have posed.

You can make this report generator program noticeably easier to understand just by restructuring it as a double loop on input, since that is the actual structure of the input file. You can make it even easier to understand, however, by constructing it around the more complex structure of the output file that it must generate. This structure can be written as:

```
zero or more page groups, each consisting of
    one or more pages, each consisting of
        a header, followed by
        1 to 40 transaction lines, followed by
        0 to 39 empty lines, followed by
        a footer, consisting of
            a page total, followed by
            either
                "more to come", or
                an account total
```

The pseudo code for this approach is shown in Figure 3.1.

I used a **REPEAT ... UNTIL** loop in this example, because the specification assures us that the loop must execute one or more times. The vast

```
status := read_line()
   WHILE (status <> end_of_file)
      <initialize account sums>
      REPEAT
         <put header>
         i := 0
         <initialize page sums>
         WHILE (status = same_account
            AND i < 40)
            <put transaction line>
            <accumulate sums>
            i := i + 1
         WHILE (i < 40)
            <put empty line>
            i := i + 1
         <put footer sums>
         status := read_line()
         IF (status = same_account)
            <put "more to come">
         ELSE
            <put grand total>
      UNTIL (status <> same_account)
```

Figure 3.1 *Pseudo code for report generator.*

majority of loops are better written as **WHILE** statements, because looping zero times happens more often than you can possibly imagine.

Notice that the only things in bizarre places in this structure are the calls to **read_line** to keep some of the predicates current. This is to be expected, since the structure reflects that of the output file, not the input. Many of you would have written this program without the outer loop, on groups of pages. Had you done so, then the code for **<initialize account sums>** also becomes orphaned from the control structure. Instead of having one right place to abide, at the top of the loop on pages within an account group, it must be replicated at the top of the program and in the footer code, where you discover that an account group has come to an end. That isn't bad, but it's not as good as it can be either.

Please understand, it is not the replication of code that I care about. That is either a good idea anyway, because different instantiations of it should evolve independently, or easily recast as multiple calls to a common function. My major concern here is the Principle of One Right Place — there should be One Right Place to look for any nontrivial piece of code, and One Right Place to make a likely maintenance change. Right-to-left design dramatically increases the chances that any changes related to the structure of the output file will be located in One Right Place within the program.

With that concrete example under our belts, we can now wax a bit more abstract. What I am talking about here is not structured programming, at least not exactly. Rather, right-to-left design tells you to look at the data that a program is to generate. Describe its structure in terms of a few basic primitive forms, recursively applied. Then write your program to reflect closely the structure you imposed on the data. If the structure of the output data is at all interesting, then you will have published an important account of it in the indentation of your source code.

The three basic structures that you should use are:

- sequence — one thing after another
- repetition — zero or more instances of the same sort of thing, the count being determined by some predicate
- alternation — exactly one of a choice of alternatives, the choice being determined by some predicate.

It has been proved, I believe, that any data structure can be composed from these three structures. I've never bothered to memorize the proof, or even the reference, because it is of no practical import whether the three structures are sufficient or not. I believe with equal faith that you can compute anything on a Turing machine, but nobody has ever offered Whitesmiths money to write a C compiler for one.

Back in the days when Dijkstra's diatribe against the **GOTO** statement was still a fresh topic of conversation (**Dij68**), completeness was an important issue. Bohm and Jacopini had proved long ago (**B&J66**) that you could model any computer program by using just three control-flow structures, and a bushel basket full of Boolean flags. Us converts waved this interesting bit of news under the noses of the unreconstructed assembly-language programmers who kept trotting forth twisty bits of logic and saying, "I betcha you can't structure *this*." Neither the proof by Bohm and Jacopini nor our repeated successes at writing structured code brought them around one day sooner than they were ready to convince themselves. But those were the good old days.

Now all I care about is how often it enhances readability to express data in terms of these three basic structures. I know there are some cases where the result just isn't worth the bother. I know also that most of the time the result is just fine.

And in case you haven't guessed by now, the program that generates structured data is a structured program. This is because you use:

- a sequence of statements — to generate a sequence of data
- a **WHILE** loop — to generate a repetition of data
- an **IF-ELSE** to generate an alternation of data

So you see, structured programming is a side effect of structuring data, in this case. And structuring data is not something you have to do only when generating reports. Look at the data-structuring capabilities of C (and Pascal):

- structs (records) — let you specify a sequence of related fields
- arrays (arrays) — let you specify a repetition of objects of the same type
- unions (variant records) — let you specify an alternation of fields

Programmers tend to be more haphazard in computing values stored in memory that when computing output. We take it for granted that memory is random access, while output can be so arbitrarily large that we'd better generate it in just the right order and get it off our hands quickly. I personally am growing progressively more pedantic about assigning to the fields of a record in the order in which they are declared, and looping over the objects in an array in order of increasing index. Why? Partly so that I can turn stores into writes to a file at a later date, should the need arise. But mostly so that I can convince myself that I haven't missed anything, just by a casual reading of the code.

I have focused primarily on the structure of generated data, because that is the simpler case. The predicates are usually the most obvious. You can also work out the structure of your input data, of course, as we did earlier. Input is fraught with an additional host of problems, however. Aside from end-of-file and read-error detection, mentioned earlier, there is the general problem of parsing the input to determine where it fits in the structure you have ascribed to it. That's where look ahead comes in, as well as other complexities such as backtracking, error recovery, and resolving ambiguities. Parsing input is the topic of a later essay. (See **Essay 5: Recognizing Input**.)

The example program I gave was not a pure example of generating data, of course. Unless you are generating a table of haversines, this is usually the case. As a matter of fact, both the input and the output to the example program contributed structure that had to be accommodated by the control-flow logic of the program. I intentionally kept the structure of the input simple enough that it mostly got lost within the structure of the output, aside from a few look-ahead reads that were hard to excuse away. When both the input and the output have nontrivial structure, however, you have quite a different kettle of fish. Then you must make a concerted effort to marry the two structures, or divorce them completely. That too is the topic of future essays. (See **Essay 9: Marrying Data Structures** and **Essay 10: Divorcing Data Structures**.)

To give credit where it is due, I should point out that there are several eloquent spokesmen for the need to structure data. Jean Dominique Warnier was perhaps the earliest to write on the subject, originally in French then later in English (**War74, War78**). His message was brought to the English-speaking world by Ken Orr (**Orr77**). The Warnier-Orr diagrams mentioned at the outset of this essay are a graphic way to represent structured data. (I'm a firm believer in indented pseudo code to represent anything structured, so I've chosen not to show them here.) Still another proponent of data structuring is Michael Jackson (not the singer). He has written quite a bit, in British, on the problems of clashes between input and output data structure (**Jac75**).

All of my references for them are fairly old now, since I have been off the lecture circuit for eight years. I know they have been writing fresher material, so you should read their latest stuff if you want to learn more. Having the privilege of the last word in this essay, however, I warn you to stay alert to where the data-structuring techniques that they describe do not work, as you read about the cases when they do. □

fterword: This is my favorite way to justify structured programming. I find that data structure offers much more guidance than a simple faith in **GOTO***-less programming. Even so, you can see that the best way to structure data does not always leap out at you. The process is guided, but iterative.*

You should also note my ongoing concern about staying current with the literature. (See previous Afterword.) There wasn't nearly as much new material as I presumed, but there was some (for example, **Jac83***).*

4 Finite-State Machines

METHOD: Bottom-up design.

DESCRIPTION: Bottom-up design focuses on the low-level operations needed to cause transitions from one remembered state to another. It can be viewed as a language-building process — a vocabulary of basic operations is first built, then used to express higher-level modules that achieve the overall result. It can also be viewed as the construction of a finite-state machine — a finite number of remembered states are identified and the rules for making state transitions form the meat of the module. The name derives from the convention of drawing hierarchical decompositions of functions with the most-general modules (the root of the tree) at the top and the most-detailed modules (the leaves) at the bottom.

Any module expressible as a structured program, and hence any module that recognizes or produces structured data, can be expressed as a finite-state machine. Hence, bottom-up design can be used in a very broad class of situations. It is most useful, however, when encapsulating some of the state memory simplifies the larger structure of the program.

DOCUMENTATION: A state diagram with transitions best captures the behavior of a finite-state machine. Unstructured flow charts and transaction lists can reflect the procedural aspects.

LIMITATIONS: Bottom-up design contributes little when there is no state memory, which is true for the great majority of modules. And if there are too many states (more than about seven) it can only be safely applied by automated techniques, such as parser generators. Otherwise the complexity quickly overwhelms you, and the resultant code looks like spaghetti.

The stored-program digital computer has three major attributes: it is fast, it is accurate, and it is stupid. The first two attributes are often used to disguise the third. Because computers can correct your spelling, beat you at chess, or compute your air fare to Toledo, many people believe that the machines know what they are doing. Those of us in the business of programming computers certainly know better. But, those of us in the business often forget that stupidity is also a virtue.

Consider the lowly program counter. It lies at the core of every central processing unit (CPU), be it on a chip or crammed into an oversize refrigerator. All the program counter does is tell the CPU where to find the next instruction in main memory. All the CPU knows about the next instruction is that it is wherever the program counter tells it to look.

Most instructions simply increment the program counter to point to the next instruction in sequence. But branch instructions can start a new code sequence by loading a new address into the program counter before the next instruction is fetched. And an interrupt can seize control from a running program for a millisecond or for a week, simply by saving the old program counter and loading up a fresh one of its own devising. When an interrupt sequence completes by reloading the old program counter, the interrupted program continues with no knowledge that it was in limbo.

Given a basic engine for executing instructions, built around a program counter, you can then proceed to make up instructions one at a time and add them to the repertoire of your CPU. You use the inherent stupidity of the CPU as an opportunity to divide and conquer. The fun comes in guessing which instructions are absolutely necessary, which are useful enough to include, and which are best left out. The last group must, of course, be adequately expressible in terms of the instructions you choose to implement, or you have a crippled CPU on your hands.

Having personally programmed dozens of different computers, designed over a span of several decades, I can testify that many of the instruction sets chosen for commercially successful computers are difficult to live with. Millions of years of programmer time have been spent doing battle with one or two widely used computers (which shall remain nameless here), instead of solving the problems at hand. Indeed, a major reason why us compiler writers are in business is that so many computers need to be paved over with a better instruction set for solving certain problems. Some of those better instruction sets are called FORTRAN, Pascal, and C.

Having also personally designed a few instruction sets, I can also testify that it is not an easy thing to get right. You have to guess the proper set of primitive operations (the instructions) for expressing a broad class of applications, most of which you certainly have not seen in any detail. You have to be ruthless in trimming little-used features, lest you use so many bits for identifying instructions and operands that even simple programs take too long to read out of memory and occupy too much space. In short, you need more experience than the vast majority of practicing programmers, coupled with an aesthetic sense that is far more art than science.

Designing programming languages is much like designing computers. You don't count gate delays or square microns of silicon, but you do worry about compiler complexity and learnability. If you include too many "instructions," as in COBOL or PL/I, the language pre-empts much of the vocabulary you'd like to use to express your program, and you never feel you understand large parts of it. If your language is too spare, as in APL or Forth, it may be difficult to express programs that can be read by others. Even if you push many of your problems out to libraries, as in FORTRAN and C, they don't go away. They simply change shape.

What does computer or language design have to do with program design? Plenty. Most of us apply the same paradigm to constructing our programs as is used in designing CPUs. We start with a program counter, build a stupid engine around it, then proceed to hang instructions on it. This is called bottom-up design.

I know you have been told in school that this is not The Way to Do Things. You must first identify the overall goal of your program, express that in a page or less of pseudo code, then proceed to refine the pseudo code by repeating the process for a hierarchy of ever more detailed modules called from the higher levels. This approach is called top-down design, and is well taught by such luminaries as Edsger Dijkstra, C.A.R. Hoare, and N. Wirth, to name a few (**Hoa69**, **WirG**, **Dij72**, **DDJ72**, **Wir73**). I'm all in favor of this approach, and plan to devote a future essay to it (**Essay 11: Who's the Boss?**). But you might also go back and read my first essay (**Essay 1: Which Tool is Best?**) concerning its limitations.

One virtue of bottom-up design is that it often works. If the problem you are trying to solve is not too complex, you can home in on a working program pretty quickly. Expressing that as structured code that is readable and maintainable requires little additional effort.

You are led naturally to bottom-up design when you start listing all the atomic operations that you must perform to solve a given problem. You also drift into this approach when you list all the variables needed to capture the state of a computation, and write down all the consistent sets of values the variables can assume. Whichever you do first, the other must follow. What you end up with is the design of a finite-state machine.

A finite-state machine is characterized by a limited amount of internal memory (the finite state), and a set of rules for making transitions from one state to another (the machine). You can think of the internal memory as an elaborate program counter, and the transition rules as the instructions, for a custom-built computer designed to solve the problem at hand. Chances are, you won't build hardware out of gates and memory chips to do the job. Instead, you will simulate this finite-state machine by writing a program in a higher-level language. There are a thousand disguises for a finite-state machine simulator, but all have the same essential shape:

```
state := STATE1
WHILE (true)
   IF (state = STATE1)
      <action #1>
   ELSE IF (state = STATE2)
      <action #2>
   .....
```

The various actions include logic that assigns new values to the variable **state**, from time to time, to put the machine through its paces.

```
state = 0
WHILE (TRUE)
   IF (state = 0)
      c := getchar()
      IF (c = '/')
         state := 1
      ELSE IF (c = EOF)
         <exit>
      ELSE
         putchar(c)
   ELSE IF (state = 1)
      c = getchar()
      IF (c = '*')
         state := 2
      ELSE
         putchar('/')
         putchar(c)
         state := 0
   ELSE IF (state = 2)
      c = getchar()
      IF (c = '*')
         state := 3
   ELSE
      c = getchar()
      IF (c = '/')
         state := 0
      ELSE
         state := 2
```

Figure 4.1 *Pseudo code for comment stripper.*

ere is a concrete, if frivolous, example. Say you want a program to remove all of the PL/I- or C-style comments from a text file. That is, the sequence /* begins a comment, and the sequence */ ends it. You want all such sequences to be dropped while you copy everything else. (This might be a useful way to process C programs whose comments are misleading.) We can identify four distinct processing states:

0) outside a comment
1) seen a / outside a comment
2) inside a comment
3) seen a * inside a comment

The pseudo code then can be written as shown in Figure 4.1.

This code assumes the existence of the C-style primitives **getchar** and **putchar**, which have special character codes for end-of-line and end-of-file. Since line structure is ignored in PL/I-style comments, end-of-line calls

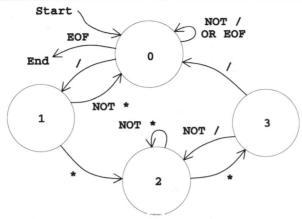

Figure 4.2 *State diagram for comment stripper.*

for no special processing here. End-of-file is represented in the program by the symbolic value **EOF**.

The only way I know to understand code like this is to trace through enough cases to convince myself that it handles everything correctly. A very useful aid is the *state diagram* shown in Figure 4.2. The circles represent the different states, and the arcs the rules for changing states. In this example, one character of input is consumed on each state transition. A state transition is thus a function of the current state and the next input character. You can also draw the state diagram first, then write the code to match. Assuming you have labeled the transitions carefully, the coding is a straightforward application of inside-out design (**Essay 2: Writing Predicates**).

*A*s an important aside, I would like to acknowledge that the pseudo code shown above is unnecessarily stylized. It is silly to set a state variable for the sole purpose of ensuring that the next time around the loop your program will select the proper choice. I am less concerned about the extra microseconds consumed by this machinery than I am about its readability. It looks at first glance as if far more is going on than there really is.

Here is the one place in all of programming where I think you can make an honest case for using **GOTO** statements. They do exactly what is needed. Consider the revised version shown in Figure 4.3.

I personally find this much easier to read, and much closer to the state diagram it is intended to model, than any contrivance that avoids the use of **GOTO** statements. Indeed, the one place we tolerate **GOTO** statements at Whitesmiths, Ltd. is in the device handlers for the Idris operating system. A device handler must typically track the state transitions of the piece of hardware it is trying to control. Hence it is written using bottom-up design and expressed as patches of code connected by **GOTO** statements. Using any other style would be dishonest and misleading.

```
NOT_IN_COMMENT:
     c := getchar()
     IF (c = '/')
        GOTO SEEN_SLASH
     ELSE IF (c = EOF)
        <exit>
     ELSE
        putchar(c)
        GOTO NOT_IN_COMMENT
SEEN_SLASH:
     c = getchar()
     IF (c = '*')
        GOTO IN_COMMENT
     ELSE
        putchar('/')
         putchar(c)
        GOTO NOT_IN_COMMENT
IN_COMMENT:
     c = getchar()
     IF (c = '*')
        GOTO SEEN_STAR
     ELSE
        GOTO IN_COMMENT
SEEN_STAR:
     c = getchar()
     IF (c = '/')
        GOTO NOT_IN_COMMENT
     ELSE
        GOTO IN_COMMENT
```

Figure 4.3 *Revised pseudo code for comment stripper.*

𝕴t is, of course, quite possible to write the comment stripper without resorting to state variables. As an exercise, you should recast the pseudo code above to eliminate the variable **state** (without using **GOTO** statements). Even though the grammar of PL/I-style comments is particularly nasty, you can still write fairly readable structured code to recognize it.

As a general rule, in fact, it is a good idea to eliminate as many switches and flags as possible from your code. Why? One of the great virtues of structured code is that you can tell a lot about the state of a computation just by knowing its textual position within your program. Instead of tracing your way through an unstructured flow chart that must be spread out over two (or more) dimensions, you have an indented listing that has only "one and a half" dimensions, so to speak. The program itself reflects a structure that closely models the structure of the problem you are solving.

But once you introduce even a single Boolean flag, the state of the computation at any point is twice as complex. It depends both upon the textual position within the program and the value stored in the flag. You have two program counters, and one of them is not so easy to inspect.

Now you see how bottom-up design earned its bad reputation. It encourages the use of redundant program counters, and/or unstructured programs, and/or GOTO statements. Small wonder that it has fallen out of favor. And if its only virtue is that it often works for programs that are small enough, that is certainly damning bottom-up design with faint praise.

There is, however, an important reason for using this approach. Sometimes you need two program counters.

We wrote the comment stripper as a stand-alone program, and acknowledged that it was of limited usefulness. There are, however, real life programs other than compilers that manipulate PL/I or C source code. They must strip comments very much as is done in this example. An important real-life difference is that comment stripping is just one of several transformations that the input must undergo, and probably one of the simplest transformations.

If performance were not an issue, and if you had a UNIX-like system at your disposal, you could use the comment stripper above as just one stage of a pipeline. Subsequent programs in the pipeline could be written to process only programs that had no comments, and each could be structured around one and only one transformation. But performance is always an issue, at some point, and few programs can be kept simple enough to devote all of their logic to one aspect of a problem.

Most programs are chock full of little finite-state machines, each keeping track of a bit of local structure, so that your program need not be polluted with all the details. Consider the primitive function **getchar**, for instance. Somewhere in the bowels of the **getchar** function, or the system facilities it draws upon, must be retained a rich assortment of knowledge about:

- which file is currently opened as the standard input
- which block within the file is being read
- which character within the block or record is the next one to read
- whether end-of-file has been encountered

and so on. We talk about **FILE** variables, about buffering, about unblocking or blocking, about queuing exception handlers, about allocating storage on a heap — all without a conscious awareness that each requires a finite-state machine with its own private state memory.

When you add a comment stripper to your program, chances are it's not as the main control module. More likely, it is an input module that you call to deliver up the next character not inside a comment. It probably looks something like the code in Figure 4.4.

```
FUNCTION get_non_comment_char()
STATIC state = 0
STATIC c

WHILE (TRUE)
   IF (state = 0)
      c := getchar()
      IF (c = '/')
         state := 1
      ELSE IF (c = EOF)
         state := 4
      ELSE
         RETURN (c)
   ELSE IF (state = 1)
      c = getchar()
      IF (c = '*')
         state := 2
      ELSE
         state := 4
         return ('/')
   ELSE IF (state = 2)
      c = getchar()
      IF (c = '*')
         state := 3
   ELSE IF (state = 3)
      c = getchar()
      IF (c = '/')
         state := 0
      ELSE
         state := 2
   ELSE
      IF (c <> EOF)
         state := 0
      RETURN (c)
```

Figure 4.4 *Pseudo code for comment stripper function.*

𝕴 have added another state which is entered whenever a subsequent call
should return the character stored in the variable **c**. Note that this
function requires private memory, for the variables **state** and **c**, which is
retained between calls to the function. It must also be possible to initialize
the variable **state** to a known value at program startup. Programming
languages that lack this form of private memory must expose such variables to functions that have no business looking at them. And programming
languages that cannot initialize private memory via static declarations
must perform explicit initializations at program startup, usually in places
far removed from the function that uses the variables. Both of these defi-

ciencies lead to program maintenance problems that make private memory deservedly unpopular among conscientious designers.

So to summarize:

- You write modules with private memory for one purpose only, to memorize where the module left off in processing some data structure when it returned control to the module that called it.

- The virtue of this practice is that it hides information about some data structure from the rest of the program, when the rest of the program has no business knowing about the hidden structure.

- The price you pay with this practice is that you are adding hidden program counters to your program, which makes it harder to read, debug, and maintain.

- If you are indeed hiding structure with private memory, the price is worth it.

- If you are not, get rid of the private memory.

The vast majority of modules you write can and should have no private memory. They should not even access global variables, if at all possible, since these merely constitute a form of private memory that is shared among several modules. (Global variables that are constant, such as read-only tables or flags altered only at program startup, are possible exceptions to this rule.) A pair of functions called **push** and **pop** can usefully hide information about the state of their stack. An **arcsine** function, on the other hand, has no business altering anything but dynamic memory that is allocated upon each invocation of the function.

When you must write a module, or group of modules, with private memory, you should use the techniques of bottom-up design to make sure you have accounted for all states and all state transitions in the cleanest possible manner. About the only thing worse than designing bottom up when you should be designing top down is designing top down when you should be designing bottom up. □

Afterword: In my lecturing days, I found it hard to convince people that opposite design approaches could be compatible. Converts to top-down design shunned any bottom-up approach. Those still wedded to bottom-up design were convinced that top-down design was slow and led to inefficient designs. I seized on the concept of "redeeming social value" as a way to sell an unpopular technique. Any approach with drawbacks must pay its way by simplifying a design in some other important dimension. Of course, all design methods have both advantages and drawbacks. Accept that about one design method and it is easier to accept it about others. Thus, I use bottom-up design as a kind of Judas goat. (My goal is to slaughter rigid ideas, not useful approaches.)

5 Recognizing Input

METHOD: Left-to-right design.

DESCRIPTION: Left-to-right design focuses on the structure of the data being input to a module. It is based on the premise that the structure of a program should closely model that of its input data. The name derives from the convention of drawing data flow from inputs on the left to outputs on the right.

The fundamental difference from right-to-left design is that input data must be recognized as valid sequences of primitive forms, which is substantially harder than generating output data as sequences of primitive forms. Moreover, every responsible module must be prepared to deal with arbitrary sequences of input, many of which are invalid. Thus, input data structure is generally represented as a grammar (a set of rules for composing valid input sequences) over a finite set of tokens (a set of primitive forms).

Numerous techniques have been developed for automatic generation of bottom-up parsers. Ad hoc input recognizers are generally hand crafted as recursive structured programs whose organization closely parallels the input data structure.

DOCUMENTATION: A grammatical description of the input, with a lexical definition of valid tokens, best captures the linguistic nature of the input. Data structure diagrams are effective as well, if error handling does not obscure the structure of valid input. Procedural representations, such as structured pseudo code or structured flow charts, may capture additional implementation information.

LIMITATIONS: Left-to-right design is an effective organizing principle only if the structure of the input dominates the problem. If the input structure is trivial, particularly compared to the calculations involved or the structure of output data, this approach is not fruitful. If the output structure is nontrivial as well, see outside-in design.

Once upon a time, reading input was an easy job, at least for the programmer. You simply required each user to punch a card giving the number of input cases that followed. Your program read that card first, then processed the number of cases specified, then terminated execution. If there were extra cases, the batch monitor skipped over them before processing the next job. If there were too few cases (possibly because your poor user failed to right justify the count in its field) your program either gobbled up part of the next job and tried to digest it, or it encountered a condition called end-of-file.

End-of-file in those days was a fatal error. The prevailing viewpoint among writers of operating systems was that no self-respecting program should ever attempt to read input data that wasn't there. Reading end-of-file was such an obvious sign of incompetence that the system wouldn't even give control back to the running program through an error handler. It was quitting time. Much the same attitude surrounded attempts to open files that did not exist, or to write on protected tapes. Anything other than complete success was classified as a disaster.

The programmer, freed of any responsibility for handling end-of-file or open failures, felt equally irresponsible about other errors. If the next input card should have two positive numbers in ten-column fields, you just tried to read it with that format. If the formatted read didn't complain, your program just bulled ahead with whatever values got stored. Never mind range or validity checks, the system will shut you down if things get too out of hand.

Thus was born the pithy dictum: "Garbage in, garbage out."

In time, this approach became less acceptable. No longer were your users so pleased to have a program that worked (sometimes) that they were willing to put up with tiresome restrictions and undiagnosed craziness.

The first thing to go, as I recall, was the practice of requiring input counts. Most users can slap a special card on the end of each data deck without feeling put out. Programmers learned a variety of ruses for marking the end of input. An input case with a well placed zero value, where a zero value did not otherwise make sense, is still one of the commonest end-of-file sentinels. Programs advanced enough to accept text input, usually as human-readable titles for cases, learned to set aside special names such as **END** or **DONE** to signal end-of-file.

(As an aside, one of my favorite stories concerns the transaction-processing system that worked beautifully for years processing domestic data within the United States. Pressed into international service, it began shutting down unexpectedly at random times. A programmer finally figured out that transactions from "Quito, Ecuador," were being taken as instructions to "Quit." Permitting abbreviations is not always user friendly.)

Operating systems eventually changed their attitude about end-of-file. FORTRAN IV got an **END=** qualifier for **READ** statements. COBOL had the **AT END** clause in its **READ** verb. And PL/I, from its outset, let you specify an **ON**-unit for **ENDFILE**. Note that end-of-file was still considered some undesirable aberration, but now it was one you could trust a user program to deal with.

The problem of signaling end-of-file in a stack of card decks still remained. It just got pushed out one level further from programmer control. The net effect was to add even stranger sentinels such as **$EOJ** to the users' vocabulary of required esoteric knowledge.

If you think we've made any progress in this area, look again. How do you signal end-of-file at your terminal? Do you type control-D, control-Z, **/***, or something weirder? Is it the same for all programs you use every day? Is there some way of crafting an input line that looks to your program like the input sentinel but is not reported to it as end-of-file? Having a standard notation for end-of-file on an interactive channel is important if you shift among several systems, or if you write programs that talk to other computers via interactive ports. Having a way of quoting the end-of-file sentinel is important in achieving transparency.

What is transparency? It is the ability to send an arbitrary message along some channel, without fear that certain messages will get lost or cause undesirable side effects. You can have a channel that treats certain input as special, yet can still be made transparent, provided there is an alternate way to spell any special input. An alternate spelling is called a *quoted message* or an *escape sequence*. The C language, for instance, makes extensive use of the backslash character within string and character constants to achieve transparency. You may not type a newline character within a string constant, but you can spell one with a backslash and a lowercase **n**, as in **"\n"**. And you can spell a backslash as two backslashes, as in **"\\"**, so that character is not lost to you either.

Most people are not sensitive to the need for transparency until its lack gets in their way. You know those plastic bars that supermarkets provide to separate your groceries from your neighbors in the check-out line? They make first rate, unambiguous delimiters. Now suppose you are seized with an urgent desire to buy one of them along with the rest of your groceries. And you have laryngitis. And no pencil or paper. The "escape sequence" you would have to contrive by pointing and grunting would certainly attract a crowd, and annoy the person behind you in the check-out line. Too bad you can't just put a backslash in front of it, on the conveyor belt.

The point is, that us humans can always pop up one level of metalanguage to deal with a communications impasse, but a computer program cannot. You can avoid transparency problems by ruling out only the most esoteric input, but sooner or later it will bite unless you plan properly from the start.

And the higher-level point is, once your program starts reading input until end-of-file, you are in the business of recognizing an input language. You can often keep that language simple, such as:

```
zero or more text lines, followed by
end-of-file
```

but it is a language nevertheless.

More likely, your input has at least some structure that your program must recognize in order to handle each case properly. A text editor, desk calculator, or most transaction-processing programs fall into this category. Possibly, your program imposes a nontrivial structure on its input, so that you or anybody else would call it a language processor. Then you're in the big leagues of input recognition.

From those primitive early days I described above, there has been a steady trend in the direction of requiring programs to recognize ever more elaborate input structure. If you've avoided thinking about this area so far, you probably won't be able to stay innocent much longer and remain a working programmer.

Once you know the shape of a problem, then you should look at the shape of known solutions for guidance in designing the program that addresses that problem. Left-to-right design says that any program that must read input is a language recognizer. You must write a grammar for the input language, then reflect the structure of that grammar in the structure of the program you write. The difficulty of this exercise is determined by the properties of the grammar you end up with.

As part of right-to-left design (**Essay 3: Generating Data**), I described the basic building blocks for structuring data. What is normally called an input record is just a sequence of related data fields of various types. Certain fields can have alternate formats, or interpretations, based on some predicate — usually determined by earlier fields in the record. And certain fields can be repeated within a record, the number of repetitions being based on some predicate — usually determined by earlier fields in the record (or a special end marker). Indeed, a typical input file is a repetition of zero or more identical records, so the outermost structure of many files is similar to the text file structure shown above. The Pascal data type **FILE** takes this repetition for granted.

These building blocks of sequence, alternation, and repetition can be used to structure any data, in principle. They are useful for structuring most data, in practice. It is the predicates for alternation and repetition that reveal how useful a given data structure is for recognizing input.

In the simplest case of reading until end-of-file, the predicate is just a little tricky:

```
WHILE (when I attempt to read input,
    I do not encounter end-of-file)
    <process the input I read>
```

Many languages do not permit you to attempt a read, store the input data if successful, and obtain a value suitable for end-of-file testing — all within the test portion of a **WHILE** statement. (C programmers delight in antics such as this.) Indeed, there is a strong school that finds offensive the calling of any function that has side effects from within a predicate. Be that as it may, it's something you have to do all the time. I always concoct read-and-test functions for any language that doesn't provide them. I find side effects within predicates far preferable to contorted control flow. Given such a function, you can write your generic input driven program as:

```
WHILE (get_input(record) <> end-of-file)
    process_record(record)
```

From these simple beginnings, you can build up most simple transaction-processing programs. Jean-Dominique Warnier (**War78**), Ken Orr (**Orr77**), and Michael Jackson (**Jac83**) all give numerous examples of how to structure input data and write programs that recognize that structure. Indeed, there are lots of simple examples of input data structure from the world of commercial data processing.

There are also lots of complex examples from the world of language translation. If you want to learn more than you should ever need to know about parsing complex grammars, read any of the several excellent books by Al Aho and Jeff Ullman (**A&U72**, **A&U77**, **A&U86**). They focus heavily on automatic generation of bottom-up parsers. (Steve Johnson's **yacc**, that comes with UNIX, is a famous example of this technology.) I think, however, that most of your input parsing needs can be met quite adequately by hand crafting top down parsers. Such techniques are also nicely covered by Aho and Ullman.

Here is a middle-of-the-road example that should illustrate several important issues in writing top-down parsers. Let's say you wish to write a simple desk-calculator program, one that performs the four arithmetic operations on numbers and parenthesized subexpressions. Each expression must be written alone on a line. For each input line, the program reads an expression, parses it, evaluates it, and prints the numeric value. You can write the input grammar as:

```
zero or more text lines, consisting of
    an expression, followed by
    an end-of-line, all followed by
an end-of-file
```

The grammar for an expression is recursive, as shown in Figure 5.1.

In the jargon of parsing technology, this is a recursive grammar with seven terminal symbols. A terminal symbol such as ' **+** ' is represented in the input as the literal character **+**, just as the terminal symbol ' **-** ' is represented by **-**, and so on. The terminal symbol **NUMBER** has its own mini grammar, enforcing the usual rules for writing decimal points and trailing exponents.

```
an expression is
        a factor, or
        an expression '+' a factor, or
        an expression '-' a factor
    a factor is
        a term, or
        a factor '*' a term, or
        a factor '/' a term
    a term is
        a NUMBER, or
        a '+' term, or
        a '-' term, or
        a '(' expression ')'
```
Figure 5.1 *Recursive grammar for an expression.*

For practice, you might try writing a grammar that tolerates all of the forms:

```
1       1.0     1e0
12      12.     0.12E+02
```

The first lesson you learn when a grammar gets even this complicated is that you want to do your parsing in at least two stages. First you deal at the character-by-character level, to group the input into a sequence of *tokens*. This is called *lexical analysis*. Here is where things like white space, comments, and other formatting niceties are made to disappear before they confuse the higher-level grammar unnecessarily. Then you endeavor to parse the sequence of tokens, which means you try to guess what the structure of the input must be and where each token fits in the structure. In this example, you could define the tokens:

```
number (with a value)
add-op
sub-op
mul-op
div-op
left-paren
right-paren
end-of-line
end-of-file
```

The second lesson you learn is that you can't always just write a structured program modeled after the grammar. For the simple, non-recursive grammars that describe a sequence of input records, you should expect few problems. Even most forms of recursion cause no problem, assuming you are programming in a language that supports recursive function calls, such as PL/I, Pascal, or C. But when you encounter left recursion, as in this example, you have to rewrite the grammar a bit. Otherwise, you end up writing code that recurses to death.

So we change the grammar for an expression to be:

```
an expression is
    a factor, followed by
    zero or more occurrences of either
        a '+' followed by a factor, or
        a '-' followed by a factor
```

And the code for parsing functions looks something like:

```
get_expr()
    tree := get_factor()
    WHILE (can_eat(add-op) OR can_eat(sub-op))
        op := get_token()
        tree := make_tree(tree, op, get_expr())
    return (tree)
```

If that transformation looks like magic to you, well it isn't. You can always take a left-recursive grammar and eliminate the left recursion pretty mechanically. And the result is still a structured program that does a pretty good job of capturing the input structure in the program indentation. Mostly it takes practice.

This is not to say that I have indulged in no magic here. After decades of writing parsers, I have learned the kind of primitive functions that give the biggest payback. Those little gems with names like **can_eat**, **get_token**, and **make_tree** make all the difference when it comes to decorating the basic program structure with nitty gritty details. I won't go into their details here, but the names should suggest much of their operation.

Which leads to the third lesson. Even if the structure of the input dominates the design, you must still know what your output looks like before you can get on with writing code. In this case, the grammar and experience tell us that you can represent an arbitrary expression by a data structure called a binary tree. The leaves of the tree hold **NUMBER**s, each of which has a value. A node with one descendant is a unary operator (**+5** or **-3**). A node with two descendants is one of the four binary operators (**3+2**, **3-2**, **3*2**, or **3/2**). There is no need to add any additional structure to represent parentheses. (Why?)

So each of the functions **get_expr**, **get_factor**, and **get_term** should return a pointer to an allocated data structure. The data structure must contain at least the fields shown in Figure 5.2.

Note that this data structure is once again composed by applying sequence, alternation, and repetition. Note also that the output of the expression parser is a data structure that exactly captures the structure of the input. There is no clash of structures. Thus, the structure of the input

```
an expression element is characterized by
a discriminant, signaling either
          a leaf, having
             a value; or
          a unary operator, having
             an operator type, followed by
             an operand pointer; or
          a binary operator, having
             an operator type, followed by
             a left operand pointer, followed by
             a right operand pointer
```

Figure 5.2 *Data structure for an expression parser.*

dominates the problem and there are no additional structuring considerations in shaping the program. (This is a partial lie, which I will address below.)

So, to summarize how far we've gotten so far:

- Left-to-right design tells you that nontrivial input data structure is a parsing problem.

- You must write a grammar that captures the structure of the input data.

- For complex input, you should identify a lexical grammar, over individual characters, and a higher-level grammar over the tokens you construct with your lexical grammar.

- If you use the three building-block forms, then you can write a structured program that recognizes the input and neatly documents the input data structure in the indentation of the code.

- You may have to modify your grammar, in a straightforward fashion, if it involves left recursion.

- You will probably have to build a nontrivial internal data structure to capture a nontrivial input data structure.

- It is important to define your internal data structure before you attempt to write detailed code from the grammar.

ow let's look at all the things that can go wrong when you attempt to structure your programs around recognizing input. As before, I am assuming that your goal is to produce an ad hoc recognizer that is organized as a collection of mutually recursive functions that parse top down. If you want to use one of the several parser generators (such as yacc under UNIX) that are widely available, please feel free to do so. You will not avoid the issues presented here, they just pop up in different places.

The first issue is ambiguity. Earlier, I gave an example of a grammar for recognizing simple expressions, the kind you might type into a pocket calculator that accepts parentheses and the four basic arithmetic operators.

When the time came to write code that implemented the grammar, I found it necessary to change the grammar to eliminate left recursion. The resultant grammar was a simple transformation of the original and, as far as I know, accepts the same input language.

What I was careful not to point out, however, was that I could have written quite a number of different grammars to satisfy the verbal description of the problem to be solved. Let's now consider a few variations.

First of all, I could have written a right-recursive grammar instead. The definitions of expression and factor would then be:

```
an expression is
    a factor, or
    a factor '+' an expression, or
    a factor '-' an expression

a factor is
    a term, or
    a term '*' a factor, or
    a term '/' a factor
```

This recognizes the same input language as the left-recursive grammar I chose to present. It does, however, ascribe a slightly different meaning to certain sentences in the language. For example, the expression:

```
6 / 2 * 3
```

is effectively parenthesized by the left-recursive grammar as:

```
(6 / 2) * 3
```

so the value is 9. The right-recursive grammar parenthesizes as:

```
6 / (2 * 3)
```

so the value is 1.

I know that common usage favors the first interpretation, but that doesn't make the second form wrong. In the first place, I forgot to specify anything about common usage in my verbal description of the problem. Any programmer would have a legitimate gripe about an analyst who forgot to write down a constraint that might be obvious to the analyst but not to the programmer. In the second place, I could have fixed up the problem in the *semantic* phase of input recognition. After all, right recursion avoids the restructuring problem that I had to deal with given the left-recursive grammar as a starting point. It's arguably no messier to rewrite the parse tree as it is formed, and stay closer to the original grammar.

With either grammar, I have put off some important constraints to the semantic phase anyway. For instance, any mathematician will be quick to tell you that the sentence:

```
5 / 0
```

is not valid in the language of mathematical expressions. Division by zero is just plain undefined. We could try to handle this by introducing a distinction in the lexical category **NUMBER**:

```
a NUMBER is either
   a NONZERO, or
   a ZERO
```

Then we could rewrite the grammar to restrict obvious division by zero. You just couldn't say it anymore.

There are problems with this approach. One is that your customer would probably prefer to have division by zero reported as, "You can't divide by zero, turkey," rather than the laconic, "Syntax error." The second is that you still haven't solved the whole problem in the syntax. Consider:

```
5 / (6 - 6)
```

or:

```
5 / (((3 + 7 + 10)
   * (1000 - 8) / 992)
   - 17 - 3)
```

(Can you spot the literary reference in this example?)

You might catch the first form by introducing the nonterminals **zero_term** and **zero_factor**, but after awhile the exercise gets tiresome. Even if you do detect syntactically that the second form is undefined, the victory is Pyrrhic. Your grammar has become so ornate that it no longer clearly documents the problem you intended to solve.

If you are going to push part of the recognition process into semantics, where do you stop? The distinction between a factor and a term is necessary to capture the difference in binding strength of the additive operators + and − versus the multiplicative operators * and /. This is not so bad, particularly since at least some people may remember those concepts from their early training in algebra. But what happens if you start introducing additional operators, with different binding strengths and different rules for grouping (left to right versus right to left)? Even with a language as simple as Pascal, the number of grammatical artifices you must introduce is uncomfortable. For an operator-rich language such as C, it is downright ridiculous.

So why not prepare for future growth by introducing a boiled-down grammar:

```
an expression is
   a NUMBER, or
   a '+' expression, or
   a '-' expression, or
   a '(' expression ')', or
   an expression '+' expression, or
```

```
an expression '-' expression, or
an expression '*' expression, or
an expression '/' expression
```

You must complete this grammar with a table of binding strengths for the various infix operators, plus grouping rules for each infix operator. Nevertheless, the resultant two-part document is probably easier to grasp by all concerned — analyst, programmer, maintainer, and user.

Once you get a taste for shifting syntax into semantics, it is easy to go into a shark-like feeding frenzy. I have seen input-driven programs degenerate into the All Purpose Input Grammar:

```
input is
    stuff, possibly followed by
    more stuff
```

The latitude you get in coding ad hoc semantic functions is wonderful for producing tailored diagnostics and context-sensitive interpretations. The only trouble is, with each simplification of the grammar your program becomes less dominated by its grammar and more by its semantics. In the technology of language recognition, there is no aspect better understood, or better automated, than parsing. It is foolish to turn your back on any discipline that can help you structure a nontrivial program.

So to summarize the problem of ambiguity:

- Left-to-right design requires you to craft a grammar that describes the input your program must recognize.
- There is usually a broad spectrum of grammars that can be used to describe a given input structure.

At one end of the spectrum, you attempt to describe all constraints on the input with syntactic rules — you endeavor to make it syntactically impossible to utter nonsense sentences. At the other end of the spectrum, you tolerate almost any utterance syntactically — you endeavor to filter out nonsense by imposing semantic checks on the input.

As a design method, left-to-right design is weaker than it first appears. With all the technology available for constructing parsers, you would think that this part of the business of writing programs would be the most cut and dried. Upon closer inspection, you find that you get far less guidance than you would like.

Remember, the purpose of a method is to tell you what to do when you don't know what you're doing. Any method that relies too heavily on previous experience isn't telling you much. It must be viewed more as an aesthetic guideline than an engineering formula.

I was fortunate that, as an employee of Bell Laboratories when the **yacc** compiler compiler was first introduced, I got to spend about a year trying it out on a number of programming tasks. That was when I learned how broad is the continuum of grammars that can be applied to any input structure. That was also when I acquired a considerable amount of my education in the pragmatics of constructing parsers.

I have learned from experience where best to draw the line between lexical analysis, syntactic analysis, and semantic interpretation. I haven't learned enough to articulate hard and fast rules to others, however. I can tell you basically to put everything you can into the grammar that looks at all grammatical. If you find yourself introducing artificial syntactic entities (nonterminals that you have trouble describing in words) just to get the parse right, back off. If you find yourself reconstructing parse trees because they aren't built quite right, take another look at your grammar.

I can't tell you much more than that.

Another issue is lookahead. One of the most important properties of a grammar is how many symbols you have to look at before you can determine which grammatical structure the symbols must belong to. Perhaps you have seen the terms LL1 and LR1. These describe grammars that require you to look at one new symbol from the input, at most, before you can decide how to parse the input. There is a vast literature on the properties of lookahead-1 grammars, so much so that you tend to forget there are other kinds as well.

Are there lookahead-0 grammars? The honest answer is, "Yes and no." You can certainly define a grammar that requires no lookahead. In fact, I began this essay by describing the traditional way programs accepted input in the days of my youth. You were obliged to punch a card (remember those?) with a number specifying how many input records follow. You were further obliged to append exactly that many input records. The program took no responsibility for the consequences of your failure to follow this recipe exactly.

That is a lookahead-0 grammar.

It is reminiscent of Queen Victoria's purported practice of sitting down, without looking back, at whatever moment the urge struck her to do so. She had every expectation that some courtier would be there on time with a chair. It is not recorded that she was ever disappointed. (This example is, more precisely, one of a lookbehind-0 grammar.)

I know of no computer programmers who have been raised to the peerage, so far. Meanwhile, us commoners have a stronger obligation to our constituencies. Even if the advertised grammar lets us off the hook regarding lookahead, we still must face the possibility that the input does not match the grammar. I like to think that I am not a dogmatic person, in most matters, but I unhesitatingly herewith present Plauger's Dogma:

No program may leave its sanity at the mercy of its input.

This can also be expressed in corollary form as:

Garbage in, diagnostics out.

What this means for lookahead-0 grammars is that they are incomplete, for the purpose of structuring a program. By the time you complete such a grammar, it necessarily becomes at least lookahead-1. You must look before you leap.

Once you have to deal with lookahead, then there is a certain amount of machinery you must master. That input stream that your program is scanning must now be elastic enough to suffer an occasional kink. In other words, your parsing code should have a number of places where it calls a function with a name something like, "Get next symbol from input stream." Lookahead is most easily handled centrally by adding a companion function with a name like, "Whoops, take this symbol back and give it out as the next symbol from the input stream."

The ANSI C library has a standard function called **ungetc** that does the latter operation for a single character read from an input stream. If that is not sufficient, or if you don't have even that machinery available, it's easy enough to create. You simply interpose a **get** function between your parsing code and the raw **get**, then team it up with an **unget** that puts returned symbols in a known place. Your **get** always looks in the known place before it tries to get a truly new symbol from the input. (See **Essay 4: Finite-State Machines** for how to design modules with private memory like this.)

If you have to look ahead more than one symbol, you simply provide for a stack (or last-in, first-out queue) of ungotten symbols. The stack must be at least as deep as the worst-case lookahead. When you write such functions, remember to have them check for stack overflow and panic loudly should it occur. That's invaluable for debugging the lookahead logic of parsers.

But what if your grammar requires lookahead of more than one symbol? This is more common than you think. Even languages as well designed as Pascal and C have occasional lapses, where the parser must look ahead two characters before it can decide. Remember the comment parser we studied in the previous essay? (See **Essay 4: Finite-State Machines**.) You have to peer past every '/' in C or PL/I before you can make a major control decision within the parser — does the slash introduce an operator or a comment? Older languages such as FORTRAN are much worse. Perhaps you have seen the classic pun:

```
DO 5 I = 1, 3
DO5J = 13
```

Since spaces are not significant in FORTRAN, you have to peer ahead quite a bit before you distinguish between a **DO** statement and an assignment.

In general, such lapses are easily dealt with by a small additional amount of lookahead, in one or two places. These are just additional kinks in the input stream, if you will. One of the virtues of using a tool such as **yacc** is that it warns you of lookahead problems, without taxing your gray cells. You can then usually isolate and deal with small lapses one at a time.

But what if you have to deal with an arbitrary amount of lookahead? It's like the old joke about the man asking directions on a subway train. "Oh, that's easy. Just watch me and get off one stop before I do." It's no fun to have to take the whole trip before you learn where you should have gotten off.

Arbitrary lookahead problems crop up all the time. The X3J11 committee almost introduced one into C when it added the option of declaring the types of arguments in a function declaration. You see, now you can write:

```
int fun1(int, int);
```

to declare the function **fun1** the new way, and:

```
int fun2(x, y)
    int x, y;
    { ..... }
```

to define **fun2** the old way. That's nice. But what happens when someone writes:

```
typedef int x, y;
int fun3(x, y)
```

Are we introducing a declaration that provides argument types, or a definition that provides argument names? If there were 30 arguments, you would have to look past all 30 in the argument list before you start seeing clues that make the correct answer unambiguous.

There are various ways to deal with arbitrary lookahead. Most people subconsciously resort to one of them as soon as they detect the problem. It never even surfaces as a lookahead problem.

You can recast the grammar to eliminate the problem. Generally, this requires the customer to specify more information up front to disambiguate the situation early. X3J11 blanched at the thought of adding yet another keyword, or grammatical artifice, so they didn't take this out.

You can accept the problem and put the burden on the implementor. This is the Algol 68 approach — make the language just barely parsable and stimulate the technology a bit. X3J11 wanted to keep a larger community of implementors (and users) than Algol 68 now enjoys.

You can simply legislate the problem out of existence by decreeing which interpretation shall be chosen up front. This is what X3J11 did. If an argument looks like it starts with a type, then it is a type. Never mind that it might be an argument identifier, in the scope of a new function, that supersedes a **typedef** in an outer scope.

Generally speaking, the third solution is the best. Most people will accept parsing by decree, if the chosen parse is the more common and if the ambiguity is sufficiently esoteric. In the case of C, there were already several places where the language is disambiguated this way, so the Committee plowed no new ground with this approach.

An issue closely related to lookahead is backtracking. If you think about what you do when you have to deal with lookahead logic, there are three general approaches.

- You can assume you know the outcome and proceed down that path. Should you find you have chosen the wrong path, you must then undo any computations you performed back to the point of your incorrect guess. This is backtracking in all its glory.

- You can tentatively assume you know the outcome, but do as little as possible to proceed with the parse. Should you find you have chosen the wrong path, you must then undo what little work you have done back to the point of your incorrect guess. This is the kind of backtracking described above, where the only damage to be undone is to the input stream.

- You can straddle the fence, deferring any commitment until you know the outcome for sure. Parsers constructed as finite-state machines often use this ploy: "Enter state 17 if you are building either a divide operator or the start of a comment."

I favor the second approach for top-down parsing, the third for bottom-up. I avoid the first like the plague. Why? Because if you must perform any nontrivial computation based on your current interpretation of the input, you must be sure to perform the inverse of that computation should you guess wrong.

The inverse will probably be nontrivial as well. And all the computations you performed going in must be inverted in reverse order going out. The chances of your getting this code right, and keeping it right under maintenance, is frighteningly small.

So the basic rule of backtracking is: Don't, if you can avoid it. If you can't avoid it, keep it simple and overt. This is where the **get/unget** function pair really pays off. It gives you a way of expressing the lookahead/backtrack machinery in a way that is contained and reasonably easy to check for correctness.

The last issue I want to mention in this essay is error handling. As I stated above, I take it as axiomatic that every program should check its input well enough to keep from going crazy. Ideally, it should also keep from *saying* anything crazy, particularly if it masquerades as sensible output. The only way to do this when recognizing input is to write code that handles *every possible sequence of input*.

What you may find, however, is that the code you add to satisfy this responsibility may swamp the code you need to solve the problem as originally presented. When that happens, much of the benefit of left-to-right design as a structuring principle gets lost.

There are ways to deal with this problem, but they constitute a whole new design method that I call easy-to-hard design. (See **Essay 6: Handling Exceptions**.) While parsing input is particularly prone to being overwhelmed by error handling, it is by no means the only aspect of program design that can suffer. So I will defer any further discussion of error handling during input parsing until the next essay. □

fterword: This essay appeared as two successive columns. I spliced them together to eliminate the artifices introduced with the original split. Parsing is an enormous subject to summarize even in a double installment. My modest goal here was to introduce the fundamentals. A nontrivial data structure should shape the structure of a program that reads it, in a fundamentally different way than it shapes a program that produces it. Too many presentations on data structuring gloss over issues such as lookahead and error recovery.

*Jon Bentley has described "little languages" that occur widely in applications programming (**Ben86**). These offer opportunities to define clean and powerful user interfaces. They also offer opportunities to structure important chunks of a program using right-to-left design.*

6 Handling Exceptions

METHOD: Easy-to-hard design.

DESCRIPTION: Easy-to-hard design adopts the viewpoint that the structure of a program should be most strongly shaped by the normal (straightforward or commonplace) situations. Errors, interrupts, limit violations, and so forth are best handled as *exceptions*, with minimum impact on program structure. The name derives from the observation that writing a program innocent of exceptions is relatively easy, so the harder problem of making a program robust in the presence of arbitrary exceptions is better deferred to last.

The goal is to ensure that all possible cases are handled safely, at the least, and gracefully if possible. The ultimate mechanism for exception handling is the *nonlocal* **GOTO**, to effect an unplanned early return from one or more levels of function call.

DOCUMENTATION: Exception lists tell what conditions are handled, and how, on a module-by-module basis.

LIMITATIONS: Exceptions raise coupling between modules and may introduce unnecessary complexity in situations where error codes are easily distinguished from valid function return values, and hence may be handled inline.

In the last essay (**Essay 5: Recognizing Input**), I spoke about the problems of parsing input to a program. I stated Plauger's Dogma:

𝔑o program may leabe its sanity at the mercy of its input.

In other words, it is professionally unacceptable to write a program that does something out of control merely because a naive (or malicious) customer contrives to type input at it that is out of the ordinary. This dogma imposes an obligation on the programmer to write parsing code that is prepared to handle every possible sequence of input. That is not an easy obligation to satisfy, but it is both necessary and possible to do so. The purpose of this essay is to help convince you that you can and should honor this obligation.

If you think, on the other hand, that this is so obvious that everyone deals with the problem automatically, try the following experiments. Choose five programs you believe in, and:

- feed each an empty input file
- ask each to write to a full, write-protected, or nonexistent disk
- feed each a text line with 1,000 characters in it
- feed each a file with 1,000,000 records in it
- offer a case of beer to an undergraduate if s/he can break it

Naturally, not all of these tests are relevant to all the programs. Some may not be possible. But it is a rare program that performs a nontrivial service and can pass all of these tests. Particularly the last one.

If you construct your input parser by using left-to-right design (**Essay 5: Recognizing Input**), there are simple techniques you can bring to bear to ensure that you have considered all possible input patterns. Left-to-right design tells you to impose a grammar on the input to a program, using as composition forms sequences, alternations, and repetitions of more basic forms. You then write a structured program using statement sequences, **IF/ELSE** statements, and **WHILE** statements to recognize these composition forms and to process them. You can be sure that your parser is complete if you make each of these forms complete. How do you complete a form? Let's look at each of the forms, in reverse order.

A repetition consists of zero or more instances of a more basic form. The number of repetitions is determined by some predicate. The predicate may be some hardwired number — the program expects one record to follow for each of the 50 states. It may be some number determined from earlier input — the program reads a line giving the count of records to follow. Or it may be determined from a limited amount of lookahead — the program reads records until end-of-file, or until a sentinel record, or until a non-numeric field is encountered.

To complete a repetition, all you generally have to do is make the predicate more suspicious. You might change, "While I haven't read 50 records" to, "While I haven't read 50 records and there are more records to read." Or you might change, "While I'm expecting more personnel records" to, "While I'm expecting more personnel records and the next record exists and has a valid personnel identification number."

You must judge whether an ill-formed record is better diagnosed in the loop as a bad member of a repetition, or whether it is better taken as proof that the repetition has ended. In the latter case, it might then be diagnosed as a bad form of the next record expected. Whatever else you look for, end-of-file must be one reason for making a **WHILE** predicate go false.

An alternation consists of two or more different forms, exactly one of which may occur next in the input. For each binary decision among alternate forms, there is some predicate that determines which form is actually present. The predicate may be determined from earlier input (the user has shifted input mode to octal). Or it may be determined from a limited amount of lookahead (the **X** coordinate is non-numeric, so treat the line as a title).

To complete an alternation, you must ensure that there is a trailing **ELSE** on the chain of **IF/ELSE** statements that look for alternatives. The trailing **ELSE** clause processes all input not handled by an earlier **IF** or **ELSE IF**. It may read, "**ELSE** we're done sooner than I anticipated, pass it on." Or it may read, "**ELSE** there must be trouble, because I can't recognize this input." As with an unexpected end to a repetition, you must judge whether the surprise is better diagnosed in the context of the alternation or in some higher context.

A sequence consists of a more basic form, immediately followed by another more basic form. You normally have no predicate because there is no choice. A print command is always followed by a filename, for instance, or a new graph title is always followed by the **X** and **Y** scale factors.

To complete a sequence, change each of the members to a completed alternation, as described above. You may have to write, "For a **PRINT** command, if there is a field following and it makes sense as a filename, take it as such; otherwise observe that the input contains an incomplete **PRINT** command." Or, "If you've got a new graph title and you can successfully read two numeric fields on the line following, take them as the **X** and **Y** scale factors; otherwise complain that the scale factors don't look good."

If you complete all your forms in this manner, nothing should get by the input parse. The price you may have to pay, however, is that you can no longer see how correct cases are handled by the code, because all the error handling dominates the structure of the program. We will discuss how to mitigate this later.

Say, for example, you want to filter a text stream for a variety of ASCII printer escape sequences. This means that, besides the usual printable characters and spacing-control characters (backspace, line feed, etc.), you can expect a variety of sequences that begin with the escape character, **ESC**. There are fixed-length sequences of one, two, or three characters, plus some that contain a variable-length list of characters with a null (zero value) character on the end. A partial grammar might read:

```
input is zero or more occurrences of
    either a non-ESC character, or
    an ESC character followed by
        CODE1, or
        CODE2 any-char, or
        CODE3 any-char any-char, or
        CODE4, followed by
            zero or more
                nonzero characters, followed by
            a zero character
```

The outer two forms are complete, since **zero or more occur-rences of** and **either non-ESC or ESC** cover all possible inputs. Once you see an **ESC** character, however, there are all sorts of fragmentary input sequences you can present that this grammar will not accept. I leave it as an exercise for you to complete the grammar so that it can serve as the basis for a bullet-proof program.

So far I have focused on parsing input as a source of errors, but there are numerous places in any program where you may be faced with alternatives you'd rather not have to deal with. Every time you add two integers, for instance, you court the possibility of arithmetic overflow. If you are accumulating a sum, you can get a silly printout. Much worse, you may end up with a dangerous limit value for a subsequent loop. Since most modern computers, and programming languages, are notoriously lax about checking for integer overflow, you must either contrive your program logic to make overflow impossible or add special checking logic to detect the occurrence in line.

Floating-point arithmetic is subject to:

- overflow, when a number gets too large to represent
- underflow, when a number gets too small
- loss of significance, when insufficient fraction bits can be retained

Most of us take for granted that a huge number, or *machine infinity*, is an adequate approximation to a result that has overflowed. Even more of us are happy to approximate with exact zero a result that has underflowed. Few of us even notice when we lose half (or all) of the significance in a calculation. A very few of us are content to have our programs terminate abruptly when any or all of these problems arise.

The point is that floating-point arithmetic is awash with exceptions, and with traditional "fixups" whose wisdom we seldom question. Certainly none of us want to replace **x + y** with:

```
ADD x TO y,
    ON OVERFLOW RESULT IS huge_val
    ON UNDERFLOW RESULT IS 0
    ON SIGNIFICANCE_LOSS print("meaningless")
```

As a general rule, however, I find that programmers err on the side of inadequate checking, and inadequate error recovery logic, when performing floating-point arithmetic.

Still another under-checked area is assignment, or type casting, that causes information to be lost. It often makes sense to assign a floating-point number to an integer by discarding all fraction bits, but not always. Rounding is often more appropriate. It is sometimes reasonable to discard significant bits when storing a large integer into a smaller one, but not often.

Some compilers give a warning message every time you write an assignment that might lose significance. If you write a type cast to reassure the compiler that you meant what you said, you lose all possibility of static type-compatibility checking. Other compilers will generate code that dynamically checks all assignments that might lose significance. If you can't afford this overhead, you may have to turn off all checking. Wouldn't it be nice if you could write something like:

```
ASSIGN y to x,
    ON SIZE_ERROR despair()
```

to get the checks only when you want them?

Still another source of errors is bad subscripts, or silly pointer values. "Safe" languages such as Pascal and Ada make a point of checking subscripts, unless you insist that all such checking be disabled at run time. Since it is difficult to check that pointers are valid, except by ruling out a special **NIL** value, such languages avoid the problem by not letting you do much with pointers. C on the other hand lets you express pointer logic that rivals assembly language in compactness, at the expense of most safety checks. Only the most conscientious C programmer will habitually write:

```
assert(&a[0] <= p && p < &a[AMAX]);
*p = 3;
```

The final exception that I will mention is the asynchronous interrupt. The commonest source of such interrupts is when you strike some magic attention key on your keyboard, such as control-C, **DEL**, **ATTN**, **ESC**, or **BREAK**. Unlike all the others mentioned above, this condition cannot be associated with any particular statement in your program. You may sometimes choose to honor such interrupts only during a read, say, but you still don't know where in the input parse an interrupt may occur. So you must either test on every read, poll for the interrupt at various places in your program, or be prepared to have the rug jerked out at an arbitrary place in your computation. None of these answers is suitable for all occasions.

Given all these opportunities for being conscientious, you can see how easy it is to completely obscure any sequence of code with error-handling logic. The ASCII escape-sequence example above doesn't get too mucked up by the addition of error handling, but sometimes a program does. What do you do then? There are several responses.

At one extreme, you can reduce the number of forms categorized as errors by ascribing useful semantics to various partial forms. If the user fails to type the name of an output file, perhaps it makes sense to write to the standard output by default. If no maxima are entered for the **X** and/or **Y** coordinates, perhaps the program should provide automatic scaling. Innumerable opportunities exist for providing shorthand by completing a grammar that would otherwise require decoration with error messages.

There is a danger in carrying this too far, however. Dennis Ritchie once wrote a powerful text editor called **QED** for the GE 635. (It is the precursor to the UNIX **ed** and its widely used screen-oriented derivatives.) **QED** had so many commands, and the input syntax was so forgiving, it was nigh on impossible to type in a sequence of characters that were diagnosed as erroneous. A common mistake was to enter plain text while in command input mode — at which point the most interesting things happened to buffers, files, and tempers. It is significant that, when **QED** became **ed**, the commands were reduced in number and restricted to one per line.

At the other extreme, you can make a virtue of necessity and shift the design focus of your parser from handling correct input as economically as possible to providing the world's most elaborate diagnostics. If you choose to do this with a program, make sure you emit diagnostics that educate the user and suggest correct inputs. Few things are more frustrating than a program that sits with its arms folded (figuratively speaking) and continually scolds you with **syntax error**.

A friend of mine, Dave Bulman, characterizes one particularly annoying class of diagnostics as, "You misspelled California." The unspoken message is, "I know what you're trying to say, but until you get it just right, I refuse to acknowledge it." Operating systems are perhaps the worst offenders in this league. I once had to live with an operating system whose commonest diagnostic amounted to, "I made a mistake somewhere, and I won't tell you where, but I'm terminating your program." A systems programmer in one of my seminars once put it perfectly — "Most operating systems act as though you're bothering them."

So if you're going to diagnose the heck out of your input, make sure your program gives constructive criticism. And if you're going to guess some meaning from fragmentary input, make sure that you guess wisely. In particular, you should never accept shorthand commands that cause data to be destroyed irrevocably. UNIX has been properly criticized for letting you type **rm *** to remove all files in your current directory, without so much as a passing, **are you sure?**

A middle-of-the-road approach is to change your mindset about what you classify as errors, and represent some of the erroneous conditions as "meta messages." You then incorporate what was once error-handling logic into the main design. This is exactly what happens when your floating-point hardware replaces an underflow with exact zero, or an overflow with a special code for infinity. The best software example I can think of is the inline handling of end-of-file that I discussed in the preceding essay. (See **Essay 5: Recognizing Input.**) A particularly clean implementation is the C library function **getchar**, which returns the special value **EOF**, that is distinguishable from any input character value, when end-of-file is encountered. C programmers habitually process end-of-file as just another input result to be handled by the parsing logic.

Indeed, C programmers seem much more willing than others to return error codes "in channel" from a variety of function calls. I know of no language that lets you declare a type such as:

```
[0 .. 255] ARE CHARACTER CODES
-1 IS END OF FILE
-2 IS END OF LINE
-3 IS READ ERROR
```

Since C provides relatively weak type checking anyway, in comparison to other modern languages, it is an easy matter to mix subranges and enumerations in this eclectic fashion.

I am all in favor of passing back error codes as meta messages, given two provisos. The first is that the error is sufficiently commonplace, and not so disastrous, that it makes sense to process it as just another case. The second proviso is that there are reasonable values left over for assigning to error codes. An early version of **getchar**, for instance, returned zero for end-of-file. You could not distinguish reading a **NUL** character from reading end-of-file. Such a loss of transparency is never worth the convenience of an in-channel error code.

But let us say that you have defaulted all you can, and diagnosed all you can, and incorporated all you can — and still the mainline computation is overwhelmed by error handling. What can you do? The answer is, separate the error handling from the mainline.

Block-structured languages are really neat for supporting information hiding and control flow, but they get in the way sometimes. From time to time, you need an escape from the pure nesting of, "I call you, you call him, he returns to you, you return to me." You want to say something like, "If you or any of your subordinates encounter this condition, just drop everything and give control back to me."

The generic name for this capability is the *nonlocal* **GOTO** *statement*. In PL/I you can do this with **ON**-units and **GOTO** statements. In Pascal, you can jump out of nested functions or procedures to a containing one with a **GOTO** statement In C you can "re-return" from a call to the magic function **setjmp** by calling the function **longjmp** with a pointer to the save area filled in by **setjmp**. In all cases, the normal nesting of calls and returns is subverted, and control reverts to a higher level in the calling hierarchy.

With this machinery, you write your program in a specific order. First you design the code for handling correct cases. (This is the easy part, which you get out of the way first.) Then you complete all control structures that parse input. If asynchronous interrupts can occur, or floating-point exceptions can occur in numerous places, add the code needed to get control when these conditions occur. Decide at what level you wish to handle each condition, then use nonlocal **GOTO** statements to transfer control there. If any of the error handling logic is too complex, introduce additional condition handlers, move the complex logic there, and put nonlocal **GOTO**s where the errors are detected. (This is the hard part, which you save for last.) And that's easy-to-hard design.

I end with two observations. The first is that COBOL, which is not my favorite programming language, probably does the best job of emphasizing the conditional nature of reads and computations. It has wonderful qualifier phrases, such as **AT END** and **ON OVERFLOW**, for handling exceptions right where they occur. And the language Ada, also not my favorite programming language, has marvelous machinery for handling exceptions in a readable fashion. Much as I respect C.A.R. Hoare in many areas, I must disagree with the unkind words he addressed to this machinery in his Turing Award Lecture (**Hoa81**).

The second observation is that I do not advocate designing programs with no error checking, then adding it later. It has been wisely and widely observed that reliability cannot be retrofit. Easy-to-hard design tells you what you can defer until later in the *design* process. You cannot defer error handling until later in the *software development* process. □

𝕬fterword: This essay has a long build-up and an abbreviated climax. It cries out for more detailed examples of handling exceptions in various languages. (It also predates the addition of exception handling to C++.) But that is the fundamental difference between a textbook chapter and an essay in a popular magazine. The latter does not have such a captive audience. Nor can it seize arbitrary amounts of paper real estate to drive home its points.

So this essay drives home the most important points first. You can't write credulous code. Writing absolutely safe code often compromises readability. Processing the nasties out of line helps preserve the relationship between the structure of the program and the overt structure of the problem.

7 Which Tool is Next?

A method tells you what to do when you don't know what you're doing. Or, to put it another way, the purpose of a method is to give you guidance in solving a problem so that you need not keep the whole picture in mind to make progress. It tells you what to do *next*.

Software development is an exercise in mastering complexity. As such, it is a nonstop battle with detail, with ruthless requirements for accuracy and completeness, that threatens to overwhelm both designers and implementors. Little wonder that each new method for aiding the software development process is greeted with an enthusiasm that often borders on religious.

It is seldom profitable, however, to confine one's tactics to a limited set of responses. For no matter how much zeal, and faith, is put behind a given approach, there will always be important situations where it is inappropriate, or simply not relevant.

In the first of this series of essays (**Essay 1: Which Tool is Best?**), I drew the analogy of picking a single tool for doing carpentry. Saws cut straight lines well, lathes shape cylinders nicely, hammers drive nails for sturdy joints. Each has its selling points.

But which tool is best for making a picnic table? Only the most loyal and persistent carpenter would stick with any one tool for the entire job, no matter how favored the tool. The sensible craftsperson learns to use many tools, each where it is most effective.

It is sad that proponents of many software development methods can't see beyond their favorite tools. What is needed, clearly, is a healthy assortment of methods, plus some guidelines for choosing the right one at the right time. Those guidelines add up to just another method, a method for choosing among methods. That's what this essay is about.

For the last several essays, I have focused on a number of design methods that I have found useful. These I have dubbed:

- inside-out design (**Essay 2: Writing Predicates**)
- right-to-left design (**Essay 3: Generating Data**)
- bottom-up design (**Essay 4: Finite-State Machines**)
- left-to-right design (**Essay 5: Recognizing Input**)
- easy-to-hard design (**Essay 6: Handling Exceptions**)

I still have at least as many methods to describe, but I thought this would be a good time for an intermission, to refocus on the overall goal.

How do you develop a method for choosing methods? There are two essential ingredients:

1) You must know the region of applicability of each method, and the areas in which it has little or nothing to contribute

2) You must learn to confine your view of a problem to its "most interesting" aspect at any given stage of solution.

An aspect is most interesting if it appears to dominate the problem, and if there is some particular method that deals with that aspect. Often it looks very much like a problem you've seen before, with a known solution you can parallel.

Here is a concrete example. Imagine that you live in, say, Concord, Massachusetts and wish to visit a friend in Rochester, New York. How do you get there?

A simple solution is: Go west, young person. Of course, a proper implementation of this simple strategy had better specify a distance, and get the compass direction a little more precise. And there is the matter of transportation. A recipe this simple can only be applied to something along the lines of a ballistic missile — which may cause trouble with neighbors at both ends of the trip, with the U.S. Air Force in mid flight, and with your general health after the landing.

More likely, you will base your solution on either flying by airplane or driving your car, then reduce the problem to a series of subproblems. This is more of a strategic decision involving relative costs, travel times, and perhaps just plain preferences. To proceed, let us assume that you have chosen to drive your car.

Applying the global go-west strategy, you consult road maps and lay out a route involving major roads that most closely approximate a straight path to your destination. The experienced traveler quickly learns that a major road going almost the right direction is faster and less subject to delays than a minor road that lies closer to the straight line. So early on in the project you must get comfortable with the notion that you will be going not exactly in the right direction for extended periods of time.

If your only measure of progress is, "How far am I from my friend's house?" then you have already learned to cultivate patience. Why? Because the research you have done on road maps has led you no closer to your goal (unless you keep your maps in the west wing of your house). You must have faith that an investment in planning early on will keep you off false trails later.

Next you must deal with getting onto that network of roads you have been studying. It is not likely that your driveway runs due west directly onto the Interstate system (at least I hope not, for your sake). So you accept the need to traverse a series of local streets and roads to get to the appropriate highway interchange. You are probably unconcerned even if you must drive ten miles *east* to get to the major highway of your choice. And all the twists and turns along the way you also take in stride, for you are sophisticated enough to know that your metric of success (distance from your goal) must be subordinated to local tactics.

Once on the highway, you can start making serious progress. But even this must be interrupted by occasional rest stops, for food and fuel as well. The wise driver knows that breaking up a trip makes it less stressful and hence safer. So you accept that progress will not always be continuous, in the interest of more certain success.

When you get to Rochester, you essentially reverse the process you followed getting started in Concord. One difference may be that, while the roads around Concord were chosen from long experience, and navigated from memory, here you are not so well versed. Hence you may have to follow directions sent to you by your friend. If you've ever tried to follow a path described only in words and sketches not to scale, you know this calls for quite another set of skills.

At last you arrive. You are weary from driving, perhaps a little stiff — and blissfully unaware of the complexities you have mastered in making such a trip. Even at that, you didn't have to deal with detours, blowouts, or No-Vacancy signs this time, but those contingencies each require separate methods as well.

From experience with other trips, you know which aspect is "most interesting" at each point — reading maps, navigating local roads, locating service stations, deciphering directions (not to mention operating the automobile). You remembered solutions that worked for your parents when they took you on trips. Once you mastered the currently most interesting aspect, the next one loomed larger in importance.

If only software development came so naturally. (Few of us, alas, have learned programming by watching our parents succeed at it!) Writing 20,000 lines of code is *much* harder than driving a few hundred miles, in terms of the complexity you must deal with. Yet developers often impose less structure for such a project than you just went through for your imaginary auto trip.

Not enough design time occurs up front, because (as Gerry Weinberg puts it so well) the boss starts asking, "Why isn't Sam coding anything?" This is the WISCA syndrome, that sabotages early planning in the interest of giving the appearance of making progress. Not enough scaffolding is put in place at the outset because it doesn't count as part of the final product. It is not "progress."

Not enough check points are specified along the way because they would delay reaching the goal. And not enough attention is given to the final packaging because it involves skills not daily exercised by most programmers. Besides, the job is always "almost done," so why delay delivery?

Worst of all, software developers are not attuned to the diversity of methods they must exercise to get the whole job done. Endorsing top-down design as a panacea for software construction woes is like saying, "Go west." Trusting structured programming to get you there is like riding a ballistic missile to Rochester, New York. The practical programmer travels safer roads and uses more varied skills.

The fundamental problem, as I have tried to emphasize with this homey example, is that we still lack the culture for developing software that is reliable and on schedule. We as a profession have certainly come a long way in the last two or three decades, but we have an equally long way to go, I believe. Other branches of engineering have a much better track record than us software developers.

It can also be stated, with good accuracy, that the average professional programmer does not have all the skills needed to do his or her job properly. To make that car trip, you had to be at various times a driver, a navigator, an accountant, and perhaps even a negotiator — among many other skills you use just staying alive in a complex society. Imagine if we placed such a premium on driving skills alone that we prepared new drivers with a week on an oval race track, then unleashed them on our streets and highways. But is that much different than teaching students how to be hotshot code writers, without teaching them about testing or project management?

No, I am not condemning the current computer-science curriculum. I believe that the colleges are teaching what has been understood well enough to be captured in usable textbooks, and that's all you can ask of them. People who write code for a living are still learning how to do it right, on the job, at the expense of their employers and their customers.

Through many years of experience, some of it unpleasant, I have learned that I lack many skills needed to coordinate a group of software developers through all the stages of a project. I am a good programmer, in some areas a very good one; but I have learned that I have many limitations. It seems, in fact, that I discover new ones almost daily. It is the difference between being a programmer and a software engineer (whatever that is).

On the other hand, I have seen people who are good software engineers. The skills they have are demonstrably real, important, and within the reach of mere mortals. While I am skilled enough to preach in one area of my profession, around these people I consider myself a rather clumsy student.

What are the skills of software engineering? I can name some of them, at least. You must understand the software life cycle, particularly the phases that occur during the software-development phase, well enough to appreciate what you should be doing in each phase. It is just as bad to start coding before you have a complete design as it is to start redesigning (or to begin designing!) in the middle of coding.

You must appreciate the importance of estimating accurately, as early in the development as possible. This does not involve taking your best guess and multiplying by π! Rather, you must learn to repeatedly subdivide each effort until you (and an honest observer) can compare each component to something you have seen done successfully before. Until you can do that, you must admit that you are still in the research phase, and you must not pretend you can give accurate schedules until that phase is complete.

You must know an accurate specification when you see one, how to fix it if it is not, and how to write one if at all possible. No project should have a serious investment of development effort until you and the customer have signed off on a spec you both can live with. Once you've signed off on it, you must resist any changes by the customer, by you, or by the programmers — unless their impact is reflected in an honest revaluation of the delivery schedule and you all can live with the change.

You must have deliverables specified so objectively that there can be no question when you are done. This is important for the mental health of your programmers — they must know when it is proper to declare victory and for cordial relations between you and the customer. (For the project you are working on right now, ask yourself if you'll know when it is complete. The answer is often sobering.)

You must know what constitutes adequate documentation for a project, both for internal maintenance and for use by the customer. There are programmers who are good at both documentation and coding, but for most nontrivial projects it is more cost effective to use writers for the writing and coders for the coding. You must also know what constitutes adequate tests, and adequate testing. It is a rare project that can leave the testing to the very end, with no preparation along the way. And it is rarer still that a software product can be kept alive without well defined procedures for regression testing, as automatically as possible.

Oh, and by the way, you also have to know how to design and code computer programs. That's my first love, and mostly what I focus on in these essays. But it's important to keep in perspective where the programming process fits in the overall scheme of things. I'm sure that some people who read this essay are of the home-hobbyist or cottage-industry ilk. They are their own spec writers, designers, coders, testers, and major customers. For them it is fair game to let the software engineering take a back seat to the more enjoyable business of crafting code. But I'm equally sure that for most of you readers the code you write contributes significantly to your income and your job security. If you ignore the context in which you write code, you risk losing the opportunity to advance in your profession (or even to stay in it!).

So when I talk about examining the most interesting aspect of a problem, mostly I mean something like, "Is it time for left-to-right design to capture the input-data structure, or can we proceed with inside-out design, to get the control flow down pat?" But on a more global scale, I mean asking questions like, "Should we even use a computer for this problem?" And, "Do we have a precise enough specification to proceed with detailed design?" And, "Is it more important to deliver something on time next month, or to add that neat feature you just thought of?"

At this point, I must confess that I can't lay down any simple mechanical rules for deciding what to do next. I could tell you to use common sense, just like driving a car cross country, but that doesn't meet the requirements of a method. I do know that, once you've accumulated enough small successes to have built up an assortment of comfortable methods, you will find it easier and easier to know which ones to apply and when.

So the best recipe I know for learning how to choose among methods is:
- Learn as many methods as you can.
- Make sure to apply each method you learn on a job small enough to be successful.
- Be on the lookout for complexity overload.

That last point is the hardest one to teach. By "complexity overload" I mean taking on a project so much beyond the biggest thing you have mastered before that you completely misjudge how big it truly is. Flush with success from your last project, it is easy for you to see the next opportunity as "just a little bit bigger." Remember, however, that people are even worse at perceiving complexity than they are at estimating probabilities. (If people could estimate probabilities at all accurately, there would be no lotteries, casinos, or insurance companies in the world.) It is altogether too easy to dismiss the blurry part of a prospectus with a wave of the hand and a confident feeling that, "I can handle those details later." A forest from a distance is a blur of green not because it is featureless but because it has millions of leaves.

One symptom that you have bogged down in complexity overload is when you find yourself doggedly applying a method that is clearly irrelevant, at least to any outside observer. It is like the mechanically inept person whose car breaks down — so he puts water in the battery and empties the ashtrays.

On the other hand, if you've accumulated enough experiences that no aspect of the project at hand is completely new turf, it is amazing how easy it is to see what to do next. You need not have done exactly that project before, or to that scale. Indeed, competitive industry and our own zeal for new experiences prevent most of us from doing the same job repeatedly. If you've seen a test-tube size version of a data-structuring problem, you can usually master a full-blown version in the real world. That's how us mammals get educated and survive.

I close this essay by reminding you of the opening sentence, "A method tells you what to do when you don't know what you're doing." That's designed to reassure you that you need not be completely clear about how to reach your goal, so long as you are clear about what the goal is. And you need not demonstrate straight-line progress to approach your goal most effectively, so long as you have some faith that you're gaining ground in some dimension. If you're going to be in the business of controlling complexity, you must accept that there are often times when it seems to control you. You don't have to know what to do, you just have to know what to do next. □

Afterword: I like the auto-trip analogy a lot. It is the best way I know to convey the fractal nature of software development. Whatever level of detail you consider, multitudinous problems confront you. The strategies you use are qualitatively similar at each level, even if they differ markedly in size. This analogy also brings home the need for a culture of software development. That culture certainly exists, and it grows richer with each passing year. But it is nowhere near as rich as the automobile culture we enjoy today.

8 Order Out of Chaos

METHOD: Chaos-to-order design.

DESCRIPTION: Chaos-to-order design applies to any situation where a sequence of data must be reordered, on the basis of some predicate applied to pairs from the sequence. The name derives from the usual assumption that the sequence that needs to be sorted may be presented in arbitrary initial order.

Sorting is sufficiently difficult technology to replicate that existing sort utilities should be used wherever possible. This is particularly true when the sequence to be sorted may be arbitrarily long. If there is any certain knowledge about the length or initial order of a sequence, however, there is a rich literature on how to take advantage of such knowledge to improve performance. A particularly important special case is *merging*, where two or more subsequences are known to be properly ordered.

DOCUMENTATION: A sort is described by its ordering rules — a list of what subfields (keys) are compared by what criteria. A sorting technique is best described in terms of its underlying algorithm, plus any tailoring done for the problem at hand.

LIMITATIONS: If a sequence needs no rearranging, sorting is irrelevant. If the rearrangements are localized in the sequence, sorting may be over-kill. If the ordering rules are not expressible as arithmetic relationships (less, equal, or greater), or if they apply to other than pairs, standard sorting technology is not applicable. And if the ordering rules may change during the sort, many popular algorithms may never terminate.

I have harped at considerable length, in earlier essays, about the importance of structuring data by recursive application of the three fundamental composition rules of sequence, alternation, and repetition. There are several good reasons for doing so:

- The vast majority of data structures encountered in real life are expressible this way.
- Human beings seem to be able to comprehend structures composed this way, with a minimum of confusion.
- This approach leads naturally to structured programs (composed of statement sequences, **IF/ELSE** statements, and **WHILE** loops), which are now widely regarded as highly readable and maintainable.

The subject of this essay is a common situation where this approach to data structuring breaks down. Such a situation arises whenever you must accept data in arbitrary order, but process it in some fixed sequence.

Consider the simple problem that arises in recognizing declarations in C. (Sorry for the language-oriented examples, but that's my primary area of activity. And no, I am not going to go into the more bizarre peculiarities of C declarations.) Let's say you want to recognize a declaration of **X** as type **int** and **register** storage class. The (unfortunately very lax) rules of C let the programmer write any of:

```
register int X;
register X;
int register X;
```

If you want to write a transformer from all permissible input declarations to a canonical output form, you must match up these three input forms with one output form. That's not too bad, just a bit tiresome. But now, let's do the same thing for the canonical declaration:

```
auto short int X;
```

By the rules of C, the keywords may occur in any order, and the keywords **auto** and **int** are optional. Now there are *eleven* input forms:

```
auto short int X;    short int X;
auto int short X;    int short X;
short auto int X;    short auto X;
short int auto X;    auto short X;
int auto short X;    short X;
int short auto X;
```

Throw in the optional keyword **signed**, now permissible in ANSI C, and you are faced with 38 possibilities! This is not the sort of thing you want to capture in a grammar using only sequence, alternation, and repetition.

A little simple arithmetic tells you that if you must recognize N distinct things in arbitrary order, there are $N!$ (N factorial) possibilities. If some of these things are optional, you must add in additional factorials as well. It doesn't take a very large value of N, or many options, for the combinatorics to overwhelm you. It's not that you can't write a grammar to capture the input data structure, it's just that it doesn't help you master complexity. Rather, it adds to it.

In real life, of course, people resort to various tricks to avoid writing grammars that explode. You can express the nonterminal **AUTO-SHORT**, for instance, by the recursive grammar:

```
an AUTO-SHORT is
    short, or
    AUTO-SHORT OTHER, or
    OTHER AUTO-SHORT
```

```
where OTHER is
  nothing, or
  OTHER auto, or
  OTHER int, or
  OTHER signed
```

subject to the semantic constraint that the final form may contain no re-peated keywords. This still is not as readable as the simple statement, "An **AUTO-SHORT** is represented by the keywords **auto signed short int** written in any order, with all but the keyword **short** optional."

In real life, of course, implementors build some form of bit vector and check it against a small set of valid patterns. This amounts to sorting the keywords into a canonical order so that valid forms are few in number. However you disguise it, a reordering is a sort. The data-structuring problem gets completely out of hand when the number of input items is open ended. But that consideration is almost academic given the combina-toric explosion that has already set in for very small numbers of items.

So the basic message of chaos-to-order design is: When you encounter a situation where data is presented in chaotic order, but must be processed in some definable order, you have a sorting problem. Forget about data structuring or structured programming for the time being. Instead, cast the problem into a form that can be handled by known sorting technology, then apply it. And keep the sort encapsulated so that changes in the sorting rules or technology do not affect the rest of the program, and changes in the rest of the program are least likely to affect the sorting aspects.

The examples above are very specialized reordering situations. It makes sense to grind out ad hoc code to do such peculiar jobs. A very high percentage of reordering problems, however, fit a more generic pattern:

1) You have some number, *N*, of items to reorder.

2) You have some predicate (set of testing rules) that depends only upon the values of a pair of items to determine their ordering (first item is less than, equal to, or greater than the second).

3) There is some way to exchange two items (swap them in memory, or swap pointers to them in memory, or rewrite items in a file).

When you see this pattern, you know there are oodles of techniques in the literature for doing the job. A straightforward presentation of some useful programs for sorting may be found in Chapter 4 of either *Software Tools* (**K&P76**) or *Software Tools in Pascal* (**K&P81**). For a clean presentation of several sorting algorithms, see *The Design and Analysis of Computer Algorithms*, (**AHU74**). And for encyclopedic coverage of sorting technology, see Volume 3 of Knuth's *The Art of Computer Programming* (**Knu73a**). I won't even try to approximate here the coverage found in any of these references.

ow comes the hardest message for the young programmer to hear. When the time comes to write a sort module, don't write your own. Sure, it's an interesting challenge. But the chances of your getting it right without a serious investment in debugging are small. The chances of your even matching, much less surpassing, the performance of an existing sort are even smaller. And the chances of your making a genuine contribution to the technology are almost nonexistent.

Sorting is big league stuff. Some of the oldest and best established of today's software companies write and sell sort packages. They make their living at shaving percentage points off the execution times of their sort packages every few years. Why? Because, the minicomputer and micro-computer revolutions notwithstanding, a significant chunk of the dollars spent on computing every year still goes toward sorting transactions in a commercial environment. We're not talking academic interest among com-puter scientists here, we're talking serious cost control and profits.

Even if you don't swim in such turbulent waters, chances are there's a sort utility, or a sort function in the library, that is already engineered better than anything you're likely to manage in the time diverted from solving the problems you're *supposed* to be working on. UNIX has a sturdy **sort** utility that often does exactly what you want to a text file, without specify-ing any options. When it doesn't, you can usually contrive a set of com-mand options that does what you want. The Standard C library has **qsort**, a very generic function for in-memory sorts. Even MS-DOS comes with a **SORT** utility, although I confess to never having used it. I favor the portable sort utility from Idris (to which I'm addicted).

So, to emphasize, there are two compelling reasons for using an existing sort instead of writing your own:

1) It's hard enough to do that you're likely to get it wrong, and/or spend a long time getting it right.

2) Existing packages are likely to do what you want.

et me give an example of the first point from personal experience. When Brian Kernighan and I wrote *Software Tools in Pascal* (**K&P81**), we naturally rewrote the RATFOR version of the quicksort function from *Software Tools* to take advantage of recursive function calls. The last lines of the function **rquick** (on p. 119) thereby acquired a compelling symmetry, as shown in Figure 8.1.

Elegant, yes? Unfortunately, no. The alternation is a waste of time, because it doesn't matter in which order you sort the subintervals on either side of the pivot element (at **i**) if you do both by recursive descent. Worse, there is a nasty *performance bug* lurking in this meretricious beauty.

Quicksort is a divide-and-conquer algorithm. You guess a pivot element, then shove everything greater than the pivot to the right and everything

```
if (low < hi) then begin
    .....
    if (i - lo < hi - i) then begin
        rquick(lo, i-1);
        rquick(i+1, hi)
    end
    else begin
        rquick(i+1, hi);
        rquick(lo, i-1)
    end
end
```

Figure 8.1 *Erroneous version of quick-sort recursion.*

less than the pivot to the left. That gives you two subintervals, on either side of the pivot, which you sort by the same technique. If you recurse only to sort the smaller of the two subintervals, then the depth of recursion cannot exceed $log_2(N)$, so the demands on a runtime call stack are nicely bounded.

If you can ever recurse to sort the larger subinterval, however, then it is possible to recurse to a depth of *N* calls. This is not so nice, since call stacks can easily require an order of magnitude more storage that the data itself. With the choice of pivot element used in **rquick**, this can happen when sorting data that has no equal elements and is already in sequence. Given small enough input, or a large enough call stack, the bug doesn't show up. But when it does, it understandably surprises the customer. That's why it is known as a performance bug. The proper way to write **rquick** is to make it a loop, as shown in Figure 8.2.

Brian and I missed the bug, obviously, thanks to a combination of superficial testing and large address-space machines. As far as I know, only one or two readers picked it up. If you've read the Letters section of any programming magazine, you know how quick some programmers are

```
while (low < hi) then begin
    .....
    if (i - lo < hi - i) then begin
        rquick(lo, i-1);
        lo := i+1
    end
    else begin
        rquick(i+1, hi);
        hi := i-1
    end
end
```

Figure 8.2 *Corrected version of quick-sort recursion.*

to pounce on anything that smacks of a bug. So that gives you some idea of its subtlety. The point is, Kernighan and I tried very hard to present a number of useful computer programs that were readable and correct. And the one we tripped up on the worst (I think) was our best version of a sort function.

The second reason for not writing your own sort is that you probably don't have to. For an in-memory sort, the only parameters a generic sort module must have are:

1) how many items to sort
2) what function to call to compare items **i** and **j**
3) what function to call to exchange items **i** and **j**

The actual algorithm for deciding when to compare and when to exchange is contained in the generic sort module. So a sort module is an excellent candidate for inclusion in a library. It requires few parameters, it performs a nontrivial function, and its performance is likely to match or exceed anything ad hoc that you write to do the same job.

If you need to sort more data than can be held in computer memory all at once, then you must resort to an *external sort*, as opposed to the *internal sort* performed by a library module. For an external sort, the basic strategy is to fill memory with chunks of data, sort the chunks in memory, write them to intermediate files, then merge the sorted chunks to produce the final output. Once again, this is heavy-duty technology; and all the earlier caveats apply here in spades. (The two *Software Tools* books show all the pieces, if you're curious.) Look for a utility that sorts files, then do your best to bend it to your needs.

A problem with prepackaged utilities, of course, is that you can seldom just drop in your own comparison or exchange functions, as for the library sort described above. Commercial packages usually offer you a plethora of sorting options, to make up for this lack of programmability. The items to be sorted must be delineated in some standard fashion, either as records (in record-structured environments) or as text lines (in less structured environments such as UNIX or MS-DOS). The ordering rules are specified in terms of keys — subfields of records — and rules for comparing the keys by pairs.

The simplest rule, for instance, is often to treat each record as a sequence of characters to be compared in native collating order for the host machine. A more elaborate rule might specify several keys, some of which are interpreted as account numbers, some as dollar amounts, and some as dates. I often find that I must experiment for about an hour with a complex sorting problem, until I get the keys and sort rules specified just right. That's still miles better than writing yet another custom sort to do the same job, with a program that is perhaps only slightly faster.

Having said all this, I concede that there are times when you really must write a specialized sort. For those cases where a standard sort *could* do the job, the only justification I can think of is when

1) you really can't get the performance you need from a standard sort
2) you're certain that the data you care about already has some order you can take advantage of

Here is an example so pedestrian that you probably have never thought of it in this light. Many data bases are still kept off line, stored as large sequential files kept in sort by account number. On a regular basis, transactions must be applied against this data base to update (or delete) certain records. This is the classic master-file update, that even Dijkstra has taken a swipe or two at.

A straightforward approach is to make data-base and transaction records look the same, except for a discriminating tag, so they can all inhabit the same file. Then you just concatenate any new transactions with the data base, sort the whole works, and pass over the sorted file to merge data-base records with their now adjacent transactions. I have often used the **sort** and **uniq** utilities of UNIX or Idris to do just this sort of operation. It saves a lot of programming for one shot (or few shot) applications.

Of course, nobody solves the problem this way for a production system. Knowing the large data base is in sort, you first sort only the new transactions. Then you merge the transaction sequential file with the data-base sequential file, applying the transactions as you match them up to produce a new sequential file. Since even the best of sorts has time complexity on the order of $N*log(N)$, and since merging is noticeably cheaper, you can win big by not sorting the entire data base. With the transaction presort and transaction merge, you have in effect replaced a single sort with a more complex operation that has better properties. At least the properties are better once you get the specialized code debugged.

I encountered another specialized sort in my first week of programming. With a minimum of help from a friend, I had contrived to write a FORTRAN program, get it to compile, and have the computer punch out a binary object deck (remember those?). With no help at all from anyone, I contrived to drop all three hundred odd cards of the deck on the floor. There was a card sorter in the room, and the deck was sequence numbered in the last few columns. So I watched a few people use the sorter for awhile, waited for the room to empty of potential critics, and went to work.

I had about thirty neat little piles (00X, 01X, etc.) laid out on a table when my friend came back. To my horror, he swept up half an hour's worth of effort into a single unordered deck. He then sorted the deck on the units column, reassembled it with that column now in order, sorted it the same way on the tens column, and again on the hundreds column. After three sorts he presented me my deck, completely restored to its original order.

What he used was a *stable radix sort*. The "radix" part was dealing the deck out into ten bins, which exhausted the space of values of each of the three sort keys (columns). The "stable" part was that sorting on the tens column didn't destroy the ordering on the units column — items that compared equal on the tens sort were never reordered. Combining those two tricks saved an incredible amount of time over building the tree of subdecks that I was working on.

That was my first big lesson in complexity theory, and in the importance of selecting a proper algorithm. It took me ten years to learn the complementary lesson, that lies at the heart of using software tools — you are better off wasting a little time by using an existing program than spending a lot of time writing a program that will only save you a little time.

There are, of course, still other reasons why you may have to write your own sorting program in certain cases. You can't safely sort by priority, using conventional algorithms, if some little demon is periodically altering the priorities during the sort. And you must be careful how you sort if you have unconventional ordering relationships. Consider the trio:

```
scissors cut paper
paper covers rock
rock smashes scissors
```

Which comes first? A more important variation of this curiosity is the problem of determining an acceptable linear ordering given only partial ordering information. In work flow, for instance, some tasks depend on the completion of others, but many are unrelated. In a subroutine library, you may have to put at the end all modules that are called by other library modules — and hope that there are no circular dependencies. These are problems that require a *topological sort*, for which technology also exists. You can often find the algorithm you need, but you're less likely to find the code prepackaged. □

Afterword: This is one of the few essays where I actively discourage programmers from doing what they love best. (The lessons of UNIX and software tools seem old fashioned in this era of event-driven mega applications, but perhaps they're not.) Still, I find that coders write ad hoc sorts almost as readily as they do Pascal parsers. I'll keep trying.

When this column first appeared, I botched the combinatoric computations and some program logic. (They are corrected here.) Naturally, several alert readers checked my work and wrote letters pointing out the gaffe. That neatly illustrated my point about how critical a technical audience can be, unfortunately.

9 Marrying Data Structures

METHOD: Outside-in design.

DESCRIPTION: Outside-in design deals with modules that have multiple nontrivial input and/or output data structures. The name derives from the view that data enters and leaves a module at its periphery, with processing occurring inside.

This approach focuses on resolving any clashes between different data structures either by marrying them into a common structure or isolating them into separate modules that communicate by a less structured intermediate data stream. A marriage of data structures is unavoidable when a merge must be performed.

If separate modules must be formed, they are organized by top-down design. The separate modules are then amenable to reduction by left-to-right or right-to-left design. One-to-many input transformations, or many-to-one output transformations, are reduced by bottom-up design.

DOCUMENTATION: If separate modules are not formed, a combined data-structure diagram best captures the underlying structure. Otherwise, other documents show the form of each module and the organization of the whole.

LIMITATIONS: If there is no clash to resolve, outside-in design contributes little. If any data sequence must be reordered, the combined structure may be too ornate. If the combined structure is much more complex than any of the separate data structures, the solution will be obscure.

Many programs are data transformers. That is, they consume one or more sequential streams of input data to produce one or more sequential streams of output data. The transformation itself is often not very ornate. In that case, the best organizing principle for such a program is to start with the structure of the data being processed and build the control flow around a similar procedural structure.

I repeat yet again the basic organizing principles of data-structured design. If you have a repetition of data structures, you process it in a loop (**WHILE** statement). If you have an alternation of possibilities in the data structure, you process it in a conditional (**IF/ELSE** statement). And if you have a sequence of different data types in the structure, you process it with a sequence of statements. A remarkably large fraction of data structures encountered in computing succumbs to this approach — which forms the basis of structured programming.

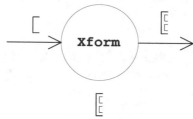

Figure 9.1 *Data transform with nontrivial output data structure.*

One broad class of programs produces structured output from fairly unstructured input. You may need to produce a paginated report, for instance, from a series of single transaction records. Or you may be generating a series of formatted screens from single-line queries typed in. For this class, the problem of producing the structured output data dominates the problem, so you build your program around the code needed to replicate that structure.

Here the hard part, once you have identified the basic data structure, is getting the predicates right. They control how many times you loop on a repetition, or which branch of a conditional to take. This I call right-to-left design (**Essay 3: Generating Data**), since it is customary to show data flow with the input on the left and the output on the right of a data transform (program) in a data-flow diagram. Figure 9.1 shows a single transform with nontrivial output structure. The resultant program structure is indicated underneath the transform. (All data structures are *highly* stylized in these figures.) The generic program structure looks something like:

```
WHILE (more_input)
    generate_output
```

where all the action is in **generate_output**.

Another broad class of programs produces fairly unstructured output from structured input. You may want to simulate a desk calculator, for instance, in one window of an interactive system. Or you may accept English-like data-base queries and generate one-sentence responses. For this class, the problem of recognizing the structure of the input data dominates the problem, so you build your program around the code needed to recognize, or parse, that structure.

Here the hard part, once you have identified the basic data structure, is getting all the lookahead and error recovery right. The code must rediscover the repetitions and alternations the user has chosen for a particular input. This is called left-to-right design (**Essay 5: Recognizing Input**), for reasons I leave to your imagination. Figure 9.2 shows a single transform with nontrivial input structure. The generic program structure looks something like:

```
WHILE (more_input)
   IF (match_input)
      generate_output
   ELSE
      put_error
```

where all the action is in the predicate **match_input**.

But what happens if both output and input have nontrivial data structure? Or, for that matter, what happens if you have multiple inputs and/or multiple outputs, and two or more of them could each serve as the principal structuring basis for the program? I have been careful to avoid such examples so far, while exploring the wonders of right-to-left and left-to-right design.

In the real world, there is no such thing as a completely trivial input or output. (The people across the street are already selling *that* program and you are trying to take their market share with a fancier version of the same thing). Even in the examples I gave, I glossed over contributions to the structure of a program from "trivial" sources. The contributions were nonetheless present.

The answer, of course, is that you must accommodate the structure of *all* the data you are processing. Otherwise the program is not doing its intended job. A program with more structure than is dictated by the problem to be solved may well have lurking bugs in the special cases. It will certainly cost you a premium to maintain. But it has a chance at serving its purpose correctly. A program with less structure than the data it must process cannot, from first principles, do the whole job.

It is still a good organizing principle to let your data structure your program. When you have multiple data structures influencing the design, you have a problem. The solution is to find a more ornate data structure that will accommodate the diverse data structures contributed from different streams. In other words, you must *marry* all of the input and output data structures to obtain the structure about which to organize the flow of control of your program. You can't simply proceed right-to-left, or left-to-right. You must approach the center of the transform from all directions at once. This approach, naturally enough, is called outside-in design. Figure 9.3 shows a single transform with nontrivial input and output structures.

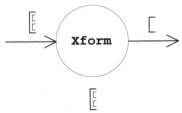

Figure 9.2 *Data transform with nontrivial input data structure.*

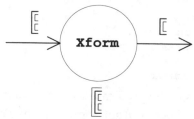

Figure 9.3 *Data transform with nontrivial input and output data structures.*

It is harder to show a generic program structure for outside-in design. Sometimes the bookkeeping involved in generating output dominates. Sometimes the problem of input recognition dominates. Sometimes the two are so intertwined as to defy decomposition. Let's look at some examples.

𝒜 data-base query language, for instance, usually permits input in a variety of forms, if only to accommodate varying numbers of parameters for different queries. Even if it is not your goal to advertise "natural English language queries" or "user-friendly input," you must still tolerate, and parse, a variety of input forms. So the input structure can be represented along the lines of:

```
zero or more requests, where
    a request is either
        TYPE1 param1 param2, or
        TYPE2 param, or
        TYPE3
```

The output, on the other hand, may be one line of text for some requests, a screenful for others, or multiple screens for still others. Let's say that the language includes the statements **SHOWFROM x TO y**, **SHOWME x**, and **SHOWALL**. Then the married structure might look like:

```
zero or more requests, where
    a request is either
        SHOWFROM x TO y, with
            zero or more
                output lines, or
        SHOWME x, with
            either
                an output line, or
                "NOT FOUND", or
        SHOWALL, with
            zero or more
                output lines
```

If you wish to structure multi-line output into screens, or if you wish to put **NOT FOUND** for any repetition of zero items, then the structure gets that much more ornate. But the basic principle is the same.

ow I know this is the sort of design work you do all the time. You don't
need any highfalutin pronouncements about marrying data structures
to figure out what to do in a simple situation like this. The point of
outside-in design, like all the other methods I have talked about so far, is
to focus your attention on the underlying principles of what you're doing.
That helps you can see where the action is (or should be).

In the case of outside-in design, you are building a combined data
structure. If you just start writing code any old way, you may well evolve
a program structure that recognizes the same input structure in two or more
places. Or it generates the same output structure in multiple ways. Or it
captures neither structure exactly right. If, on the other hand, you know
your goal is to produce a marriage of input and output structures, then you
have a check list of what operations must be performed and where in the
program they should appear.

Almost as bad, many programmers have unwittingly fallen into the
habit of writing all transforms as if they were either report generators or
parsers. You construct report generators by applying right-to-left design,
which is fine if the input is not too fancy. If it is fancy, however, you will
find read-ahead code stuck here, push-back code over there, and partially
parsed data stuck in side pockets all over the place. Report generators do
not accommodate parsing at all well.

If you are a parser freak, on the other hand, you apply left-to-right
design. This is fine if the output is closely related to the input. If it is not
closely related, you will have an assortment of partially filled buffers, state
flags such as

page_done   **buffer_empty**

and counters such as

column_number   **line_number**

sprinkled about the program. Parsers do not construct output at all well.

If you consider all your data structures at once, however, you are less
likely to produce an unmaintainable travesty. You may well end up with
an output-driven program (report generator) anyway, because that is the
best compromise. Or you may well end up with an input-driven program
(parser), because that minimizes maintenance. In either case, however, you
will have made an informed choice, instead of lucking out or losing out.

ere is a simple variant on the previous example, which shows some
aspects of a hybrid solution. Let's assume that input consists of ac-
count-number records each followed by zero or more transaction records
for that account. A transaction record may contain zero or more items of
that transaction type (whatever an item may be). We wish to produce a
report that starts a new page for each account number. The report may have
multiple pages per account. It lists up to 50 transactions per page. And it is

wide enough to accommodate the maximum number of possible items in
the columns of one report line. The input structure is:

```
zero or more groups, each with
    an account record, plus
    zero or more transactions, with
        a transaction type, plus
        zero or more
            items
```

The output structure is:

```
zero or more accounts, with
    one or more pages, with
        a page header
        zero to 50 lines, with
            the transaction type, plus
                zero or more
                    item columns
        a page footer
```

These structures marry fairly easily, as is often the case. (Nothing magic
here — people tend to keep the input structure in mind when contriving
output structure, and conversely.) Here is a program that handles the
problem:

```
got_one := get_rec(rec)
WHILE (got_one)
    IF (rec.type <> ACCTNO)
        put_error(rec)
    page := 1
    DO
        put_header(rec.acct, page)
        line := 1
        WHILE (got_one AND line <= 50
            AND rec.type = XACTION)
            start_line(rec.xaction)
            col := 1
            WHILE (is_item(rec.item[col]))
                put_col(rec.item[col])
                col := col + 1
            line := line + 1
            got_one := get_rec(rec)
        put_footer(page)
        page := page + 1
    WHILE (got_one)
```

If you had to characterize this structure as one or the other, it is more of
a report generator than a parser. Why? Because everything is in its expected
place for generating the output. Counters are incremented where you

expect and program structures mimic the output (**zero or more** becomes **WHILE, one or more** becomes **DO-WHILE**).

On the other hand, the lookahead required for parsing occurs in two places, a primer at the top of the program and a refilling read down where the last of the input record is consumed. That's not too unusual for parser logic, but the output generation code puts some perceptual distance between the parsing bits. The distance is enough that output generation certainly lays more claim to the program structure.

On the third hand, the overall structure of this program looks remarkably like the generic solution given earlier for programs produced by left-to-right design. You can argue it either way. What is important is that the check lists for both report-generator and parser logic are easily verified. You have reason to believe that the program structure might be correct and complete. That is the goal of outside-in design.

So far we have examined only programs with a single input source. As soon as you introduce a second input stream, a whole new class of issues presents itself. If the input streams don't interact, you must ask why a single program is being called upon to process them. If they do interact, you must determine the predicate that selects when you draw upon each stream to produce the combined data flow to be processed.

If the data streams have identical structure, then the program is performing a simple merge. Figure 9.4 shows two identical streams combining into one at a transform, making a simple merge. Merging was touched upon as one aspect of chaos-to-order design (**Essay 8: Order Out of Chaos**). While merging offers a number of interesting challenges, better designers than I have contributed more to that technology than I can begin to even summarize here. What you need to know is, as soon as you see a merge point in your data flow, it is time to dig up a merge utility if possible, or look up an appropriate merge algorithm if necessary.

What if you have multiple input streams converging at a single transform? A number of merge algorithms work fine with an arbitrary number of inputs. If you can't apply one of these, for whatever reason, you can always factor a multi-way merge into two or more two-way merges. Figure 9.5 illustrates the data flow for such a compound merge. If you are implementing this as a UNIX-style pipeline, then the amount of extra work is

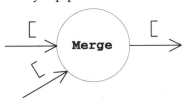

Figure 9.4 *Data transform performing simple merge.*

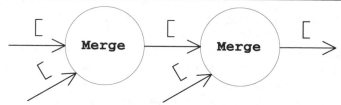

Figure 9.5 *Data transform performing compound merge.*

minimal. You simply mention the extra merge as another stage in the pipeline, using the same utility for both:

```
gen file1 | merge file2 | merge file3 | use
```

Organizing a single program that implements a compound merge, however, has some interesting problems, which I will defer until a future essay on top-down design. (See **Essay 11: Who's the Boss?**.)

An interesting variation occurs when you have two or more distinct streams you must bring together before you can process either. This commonly occurs in the classic master-file update. Here you merge a stream of transactions, sorted by account number, with a stream of master-file records, sorted the same way, to produce an updated master file.

I described master-file update as a special form of sorting in the previous essay. (See **Essay 8: Order Out of Chaos**.) Figure 9.6 shows a transform that performs an update merge. It looks the same as a simple merge (Figure 9.4), except that the input data structures differ.

What makes the update merge interesting is not so much the problem of marrying diverse data structures. They are simply concatenated long enough for a transaction processor to digest them and emit an updated master-file record. No, the challenge comes in bringing the streams together in such a way that all special cases are properly handled:

1) If no transaction corresponds to a given master-file record, then the record is copied unmodified.

2) If no master file record corresponds to a given transaction, then the transaction either creates a record or it is erroneous.

3) All transactions that correspond to a given master-file record must be applied in sequence. A transaction that calls for a record to be deleted produces no updated record.

4) If the transaction file is exhausted before the master-file, remaining master-file records must be copied unmodified, as in 1) above.

5) If the master file is exhausted before the transaction file, remaining transactions must be processed as in 2) above.

6) If either file is not in sort, then the program should stay sane at least, and diagnose the disaster at best.

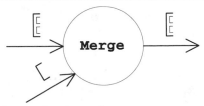

Figure 9.6 *Data transform performing update merge.*

𝕴 have given this problem, in one form or another, to hundreds of students in week-long seminars. They worked in groups of three to six people, over a period of about ten hours. In that environment, about half the students came up with reasonable solutions. The successful students produced every structural variation (and every bug) that you can imagine. As the simplest nontrivial data-flow problem most programmers encounter, master-file update is a good vehicle for conveying a variety of sermons.

Interestingly enough, the most successful group consisted of commercial COBOL programmers. Why? Because programs like this are their stock in trade. At least they were before on-line data bases came to dominate commercial data processing. Nevertheless, I am still surprised regularly when I trip across a program with the same morphology as master-file update that is still in use in some well traveled corridor of contemporary computing.

There are two general shapes for performing a merge of this sort. Leaving out all but the grossest details, the simplest looks like:

```
WHILE (more of both)
    IF (master.no < xaction.no)
        <put master>
        <get master>
    ELSE IF (master.no = xaction.no)
        <apply xaction to master>
        <get xaction>
    ELSE
        <do xaction>
        <get xaction>
WHILE (more master)
    <put master>
    <get master>
WHILE (more xaction)
    <do xaction>
    <get xaction>
```

The second variation relies on a clever trick beloved of COBOL programmers. It assumes that end-of-file on either stream can be represented as an ordinary record with an account number higher than any input value for that field (a.k.a. **HIGH-VALUES**):

```
WHILE (both not HIGH-VALUES)
   IF (master.no < xaction.no)
      <put master>
      <get master>
   ELSE IF (master.no = xaction.no)
      <apply xaction to master>
      <get master>
   ELSE
      <do xaction>
      <get xaction>
```

In either case, it is clear that the details must be filled in carefully if you intend to satisfy all of the requirements enumerated above. The most important thing, as always, is to recognize the shape of this problem when you see it. That way, you will know immediately the shape of the solution required. And you will know what to look out for when generating a program of the requisite shape.

You encounter another broad class of situations when doing outside-in design. These are characterized by multiple data structures that *do not* lend themselves to being married. When you encounter these, you must apply a completely different set of approaches. But that is the subject of the next essay (**Essay 10: Divorcing Data Structures**). □

A̶fterword: This essay and the next are my reaction to data-structured design as traditionally taught. Both Michael Jackson (Jac75, Jac83) and Ken Orr (Orr77) have earned ardent followings by teaching this powerful approach to program design, and justifiably so. Many commercial programs structure naturally around nontrivial data flow. Unfortunately, that feeds the inevitable tendency to make this a one-size-fits-all design method. And it obscures the relationship between data-structured design and other methods.

I prefer to peel data-structured design apart into its component approaches. Output-driven design is the simplest, followed by input-driven. This essay shows both as special cases of marrying data structures. Doing so, I believe, takes some of the magic out of the lookahead logic and other warts needed to make data-structured design work in real life. The next essay shows where things get really nasty.

10 Divorcing Data Structures

In the last essay I introduced outside-in design, which focuses on the problem of structuring modules that have multiple nontrivial data structures being input or output. (See **Essay 9: Marrying Data Structures**.) The examples I gave all involved marrying the multiple structures from the outside to form a composite data structure that shaped the code inside the module. Thus the name outside-in design.

I continue the discussion of outside-in design with a hard look at the many cases where such a marriage of data structures doesn't work. To say that the marriage doesn't work is not an absolute statement. Rather, it involves a judgment that the resulting structure is so complex that it doesn't help control the complexity of the problem to be solved. It adds to it.

So what do you do? The answer is best summarized in the Brian Savage cartoon shown in Figure 10.1. (I am a sucker for a well aimed cartoon, and Savage often lives up to his name.) Indeed, if you can't get along, why not get a divorce? That's all there is to it.

Figure 10.1 *"What's the big problem? If you can't get along, get a divorce."*

Figure 10.2 *Data transform with clashing data structures.*

In programming terms, you must put some distance between the various data streams that don't fit together well. Where originally you had a single module, replace it with two or more. Each of the new modules inherits just one of the troublesome data streams. Naturally, you must connect these multiple modules by introducing new data streams. Otherwise they could not possibly cooperate to perform the task specified for the original module. The real design work comes in specifying the structure of the newly introduced streams.

What you need to do is determine a simpler structure that is common to the more complex structures. You want this structure to be as complex as possible, to stay close to the original data structure, yet simple enough to marry nicely with two or more of the more complex structures you started out with. You see, you can't get away from the necessity of marrying all of the data structures for streams that enter or leave a single module. All you can do is break a difficult problem up into two or more simpler problems.

Figure 10.2 shows a simple example where input and output data structures clash. The clash is illustrated symbolically by an input structure that repeats in groups of threes and an output structure that repeats in groups of twos. Since 2 and 3 are relatively prime, the simplest structure that accommodates both is a repetition of groups of sixes. That's not an awful data structure, but it's certainly not a compelling design to repeat any code in six variations. And as with all combinatorics, things get bad very fast with more factors.

Figure 10.3 shows the obvious way to resolve this structure clash. You break the original module into two, and connect the two with a stream whose structure is a simple repetition of the common atomic structure. Now you have two simpler problems. The left module in the data stream is a classic input-driven form, reducible by left-to-right design. (See **Essay 5: Recognizing Input**.) It is a parser that must produce single records as they are recognized.

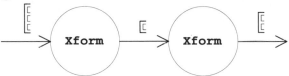

Figure 10.3 *Resolving the structure clash of Figure 10.2.*

The right module in the data stream is a classic output-driven form, reducible by right-to-left design. It is a data generator, or report writer, that must compose more complex forms from a stream of single input records. (See **Essay 3: Generating Data**.)

*F*or a more concrete example, consider a text formatter. Shorn of its whistles and bells, a text formatter spends much of its time reading lines of text written any old way and composing them into lines of more or less uniform width. In the absence of any hyphenation algorithms, output lines are split between words. You start a new line after you have placed at least one word on a line and before you place a word that will make the line too long. With this simple rule, and a fairly moronic definition of what constitutes a word, you can do a remarkably pretty job of formatting text.

The structure clash is obvious. There is no predeterminable relationship between the words presented on any one input line and the output lines they generate. A given input line could complete one line, generate several more whole lines, and/or provide the beginning of yet another. I have seen programs which nevertheless read lines, unpack them into words, repack words into output lines, and put out the lines, all in one giant control loop. What such programs lack in aesthetics, they make up for in job security for the original authors.

How to resolve the structure clash is equally obvious. You want an input module that reads lines of text and delivers up separate words. You also want an output module that eats words one at a time and produces lines to be written out. The intermediate data stream you introduce is a sequence of zero or more words.

Of course, you could also introduce an intermediate data stream that consists of individual characters. In a UNIX-like environment where each of the modules is a separate program and the two are connected by a pipeline, this is a compelling solution for the intermediate stream. But that is mostly because UNIX traffics heavily in unstructured streams of individual characters. You always have more machinery to help you out if you adopt the local lingua franca.

If both modules are within the same program, however, it may be harder to justify introducing a character stream. I am assuming that there are ways in which the line structure of the input affects how you break the input into words. (You may tolerate hyphenated words split across input lines, for instance.) In that case, you may find yourself recognizing words, then decomposing them for transmission, in the input module. Meanwhile, the output module is reconstituting words from the connecting data stream so that they can be properly packed into output lines. This is make work.

And even if you don't object to communicating via streams of characters, you would probably balk at communicating via bit streams. Everyone draws the line somewhere.

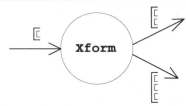

Figure 10.4 *Data transform with clashing output structures.*

Examples abound, in fact, where input data structure clashes with output data structure. Disk files are almost invariably composed of a sequence of fixed-size blocks. If a file contains variable-length records, be they text lines or more structured entities, it is commonplace for records to span block boundaries. You have a clash just separating out the record structure.

A program that reads one disk file and writes another faces multiple clashes. It must read disk blocks, compose input records, perform its principal business of transforming input records to output records, then sprinkle output records across a different pattern of disk-block boundaries. Small wonder that most of us lean heavily, and gratefully, upon operating systems and libraries to handle most of this business for us under the hood.

A programmer's vocabulary is replete with jargon for various stylized ways of resolving structure clashes. We speak of blocking and deblocking, packing and unpacking, buffering and unbuffering. Think of all the programs that compose screens, or paginate output, or assemble packets for transmission. Each is isolating an output stream with nontrivial data structure from an input stream with an unrelated nontrivial data structure.

Structure clashes don't just occur between input and output structures. Figure 10.4 shows a stylized example of a module that accepts relatively unstructured input, but must produce two output streams each with its own peculiar structure. If the two output structures do not marry easily, you have just as much trouble arriving at a clean data-structured organization of the module as when input and output structures clash.

Figure 10.5 shows a data flow you can introduce to resolve the output structure clash of Figure 10.4. This time we add two modules, because the original module still has plenty to do in splitting the data stream. It is generally best not to pollute it with the problem of handling one of the nontrivial output structures as well.

Splitting modules this way is just another application of the principle of information hiding. D.L. Parnas deserves credit for expressing this principle most clearly (**Par72**). Each module is responsible for the detailed knowledge of one (and preferably just one) data stream. Ideally, everyone else calls upon one module to generate data for that stream, and upon a companion module to consume data from that stream. Information about the structure of the stream is shared between these two modules, but

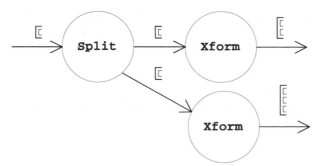

Figure 10.5 *Resolving the structure clash of Figure 10.4.*

hidden from the rest of the universe. That way, changes in the structure of the stream can safely be effected by changing just the producer and consumer modules. Nothing else should be perturbed by the change.

The price you pay for working with more tractable modules, of course, is that you have more of them. You must be sure that, given your implementation of data streams and modules, you do not lose too much performance for the elegance you gain. So lets talk about implementations for awhile. Systems analysts have learned to deal as much as possible in drawings with neat circles connected by arrows. This is the most abstract way of representing the flow of data and the transformations that must occur upon that data to get the job done. You have maximum freedom to understand and refine the fundamental data flow at this abstract level.

The job of the systems analyst can be summarized in four steps:

- Determine the *current physical* data flow in the system under study. Draw a physical data-flow diagram, showing paper flow, phone lines, and all other ways that communicate data.

- Determine the *current logical* data flow. Redraw the physical data-flow diagram as abstract data streams and transforms.

- Determine the *desired logical* data flow. Alter the current logical data-flow diagram to simplify communications, add new functions, resolve structure clashes, etc.

- Determine the *desired physical* data flow of the improved system. Draw a new physical data-flow diagram, showing implementation decisions for the desired data-flow diagram.

We tend to take for granted that the result of a systems analysis will be a computer program (or suite of programs) that performs all of the functions identified in the analysis. A good analyst will keep in mind that there are many ways to implement parts of a system that are better handled outside the computer. (A very good analyst will keep open the possibility that the *entire system* might be better handled outside the computer.)

Here, for instance, are a few ways to implement a data stream:

- arguments to a function call, or the return value from a function call
- data written in a globally accessible location
- data read from or written to a disk file
- data passed along a pipeline
- data read from a serial communications link, or a network
- a truck full of magnetic tapes
- a (voice) telephone call
- a letter, sent once a month
- a standard form filled out and pasted to the outside of a crate
- a few words shouted over a partition

Similarly, you can implement a data transform in many ways:

- a main routine
- a subroutine
- a program in a pipeline
- a separate microprocessor connected via a data link
- a cam
- a human being
- a trained seal

To stretch your imagination a bit, try drawing a hydrocarbon-flow diagram of a 1970 VW Beetle. Identify all the different kinds of logic used to turn gasoline into kinetic energy and exhaust. Some of the transforms are mechanical, some fluid logic, some electrical, and some chemical. Who knows, you may find a better implementation for your IBM 3270.

Back to computers. Even if you confine your attention to data-flow diagrams implemented entirely as single programs, you have much more freedom than you may realize. The data-flow approach tells you to allocate one function for each transform in the data-flow diagram. It also tells you to communicate data as much as possible via arguments to the functions and values returned by calling functions. Most important of all, it tells you that the backbone of your program is its data flow. The hierarchy of functions you contrive to implement your program must have the same connectedness as the original data-flow diagram.

This raises an interesting issue. What you start out with is a bunch of circles connected by arrows. These circles sprawl across a two-dimensional sheet of paper. (More complex systems may require arrows to cross over each other, or layered data-flow diagrams, so even two dimensions may not be enough to represent the data flow.) Your job is to map this network onto a tree of functions. A tree has only one root, the main routine that controls everything. To do the job, you must either introduce yet another

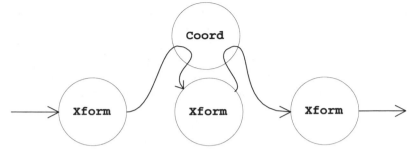

Figure 10.6 *Data flow with added coordinator transform.*

module whose sole purpose is to coordinate all of the data transforms as subfunctions, or exalt one of the transforms above all the others. It would be nice to have some guidelines in choosing among the alternatives.

Introducing a coordinator at the top is generally the least desirable approach. What you are doing in effect is writing an additional data transform on your data-flow diagram, then looping all of the arrows through that single transform, as shown in Figure 10.6. You then appoint the new transform as the top function in the hierarchy. That violates all sorts of design principles, not the least of which is information hiding.

On the other hand, this is exactly what the UNIX operating system does for you when you write a pipeline. The shell parses the command-line description of the pipeline, sets up all of the data streams, and starts each data transform going as a separate program. All data streams loop through the UNIX resident, which calls upon each of the data transforms to resume its activities when it can make additional progress. This wins, in many cases, because UNIX doesn't know any of the internal structures passing through the pipelines that it is administering. Each looks like a simple stream of characters being administered by a standard central service.

If this implementation of data streams has acceptable performance, and if the connectedness of the data-flow diagram can be modeled by the simple bits of plumbing provided by UNIX, then you can arrive at a quick solution. Many a program has been lashed together in this fashion long enough to tune its specification and prove its worth, before investing in more expensive C code. Many a production system in use today is still implemented in terms of UNIX shell scripts that build pipelines, because the solution is maintainable and has performance that is quite good enough.

But let's return to the construction of a single computer program from a data-flow diagram. To build a tree of modules, you need to pick one of them and place it at the top of the tree. You would like to have some guidance in picking the module that goes at the top. You would also like to have some guidance in deciding how to hang the remaining modules off the one at the top — in short, a design method.

The design method that addresses this problem is not outside-in design. What outside-in design does for you is to show you how to break complex modules up into simpler modules, so that each module is easier to implement. It also leads to modules that better specialize in the important business of information hiding. Given a data-flow diagram, you apply outside-in design repeatedly until all of your modules can be structured by left-to-right or right-to-left design. How to organize all of the (now more numerous) modules into a function-call hierarchy is the topic of the next essay, on top-down design. (See **Essay 11: Who's the Boss?**)

To get some sense of the impact of hierarchical organization on the implementation of each module, meditate upon the following simple problem. Let us say you need to implement the function that performs the rightmost data transform in Figure 10.3. It takes as input a repetition of atoms and produces groups of atoms as output. To be more concrete, consider the earlier problem of consuming words of text and producing justified lines. Try writing the control structure for this module as:

- an input module you call to get justified lines of text
- a control module that gets words from a subfunction and delivers justified lines to another subfunction
- an output module you call with single words, that calls a subfunction whenever it completes a justified line

For extra credit, you can try the same exercise with the cluster of data transforms shown in Figure 10.5.

To give credit where it is due, I should point out that what I call outside-in design was pioneered by J.D. Warnier (**War74, War78**). More recently, Michael Jackson (**Jac75, Jac83**) and Ken Orr (**Orr77**) have separately written quite a bit on various aspects of this approach to designing computer programs. What is known as the Jackson Design Methodology is largely outside-in design. Those sketchy little data structures I write on the data flow diagrams are handled in much greater detail as Warnier-Orr Diagrams. Data-flow analysis has seen many contributions from Chris Gane, Trish Sarson, and Ed Yourdon, among others (**G&S77, Y&C79, W&M85, H&P87, Y&C89**).

Indeed, this essay comes closest, of all that I have written so far, to the mainstream of programming-design methods. With the next essay, I jump right into the middle of the mainstream, with both feet. □

Afterword: This essay hovers somewhere between the trivial and the profound. I wanted to emphasize that programmers resolve structure clashes almost intuitively. At the same time, I wanted to show the central role the clash resolution plays in the sophisticated discipline of data-structured design. All of these approaches start coming together now. And clash resolution is right in the middle.

11 Who's the Boss?

METHOD: Top-down design.

DESCRIPTION: Top-down design focuses on the decomposition of a program into a hierarchy of modules. It can be viewed as a process of stepwise refinement, from the most general to the specific. Or it can be viewed as a technique for mapping a data-flow network into a hierarchy of modules. The name derives from the convention of drawing hierarchical decompositions of functions with the most general modules (the root of the tree) at the top and the most detailed modules (the leaves) at the bottom.

Mapping data-flow networks is a safe way to evolve a hierarchy of modules, because it offers a number of models for proven solutions based on frequently occurring network topologies.

DOCUMENTATION: A data-flow diagram retains the most information about a modular decomposition. At the procedural level, a structure (or HIPO) chart documents the modules and data interfaces of a hierarchy.

LIMITATIONS: Without a clear understanding of the flow of data, at the appropriate level of abstraction, top-down design offers little guidance and leads to an excess of modules. Recursion can tie knots in a structure chart.

When I discussed bottom-up design several essays earlier (**Essay 4: Finite-State Machines**), I probably annoyed some people by focusing on the construction of finite-state machines. I know that a number of other design methods are generally subsumed under that rubric, but I felt few qualms about using the name for finite-state machines alone.

In this essay, I expect to annoy even more people by discussing top-down design almost purely in terms of data-flow analysis. I know that for many readers top-down design is a blanket term that covers any of several Right Ways to Do Things. It is stepwise refinement, it is prototyping, it is goal-directed programming. I am willing to stipulate that top-down design is indeed all of these things, provided that you are willing to concede that more guidance may be needed to turn an approach into a design method. In my experience, the greatest guidance in elaborating a top-down design comes from an analysis of the flow of data through the program you are trying to build.

The goal of top-down design is to produce a list of all the functions (routines, procedures, subroutines) that are required to perform a set of operations within one computer program. A computer program has one main function that gets control when the program starts up. The main function calls in turn all of the other functions, exchanging data in the form of arguments, function return values, and access to shared global data. So at this level of abstraction the list of functions should be accompanied by:

- a list of the data passed into each function when it is called
- a list of the data passed back from the function when it is called
- a list of the shared global data that may be accessed or modified by the function when it is called
- a brief (often one sentence) description of what each function does
- a list of the functions called in turn by each function

Essentially all of this data can be captured on a diagram called a *structure chart*. IBM popularized a more stylized version of the structure chart as a HIPO (for Hierarchy with Input, Process, and Output) chart. Figure 11.1 shows a small structure chart. Each box represents a function, each large arrow a potential call to that function from another function. Each small arrow is a data item that is read (down arrow) or written (up arrow) by the called function. As you can see, you can pack quite a lot of useful information into a structure chart.

The structure chart is an excellent document for capturing the initial design of a program. You have something concrete that is detailed enough to evaluate, yet abstract enough to keep you out of the mire of implementation details. It is close enough to our everyday experience of writing code that many of us can evaluate the likely success of the coding effort just from the data-flow and function descriptions. There are also a number of criteria for measuring design quality that are applicable only after a structure chart has been generated. (See **Essay 15: Which Tool is Last?**)

The structure chart is also an excellent document to maintain throughout the lifetime of a program. Changes do occur in the number and nature of functions that constitute a program, but such changes are fewer in number than those that leave the structure chart unchanged. The maintenance effort in keeping the structure chart current is well repaid. You have a quick

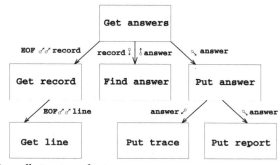

Figure 11.1 *A small structure chart.*

overview of the program, and a handy road map to the functions and data that are likely to be affected by a given change. If the structure chart for a program is at all nontrivial, it is well worth generating and keeping alive.

So how do you go about making this marvelous document? The easiest way is to write the program, get it working, then document what you did. That puts the structure chart in the same category as, say, a cross reference of all identifiers defined in your program. It helps with the maintenance, but not with the design. If you want to generate a structure chart as part of the design creation and evaulation process, however, you need a bit more guidance.

The HIPO approach is one attempt at giving added guidance. It tells you to write the main function box at the top of the page. You then describe its function the same way you would describe the overall function of the program. It could be, "produce graphs." Or, "update database from transactions." Or, "perform Fourier analysis on spectra." You then identify three subfunctions that:

- obtain input, at the appropriate level of abstraction
- process the input to produce output
- deliver the output

For each of these subfunctions, you then apply the same paradigm. For input functions, you ask yourself what three subfunctions are appropriate to obtain (somewhat less refined) input, do the process, and generate the (refined) output. For output functions, you ask yourself what three subfunctions will result in the production of somewhat more refined output. And for process functions, you're on your own.

Eventually you should get to a level where input/output can be performed in terms of the input/output services of the programming language you are using. Similarly, all processing can be performed in terms of statements in the language or calls to standard library functions. In real life, you probably discover the need for a few common subfunctions along the way. You stop what you're doing and go specify them. This is a way of bringing the bottom up to meet you, as it were, while you're mostly progressing top down. Nothing to be ashamed of, everybody does it.

Also, in real life, you shouldn't be too religious about decomposing each module into three subfunctions, for input, process, and output. Often one or two of these subfunctions becomes trivial long before you get to the bottom-most module for the third. If you find yourself making up silly little functions just to keep the hierarchy balanced, then you've fallen into the HIPO trap. As we shall see, there is no particular virtue in having structure charts that are symmetric. There are more fundamental forces at work in shaping the hierarchy of a program.

There's a more important limitation of this approach to top-down design, as I have said before. (See **Essay 1: Which Tool is Best?**) It's easy to get lost on the way down. If the problem is small, you can usually succeed — but then the design method doesn't help all that much. If the problem is familiar, you can also succeed — but then you are primarily imitating a past design. What you need for big-league problems is a set of guidelines that:

- let you make small problems out of big ones
- let you identify familiar problems within unfamiliar ones
- let you organize the smaller pieces into a coherent whole

This is where data-flow analysis moves to the fore in top-down design. With this approach, you first develop a data-flow diagram for the problem to be solved. You then derive the structure chart almost mechanically from the data-flow diagram. The hardest part of the design, in fact, is hidden in that word "almost." Of the many structure charts you can derive from a given data flow, you need some guidance for determining which is best.

A data-flow diagram is nonprocedural. It deals with the connectedness of the problem, in terms of the data transformations that must occur, without committing to any particular hierarchical decomposition into functions. It is a natural by-product of the analysis phase, before program packaging decisions come into play. It is often easier for civilians to understand a data-flow diagram, well enough to perform a constructive review, than to understand a procedural description that implements the data flow.

I talked quite a bit about how to refine data-flow diagrams in the previous two essays, on outside-in design. (See **Essay 9: Marrying Data Structures** and **Essay 10: Divorcing Data Structures.**) There I focused on breaking up the data-flow transforms into subnetworks of simpler transforms. Each simpler transform can be implemented with a single function whose structure is dictated by the structure of the data streams flowing in and out of the transform. You should always apply outside-in design repeatedly to a data-flow diagram, until you can make no further improvements. Only then do you begin top-down design.

In the previous essay, I stopped just short of showing how to turn data-flow diagrams into structure charts. Now you are ready to learn the great secret. All you do is grab the data-flow diagram by one bubble and shake it hard. The result, every time, is a structure chart that you can implement, that does the job, and that has the minimum connectedness required by the problem to be solved.

Figure 11.2 shows a typical data-flow diagram that can result from data-flow analysis, plus the application of outside-in design. The double arrow indicates the module (labeled **C**) I chose as the grabbing point. With a flick of the wrist, Figure 11.3 results. Outside-in design assures that each box in the structure chart performs just one function. Moreover, that

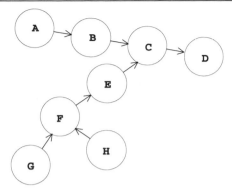

Figure 11.2 *A typical data-flow diagram.*

function can be implemented by code whose structure captures the structure of the data flowing in and out (as arguments or calls to subfunctions). Data-flow analysis assures that all necessary data sharing is present, and no more. This is not just a top-down design, it is probably a good one.

𝕴 haven't told the whole story, of course. I gave no justification for my choice of bubbles to grab in Figure 11.2. The one I picked (labeled **C**) gave a nice looking structure chart, but who is to say that it is the best? I could have picked the bubble below and to the left of my actual choice (labeled **E**), or the one below that (labeled **F**). Indeed I have seen programs based on those choices, and they work.

I could even have picked one of the ones out on the fringes, and I could make any of them work as well. Figure 11.4 shows the structure chart you get if you choose the fringe module at the lower left of the diagram (labeled **G**). Such modules are seldom chosen in real life to serve as the main function of a program hierarchy, but people equally seldom explore why that is so.

Believe it or not, you can truly pick up a data-flow diagram by any of its bubbles, shake it out, and write a program that works from the resultant structure chart. What you find, however, is that some of the structure charts

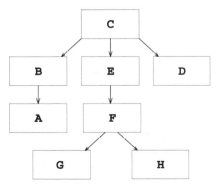

Figure 11.3 *A structure chart from Figure 11.2.*

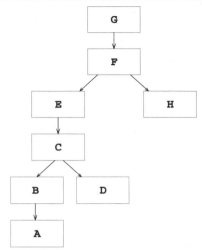

Figure 11.4 *Yet another structure chart from Figure 11.2.*

require more exotic coding than others, to get the data to appear in the right place at the right time.

Data-flow diagrams with merge points, like the two in Figure 11.2, cause one set of problems. Merges are reasonably well understood, but still easy to get wrong. Most people automatically make a single merge point the main function of a program, and with good reason as it turns out. Data-flow diagrams with loops in them are often even more troublesome, for you have data that both merges and diverges at different points in the diagram. Designers usually fall back on various ad hoc structures to implement such data flows, and they often introduce an excess of data coupling between modules as a result.

So it turns out that all of the bubbles in a data-flow diagram are equally valid candidates for serving as the main function of a program hierarchy. But, just like the pigs and the other animals in George Orwell's *Animal Farm*, some are more equal than others. The data-flow diagram is great for showing what data must flow to what modules to get the job done. What the data-flow diagram doesn't tell you is how to coordinate the flow of data between modules. That's where you have to get procedural. And it is the procedural criteria, in the end, that determine who should be the boss.

All sorts of hairy issues can crop up when you try to get the coordination right in a hierarchy. I just touched on some of them in conjunction with merge points and loops in data-flow diagrams. Most of the everyday issues, however, are really quite pedestrian. They have nothing to do with fancy connectedness. Rather, they arise out of the very modules we write all the time to resolve structure clashes, to buffer or unbuffer data.

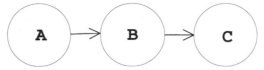

Figure 11.5 *A simple data-flow diagram.*

In the previous essay, I asked you to consider the effect on a module of making it variously an input function, a main function, or an output function. Figure 11.5 shows a very simple data flow diagram that could force you to confront such effects. Depending upon which of the three bubbles you choose as the boss module, the central module (labeled **B**) can occur in any of three positions in the resulting hierarchy. Figure 11.6 shows all three possibilities.

Let's assume that **B**'s role in life is to gather up several records from **A**, assemble them into a combined datum, and deliver a stream of such combined data to **C**. If **B** is an input module, then **C** calls it every time it needs another combined datum. **B** calls in turn upon **A** repeatedly until it has assembled a complete record, then returns control to **C** with the combined datum as the function return value.

If **B** is the main module, it is built around a loop. While there are more input records obtainable from **A**, the main module assembles some of them into a combined datum, and calls **C** to dispose of the combined datum. Finally, if **B** is an output module, it is called by **A** every time **A** has constructed a record. **B** must maintain enough private memory to hold a combined datum, with notes detailing the state of that combined datum. **B** adds the newest record to the combined datum, calls **C** if the combined datum is complete, then updates its private memory so that it knows where to pick up the next time it is called. **B** then returns control to **A**.

Of the three implementations, the last is probably the most ornate. You can't avoid having private memory when **B** is an output module. You should know by now that having private memory incurs a maintenance cost that had better pay for itself by decreasing complexity somewhere in the design. If there is an alternate hierarchy that doesn't need private memory, it should be favored.

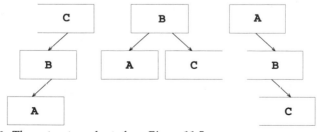

Figure 11.6 *Three structure charts from Figure 11.5.*

By this criterion, the implementation that has **B** as the main function is probably the least complex. (It may lead to higher cost for the other modules, but we'll get to that in a moment.) The implementation that has **B** as an input module can be equally as simple, provided there are no lookahead issues in recognizing the end of a group of records that constitutes a combined datum.

If you must lookahead, then you need some form of push-back as well. That means that either **A** or **B** must have private memory to the tune of one input record, plus state information, to assist the input parse. So once again, **B** is the least complex if it is the main function.

You should not be surprised to learn that *all* modules are least complex when implemented as main functions. That is one of the reasons why UNIX-style pipelines are often so cheap to code and maintain. Each module gets to be the boss of its own little data transformation, and the operating system solves most of the coordination problems in a standard way. But if you're bent on implementing a data-flow diagram as a single hierarchy of modules (a single program), then only one module can be the boss.

That's not as bad as it sounds. As this little example shows, **B** is almost as simple when it is written as an input module. And it is not all that bad as an output module. Chances are the other modules in the data-flow diagram have different problems. You should be able to guess the properties of a module that unpacks records, for instance, rather than packing them as **B** does. An unpacker has to have private memory as an input module, is simple as a main function, and is equally simple as an output module. None of the implementations are all that hard to write or to maintain.

So the seat of the pants rule for picking the best bubble to grab is really quite straightforward — locate the one that has the most complex structure and make it the boss. Chances are, one module stands out from the others in this regard. And chances are, all the others can be implemented reasonably well wherever they fall on the hierarchy.

You will find that this straightforward rule usually selects modules somewhere near the center of a data-flow diagram. The fringe modules are usually the easiest to simplify by outside-in design, so they present the fewest problems by the time you get to top-down design.

Several major schools of software design are covered by the approach I've outlined in this essay and the one before. Each uses a different vocabulary, and each devotes considerable attention to details I have just touched on fleetingly here. I plan to spell out the parallels with other schools, and some of those details, in the essay that follows. (See **Essay 12: By Any Other Name**.) □

$\mathcal{A}$fterword: I developed the grab-and-shake approach many years ago, while I was teaching seminars at Yourdon inc. I taught it to several other seminar instructors who have gone on to write any number of books. Nevertheless, I have never seen the approach captured in print outside these essays. Larry Constantine is the first person I know to use data flow as a guide to constructing structure charts. The detailed analysis of module complexity as a function of position in the chart is my small addition.

12 By Any Other Name

In the previous essay, I discussed how you can use data-flow diagrams to guide you when doing top-down design. (See **Essay 11: Who's the Boss?**) The goal of top-down design is to produce a structure chart, documenting the modules you need and how they call each other. Your basic approach is to grab the data-flow diagram by one bubble and shake it hard. The result is always a structure chart that implements the data flow with a minimum of modules and data interchange.

What is harder to minimize is the complexity of each module. If a data transform maps to any module except the main, or topmost, module, it may have to retain private memory between calls. It's not so bad if that private memory is mostly remembered data, such as a partially consumed buffer or a partially complete output screen. It can be much worse if that private memory contains nontrivial state information. You are then in the business of writing a program with multiple program counters, each implemented in a different way.

In this essay, I want to explore further the methods for picking a good top and for living with the consequences. Along the way, I will show how these methods relate to an assortment of design disciplines that have been put forth in the past. My goal is to show you how each of the older design disciplines is successful in dealing with certain classes of problems. I also want to show you how the older disciplines all hang together, in terms of the various design methods I have been talking about so far.

One of the commonest program structures encountered in commercial programming is the *transaction center*. At a transaction center, input data is divided into a variety of classes, each of which is handled by separate code. If you have to maintain a specialized data base, for instance, you may well conceive a single program that performs all data-base accesses. The program reads a series of transactions, each of which contains a command plus any necessary additional data. At the very least, you need commands to create, delete, and read items in the data base. You may also want others. The transactions differ considerably in effect, but all result in (possible) changes in the data base and (possible) additions to the output report.

How do you design a transaction-centered program? First you recognize that the data-flow diagram has a familiar shape. Figure 12.1 shows a data-flow diagram with an obvious transaction center. Transactions are distilled from the input, then divided into a number of separate streams.

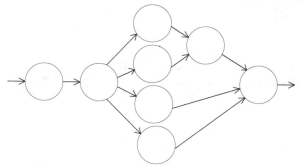

Figure 12.1 *Data-flow diagram with a transaction center.*

Each of these streams performs a series of distinct transformations, but all results are merged to produce a common output.

𝕴f you grab the data-flow diagram by the bubble that separates the transactions, then you get the classic transform-centered structure chart shown in Figure 12.2. The main module obtains transactions and fans out control to one of a group of subfunctions to perform each transaction. These call in turn upon a small group of common action functions. All data-base operations, for instance, can be implemented in terms of atomic functions that insert, delete, and read items. The net result is that the structure chart fans in at the bottom to just those functions that define the interface to the data base, or produce the output report.

Yourdon and Constantine discuss transaction centers at length in their book *Structured Design* (**Y&C79, Y&C89**). They refer back to an even older technique with the acronym SAPTAD. I always forget what the SAP stands for, but the TAD reminds you to address in turn all the Transactions, their Actions, and the resultant Details. If the most interesting part of your program is a transaction center, then SAPTAD tells you how to elaborate the design.

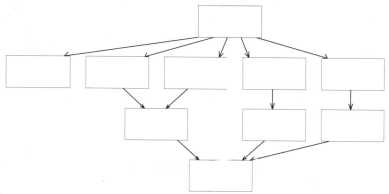

Figure 12.2 *Structure chart for the transaction center in Figure 12.1.*

A transaction center is at its best when it encapsulates information. If you provide a complete set of operations for accessing your data base, for instance, then no other program need know the internal structure of the data base. No other program *should* know the internal structure, in fact. Otherwise, you have greater maintenance problems when you (inevitably) alter the structure of the data base at some future time.

A transaction center is less useful if the commands are a hodgepodge, or if there is no information to hide. Back in the days of batch programming, and in the early days of time-sharing, there was a strong tendency to write large, monolithic programs. The mind set was that it costs so much super-structure to build any program, and it costs so much to start a program running, that you need to get your money's worth. Many programs became transaction centers just to handle all the myriad alternatives you might want to handle in conjunction with the specific business of the program.

Now that we have better support for reusable modules, it's easier to write a suite of small programs that share common access modules for a given data base. And now that we have user-cordial, if not user-friendly, operating systems, it's easier to run a program to do just one transaction and then exit. That's not to say that transaction centers are a thing of the past, but they do seem to be more wisely employed these days.

Now let's look at an operation called *program inversion*. In the previous essay, I talked at some length about how to implement a data transform when it appears in different places in the structure chart. It is easiest to make a data transform into a main module. You can directly apply:

- right-to-left design (**Essay 3: Generating Data**),
- left-to-right design (**Essay 5: Recognizing Input**)
- outside-in design (**Essay 9: Marrying Data Structures** and **Essay 10: Divorcing Data Structures**)

It is also always possible to make a data transform into either an input or an output module. To do so, however, you have to modify the straightforward structure of the module as main module. That's not always easy.

Let's look at the simplest case first. A generic data transform looks like:

```
WHILE (more_input)
    get(input)
    transform(input, output)
    put(output)
```

That's how it reads as a main module. If it appears on the input leg of the structure chart, however, you must alter it to look like:

```
get_transformed()
    get(input)
    transform(input, output)
    RETURN (output)
```

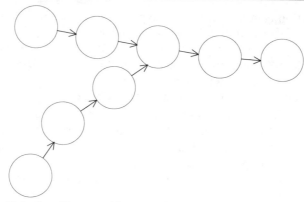

Figure 12.3 *Data-flow diagram with a central merge.*

The main module becomes a function that returns a generated output datum. Wherever you had to output a datum in the main module, you replace the output statement with a **RETURN** statement that returns the latest generated value.

On the other hand, if the module appears on the output leg of the structure chart, you must alter it to look like:

```
put_transformed(input)
    transform(input, output)
    put(output)
```

The main module becomes a function whose argument is an input datum. Wherever you had to obtain more data in the main module, you return control to the caller.

Looks simple, no? Then let's try a more difficult case. A variation of the transaction center is the merging central transform, where two or more data streams must be merged to produce a stream that is further transformed. Figure 12.3 shows a data-flow diagram with a merging central transform. On more than one occasion I have described the classic master-file update, where you merge a sorted stream of transactions with a sorted sequential file of master records. You then do one of three things:

- If no transaction matches a master record, you copy the master record unchanged.
- If no master record matches a transaction, you create a new master record from the transaction (or generate an error report if the transaction does not call for a record to be created).
- If a transaction matches a master record, you apply the transaction to produce an updated master record (which may be the same as the original record if the transaction is merely an inquiry).

```
read(T)
read(M)
WHILE (more_T AND more_M)
    IF (T.key < M.key)
        update(T, NULL)
        read(T)
    ELSE IF (T.key = M.key)
        update(T, M)
        read(T)
    ELSE   {M.key < T.key}
        update(NULL, M)
        read(M)
WHILE (more_T)
    update(T, NULL)
    read(T)
WHILE (more_M)
    update(NULL, M)
    read(M)
update(NULL, NULL)
```

Figure 12.4 *Pseudo code for a merge main function.*

Figure 12.4 shows the pseudo code for a main module that does the merge. The actual update is performed by the function **update**, which accepts a **NULL** argument in place of either the transaction record or the master record. When both arguments are **NULL**, **update** knows to drain any buffered output, since no additional input remains. Note that when a transaction matches a master record a new master record is not immediately obtained. This supports the (very reasonable) possibility that multiple transactions may be applied to the same master record. Writing the master record too soon is an all too common bug.

ow that we know how to do a merge as a main module, let's look at another form. If we decide to put the merge on the input leg of the structure chart, then we must alter the control flow along the lines of the simpler example above. Every time the main module calls **update** to output something, the input function must return to the caller. Every time the input function is called again, it must pick up where it left off. The result is certainly messier than the simple example, but it can be done.

There is even a fairly straightforward, if inelegant, way to do it. You should recognize this as a module that must retain its own program counter, to keep track of where it is in the combined data structure that it must track. In other words, you must turn the module into a finite-state machine. I covered how to do that under bottom-up design. (See **Essay 4: Finite-State Machines**.)

```
get_pair()
   STATIC pc := 0

   GOTO pc
0:
   read(T)
   read(M)
   WHILE (more_T AND more_M)
      IF (T.key < M.key)
         pc := 1
         RETURN (T, NULL)
1:
         read(T)
      ELSE IF (T.key = M.key)
         pc := 2
         RETURN (T, M)
2:
         read(T)
      ELSE   {M.key < T.key}
         pc := 3
         RETURN (NULL, M)
3:
         read(M)
   WHILE (more_T)
      pc := 4
      RETURN (T, NULL)
4:
      read(T)
   WHILE (more_M)
      pc := 5
      RETURN (NULL, M)
5:
      read(M)
   pc := 6
6:
   RETURN (NULL, NULL)
```

Figure 12.5 *Pseudo code for a merge output function.*

ssuming you can program in a language sufficiently tolerant to permit
GOTOs into blocks (C is such a language, sadly), you can simply write
code similar to Figure 12.5. The **STATIC** variable **pc** is set to its assigned
value at program startup. Afterward its current value is remembered
between calls to the function.

The last label is not misplaced, by the way. Why do you think it has been
moved up?

```
get_pair()
   STATIC state := NEED_TM

   IF (state = NEED_TM)
      read(T)
      read(M)
   ELSE IF (state = NEED_T)
      read(T)
   ELSE IF (state = NEED_M)
      read(M)
   {ELSE
      nothing to read}
   IF (more_T AND more_M)
      IF (T.key < M.key)
         state := NEED_T
         RETURN (T, NULL)
      ELSE IF (T.key = M.key)
         state := NEED_T
         RETURN (T, M)
      ELSE   {M.key < T.key}
         state := NEED_M
         RETURN (NULL, M)
   ELSE IF (more_T)
      state := NEED_T
      RETURN (T, NULL)
   ELSE IF (more_M)
      state := NEED_M
      RETURN (NULL, M)
   ELSE
      state := DONE
      RETURN (NULL, NULL)
```

Figure 12.6 *Revised pseudo code for a merge output function.*

This pseudo code is moderately ugly, as I warned, but it works. With a bit more effort, you can make the more readable transformation shown in Figure 12.6.

I won't show you how the merge looks as an output module. You might try your hand at it, to see if you understand what's going on here. The point I want to demonstrate is that the merge gets noticeably messier when you make it other than a main module. There is a straightforward, almost mechanical, way to transform the module, but the result is less readable. There are creative ways to transform the module and keep it readable, but creativity requires work without guidance.

Most people who preach the use of data-flow diagrams as design aids tell you simply that a merge point should be at the top of the hierarchy you derive. You grab the data-flow diagram by the transform center and shake it out. Perhaps now you can see why this is almost always a good idea. You can also see when it might not be a good idea:

- If your data-flow diagram has more than one transform center, you must either make one the boss or introduce an artificial coordinator.
- If your data-flow diagram has a data transform which is even more difficult to structure than the transform center, you may be better off making that the main function.

Michael Jackson talks quite a bit about this process of restructuring modules that cannot be main modules (**Jac75**, **Jac83**). He calls the restructuring *program inversion*, which is reasonably descriptive. He also believes strongly in what I call right-to-left design, or letting your output data structure your program. Curiously enough, he pays less attention to left-to-right design, or letting your input parse structure your program. But he also teaches quite a bit about marrying data structures and resolving structure clashes, the yin and yang of outside-in design. Perhaps now you can see why Jackson's approach is often successful.

Jackson's approach is, of course, not fruitful for some design problems. That's okay, because no method is always relevant. There is, however, a class of relevant programs where program inversion breaks down. So far, the most complicated problem I've shown requires that only a single module be inverted. That is, an input module has all of its output statements in the module proper, so these can simply be turned into **RETURN** statements. Equally, an output module has all of its input statements in the module proper, so these can simply be turned into **RETURN** statements.

But what happens if the transform is sufficiently complex that several modules participate in the input (or output)? If an input module calls a submodule to generate part of the output, you can't just have that submodule return control to the original caller. You must also provide some way to have the next call from on high get control back to the point in the submodule where you left off work. I'm not saying you can't write it — the biggest problem with programming is that you can do anything. You just end up with something that's hard to write, read, and maintain. That's all.

The machinery for handling this particular control problem has been invented, several times in fact. What you need is the ability to write *coroutines*. A program structured into coroutines has multiple control stacks, one for each thread of control. When one coroutine (co)calls another, your program stacks the current state of the caller just as on a normal call. But it then switches to the saved control stack of the callee, so that it can pick up right where it left off, after its last cocall. With coroutines, you can indeed return to a caller from within a submodule, then get control back at that point on the next cocall.

Only a few modern languages support coroutines, and none of the widely used ones do. Ada has machinery that supports coroutines, after a fashion, but then Ada has a little bit of everything. There are serious problems in implementing coroutines, problems that can only be solved by consuming program space for multiple stacks and/or execution time for switching more elaborate contexts. It is little wonder that languages supporting coroutines have seldom proved competitive with simpler ones.

An operating system that supports multiple processes, however, has almost all the machinery needed to implement coroutines. At the risk of being tiresome, I point out yet again that the UNIX pipeline mechanism is just the added bit you need to finish the job. All the popular UNIX shells (command interpreters) make it easy for you to type a line of text that starts up two or more autonomous processes linked together by their standard data streams. If you can afford the time overhead of communicating via pipelines, UNIX hides the complexity for you.

You can even implement coroutines on single-thread systems, if the total program need not be interactive — if you don't need to obtain the first output before the last input is read. Even a system as simple as MS-DOS lets you specify pipelines just like UNIX does. The only difference is that MS-DOS runs the first program in the pipeline to completion, saving its output in a temporary file on disk. It then runs the next program in line, feeding it input from the temporary file. After the second program terminates, the temporary file is quietly discarded. If you can afford the pipeline overhead, and the extra demands on disk space, and the non-interactive behavior, you've got coroutines.

In summary, there is nothing new about using data-flow diagrams to guide top-down design. What may be new is the realization that top-down design needs some guiding principle to make it a design method, rather than just a good idea. There is nothing new about choosing the central transform in a data flow, when picking the top module for a structure chart. What is new is a more detailed understanding of the forces that favor choosing the central transform. And there is nothing new in the technology for inverting modules that cannot be at the top of the structure chart. What is new is a realization that inversion has several degrees of difficulty:

- It can be so easy that you hardly notice that you're doing it.
- It can be hard enough to require a mechanical transformation to a finite-state machine.
- It can be so hard that only coroutines do the job properly.

I end by emphasizing that top-down design is one of the most powerful approaches to designing programs that I know. Despite all my disparaging remarks, I use it frequently and encourage you to do the same. Just remember that there are two difficulties in practicing top-down design:

- finding the right top
- working your way to the bottom

Otherwise, it's a snap. □

Afterword: This essay is my attempt to tie together the major approaches to designing computer software — stepwise refinement, structured design, and data-structured design. To me, it is obvious that all are more alike than different. The most interesting parts of the problem are what determine the best approach. I just wish it were more obvious to others who preach the gospel of disciplined software design.

13 Searching

METHOD: Order-to-chaos design.

DESCRIPTION: Order-to-chaos design deals with the problem of looking up an arbitrary sequence of items in an ordered collection of data. The result of each such search may be to insert, delete, replace, or simply read all data from the collection which satisfies some predicate. The predicate is generally applied to the lookup item and the data in the collection. It may also involve the position of the data. The name derives from the assumption that lookup data is less ordered than the collection.

Numerous techniques exist for ordering and searching collections of data, with various tradeoffs among access time, ease of update, and storage space. Common to all techniques, however, is the need to encapsulate all accesses in a minimal set of cooperating modules.

DOCUMENTATION: Data-linkage diagrams show the paths along which a collection can be searched. Data-structure diagrams document the composition of the data. Module specifications describe access functions.

LIMITATIONS: If you guess wrong about the pattern of accesses, you may impose inappropriate structure on the data. Encapsulating a data collection with a trivial pattern of accesses may introduce higher coupling than necessary.

everal essays back, I discussed sorting at some length. (See **Essay 8: Order Out of Chaos.**) I talked about why sorting falls into a special category of programming. I discussed a few approaches to sorting. And I gave my usual sermon about why you should avoid writing your own sorting code. The one thing I failed to do was discuss why you might want to sort in the first place.

Several people wrote letters when that essay appeared in print. I botched some arithmetic on combinatorics, and I got a test wrong way 'round in an algorithm. (All such errors are corrected in this collection.) That was plenty of fuel for programmers who delight in catching their brethren out on matters of verifiable fact. (What can I say? I've been known to indulge in the same pastime myself.) There was not a single complaint, however, that I failed to justify the need for sorting as part of the discussion.

I have become sensitized to issues of this nature lately, in my role as president of a software company selling into a marketplace that has become increasingly competitive. As I have learned more and more about marketing, I have learned to distinguish between features and benefits.

What is a feature? It is a gadget, a refinement, a characteristic of the product that the vendor chose to add. The vendor added it for any of several reasons:

- It was fun to do.
- It seemed like a good idea.
- The need for it was obvious, at least to the vendor.

The description of features makes for all the fine print you read in ads written by techies to clutter (and pay for) computer publications.

What is a benefit? It is a gadget, a refinement, a characteristic of the product that the buyer wants. The buyer wants it for any of several reasons:

- It is fun to have.
- It seems like a good idea.
- The need for it is obvious, at least to the buyer.

The absence of clear benefits in ads and product literature makes for all those annoying reviews that clutter (and justify) computer publications.

𝕴 trust the distinction between features and benefits is now clear. If the vendor puts it in the product, it is just a feature. Only if the buyer knows that it is there, knows what it is for, and knows why it might make life better — only then is it a benefit.

If you paint the product orange, that is a feature. If the buyer knows that painting the product orange reduces eyestrain and improves worker productivity, that is a benefit. If the product fits in a shoe box, that is a feature. If the buyer knows that your smaller product will cut shipping costs and the need for warehouse space, that is a benefit. You get the drift.

It is amazing how easy it is to lose track of the distinction, however. Once you become immersed in your trade, you associate more and more with people who share your peculiar culture and vocabulary. Features automatically turn into benefits. You forget that a significant portion of your customer base has only casual contact with your area of expertise, and they want to keep it that way. That's how you end up with ad copy that reads something like, "The doors are blue, with green diagonal stripes, and you know what that means!"

When you buy a vacuum cleaner, for example, you probably don't want to research the current state of the art of suction engineering. You may try to dig up a recent *Consumer Reports* article, but that's about the limit of interest for the average civilian. Mostly, you want some assurance that the model you pick:

- has the tradeoff you want between economy and quality
- is appropriately priced
- meets or exceeds industry averages for performance

That's about it.

What does all this have to do with software in general, and with sorting in particular? Plenty. If you are a serious programmer, one who is programming on purpose, then you are in a competitive marketplace. Time is your principal asset, and complexity is your bane. You don't waste time adding complexity to the products you make just because it's fun, or it seems like a good idea. There must be an obvious, measurable benefit to everything you do.

Sherlock Holmes went one step farther — he refused even to learn about anything that was not of obvious application to his trade. He once told Watson that whether the Earth revolved about the sun, or the sun about the Earth, was of no interest to him. He chose not to clutter his mind with facts that did not help him solve cases. I don't know whether Arthur Conan Doyle actually espoused this approach to life, or whether he described this incident just to shed further light upon the fascinating character of Holmes. It certainly shows a professional dedication that is extremely benefits oriented.

You can learn all sorts of things about sorting, and you can apply them at the least excuse to every program you write. But unless you have a good reason for every time you reorder data, you are focusing on the feature instead of the benefit. And when you think about it, there is only one reason you ever have for sorting data — to make it easier to search for something later.

If you're never going to look at the data again, there is no need to sort it. And if you don't care what order you consider the data in future, there is no need to sort it. Only when you need to revisit the data — and you perceive a need to reduce the cost of access for certain patterns of queries — only then does sorting pay off.

Sorting, therefore, is a prelude to searching. Or contrariwise, searching is an epilogue to sorting. You need to consider both operations together to make proper design decisions about either. And, of course, you must be sure there is some measurable benefit to any searches you do, as well as any sorts.

So, let's assume from here on that you have a legitimate need to search a collection of data from time to time. This imposes at least three obvious constraints on how you represent the data:

- You have to know how to find it all.
- You have to know when you've found what you're looking for.
- You have to be able to do what you want to do with the data once you've found it.

You must satisfy these three constraints irrespective of any performance goals. Otherwise you can't do the job at all.

To see how the constraints interact, consider a simple situation. Say you have a list of several hundred customers. If you want to access it from a computer program, you must put it in machine-readable form. The easiest way is to use a text editor to produce a sequential text file. You need some sort of delimiter to separate customer records. For small enough records you can type one-line records and use the line terminator as a delimiter. To look up a customer by name, say, you need a program that reads the customer file one line at a time, knows which part of the line contains the customer's name, and does a comparison between the search name and the customer's name.

It is then easy enough to scan the file from front to back to get the goods on any particular customer. Adding customers is easy, provided you are content to add them at the end of the file. Deleting customers is tiresome. You must either rewrite the file to percolate down records after the deletion, or have some way of marking certain records as dead. If you choose the latter course, you must plan to squeeze out the dead records, from time to time, before wasted disk space and longer access times become a problem. But these are performance issues. The point is, you can do everything you have to do with this simple organization.

You could also allocate a fixed amount of space for each customer record, large enough to hold the largest record. That would make it easier to delete records. You just move the last record into the hole and shorten the file by one record. If you perform a lot of deletions, it might make sense to trade off extra disk space this way for a simpler deletion algorithm. It would also open the door for various speedups, since it is much easier to locate and rearrange fixed-length records than varying-length ones. Once again, however, we are talking performance. Switching from varying-length to fixed-length records is not necessary to do the job, just (possibly) to do it better.

To know whether you can do the job better, you have to know what the job is. As I stated earlier, you must know how to locate existing data (or decide where to put new data), and you must be able to operate on the data. Locating data involves examining data until you have satisfied some predicate. Two possibilities are:

- You are looking for a particular datum, part of whose contents (called a search key) matches a pattern provided as part of the search.

- You are looking for an extremum, that datum whose search key is smallest (or largest) among the relevant data in the collection.

Operations on a collection of data can generally be characterized as:

insertions — you have new data to add

deletions — you wish to discard existing data

replacements — you wish to insert new data in place of existing data

reads — you wish to examine existing data

All data collections are read from time to time. (Otherwise, why bother keeping the data?). Once initially constructed, however, different data collections may require different combinations of insertions, deletions, and replacements, including none at all. You may speed up insertions and reads, for instance, by switching to a data organization that is miserable at deletions. This could lead to simpler code if deletions never occur, or to better overall performance if deletions are rare. Or you may know that you will only delete the smallest datum, at any given time, so you can choose an organization that favors this operation at the cost of others.

The point is, you need certain knowledge that one or more of these operations will never occur before you can safely omit the code that supports the operation. And you need some reliable conjecture about the pattern of possible operations before you can make performance tradeoffs with any wisdom. Once you have that reliable conjecture, you will find that the literature abounds with methods for organizing data. (I just caught up on reading the last two years' worth of *Communications of the ACM*. You'd be astonished at all the things you can do with partially ordered heaps, lists, and trees.) You can tradeoff access time against insert time, or insert time against delete time, or enhance any group of properties at the cost of the remainder.

About the only thing you cannot do is spit in the eye of information theory. If you need to determine the smallest of a set of N records, for example, then some operation is going to take time proportional (at least) to $N*log(N)$. You can sort at insert time, and read in constant time. Or you can insert in constant time, and sort when you read. Or you can divide the work between the two. Sooner or later, however, you pay the piper.

It's kind of like pushing down on the bedsprings that stick up from an old mattress. Given enough hands and feet, you can hold down all the bedsprings you want to. The more you want to hold down, however, the more force you have to bring to bear. And various conservation laws ensure that some unattended bedsprings will eventually pop up, by way of compensation.

The best thing to try first, in fact, is the solution that requires you to push on no bedsprings at all. My personal list of addresses and telephone numbers, for example, is implemented just the way I described the customer list earlier. It is a text file of about 200 lines, which I keep under the Idris operating system, which in turn runs under MS-DOS on my Compaq Deskpro 386. The command:

```
Phone <pattern>
```

is actually a shell script, which in turn uses the utility **grep** (well known to users of UNIX) to select and display records that match **<pattern>**.

Unfortunately, there are some conceptual flaws with this approach. Two important ones are:

- **grep** doesn't know the structure of a record, so it occasionally gives "false positives" by matching a key intended as a surname to some other field, such as a street name.
- The average access time is proportional to the number, and size, of records in the file.

The first flaw is easy to live with, since I use **Phone** only as an interactive filter, never to provide uninspected input to another program. The second is equally innocuous, since **grep** is more than fast enough to scan 200 names on my older IBM PC/XT. On a Desqpro 386, it has growth capacity to spare. So even though **Phone**:

- invokes a shell
- which reads a script
- which invokes **grep**
- which performs pattern matches on every line it reads
- which calls for data blocks to be read by Idris
- which calls for data blocks to be read by MS-DOS

the script is fast enough to do the job. By making use of considerable canned complexity, and by overwhelming a bad algorithm by brute force, I avoid having to add complexity to this little collection of data.

If I ever acquire enough friends and business contacts to saturate this simple system, only then will I reconsider how it is organized, accessed, and maintained. At that point, I will probably break down and acquire one of the excellent data-base management systems now available for personal computers. That introduces lots of implementation complexity, and gives me better performance than I probably need. But it once again sidesteps any complexity that I personally would have to create and maintain.

Whatever I do, you can be sure that I will confine any knowledge of the structure of the data collection to a minimum number of modules. That way, I can change representations as the mood strikes me, knowing each time that the code I must alter is minimal and clearly bounded. Searching, because it involves so few primitive operations, is a prime candidate for information hiding.

There are several important principles at work here:

- An algorithm with poor asymptotic performance often out performs a better one, for small amounts of data, because it is simpler and has less overhead.
- The crossover point between a simple algorithm and a more sophisticated one may well involve far more data than you need to handle.

- An algorithm with poor asymptotic performance is often good enough even in regions where it is outclassed by a better one.
- An algorithm that is already implemented is much cheaper to employ than one you have to write code for.
- Complexity is an asset if someone else is responsible for creating and maintaining it, a liability if you have to create and maintain it yourself.
- No algorithm is so wonderful that it is not a candidate for future change, so you may as well contain the damage that will cause right from the start.

Sometimes, of course, you can't avoid pushing on the odd bedspring. One of my favorite examples comes from the external sort that Brian Kernighan and I presented in Chapter 4 of *Software Tools* and *Software Tools in Pascal* (**K&P76**, **K&P81**). The problem is to merge **N** files, each of which is in sort, to produce a single output file. One way to do it is:

- Read a record from each file, and tag each record with the file it came from and whether it is end-of-file.
- Sort the records to identify the smallest one, sorting end-of-file higher than all other records.
- If the smallest record is end-of-file, then stop, else put it out.
- Replace the smallest record with another record from the same file, as in the first step, then go back to the second step.

This seems to be the irreducible minimum to do the job. You need an internal data structure that can represent **N** records, each with a file tag and an end-of-file indicator. You need to be able to sort the data structure, find the smallest record, and replace the smallest record.

But wait. Once the first set of records is in sort, all you ever do to perturb the order is replace the smallest record. You should be able to reorder the new set with far less effort than a full blown sort would expend.

Indeed, this is the case. You can organize the records into a *heap*, which is a balanced binary tree each of whose nodes is less than any of the records in its subtrees. Nothing is promised about the relative ordering of the subtrees of a node. Figure 13.1 shows a small heap, with six items.

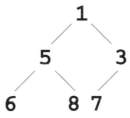

Figure 13.1 *A small heap.*

One of the desirable properties of a heap is that you can represent it neatly as an array (or as an array of pointers), assuming that its size is reasonably bounded. In this case:

- If **(2*i+1 < N)** then **heap[2*i+1]** is the root of the left subtree of **heap[i]**.
- If **(2*i+2 < N)** then **heap[2*i+2]** is the root of the right subtree of **heap[i]**.

So the heap shown in Figure 13.1 can be represented by the array:

    1 5 3 6 8 7

*A*nother desirable property of a heap is that you can find its smallest entry in constant time — it is at the root of the heap, or **heap[0]** in the array representation. Still another desirable property of a heap is that it is easy to reestablish its integrity after you replace its smallest entry:

```
i := 0
WHILE (heap[i] has subnodes
    AND either is smaller than heap[i])
    <swap heap[i] with the smaller subnode>
    <set i to the index of that subnode>
```

Since a heap with N items can have no more than $ceil(log_2(N))$ levels, the heap is re-established in time proportional to $log(N)$.

For example, say the first record, with value 1, is replaced by a record with value 9 in the heap of Figure 13.1. The array evolves through the stages:

    9 5 3 6 8 7
    3 5 9 6 8 7
    3 5 7 6 8 9

and it is once again properly ordered.

All that remains to complete the merge is to write code that will build the heap in the first place. It is easy enough to write the code that builds a heap, but even that can be avoided. All you have to do is fill the array with a record from each file, then sort it with a conventional sort. It so happens that an array that is completely in sort also satisfies the ordering requirements of a heap, and then some. Sure, it's overkill, but a sort utility already needs an internal sort function, and it's an operation you only do once per external sort.

Using a general sort function to build a heap nicely satisfied several of the principles I outlined above:

- It recycles canned complexity from somewhere else.
- It is a suboptimal algorithm used in an arena where it is good enough.
- It is overkill with an insignificant time penalty.

Now *that's* programming on purpose. □

fterword: My original plan in writing this essay was to show half a dozen clever ways to optimize accesses to a data base. Then I realized that I would be replicating a common intellectual trap. It's easy to get caught up in the features of algorithms without a thought to their true benefits. Thus, I decided to focus on why you might want to sort or search in the first place. I'd still like to show all those clever ways to access a data base, however.

14 Synchronization

METHOD: Hard-to-easy design.

DESCRIPTION: Hard-to-easy design focuses on safe cooperation among sequential processes. When independent agents endeavor to share data, synchronization is required to prevent race conditions and data corruption. When synchronization is poorly implemented, lapses and deadlock may occur. The name derives from the observation that synchronization is hard to get right, and best dealt with early on in the design process.

The primitives used to effect synchronization vary widely among different systems. Often, safe operation can be achieved only at the cost of overall system performance. Thus, synchronization requirements should be kept to a bare minimum.

DOCUMENTATION: Timing diagrams show the critical transitions that assure proper synchronization.

LIMITATIONS: You cannot always separate synchronization from background computation, particularly in real-time systems with sophisticated feedback. It is hard to avoid all possibility of deadlock in a complex system.

Once upon a time, computers were fairly simple. When your program wanted to read a card, it issued a **READ** instruction to the card reader, then proceeded to twiddle its thumbs. Nothing else happened while the picker separated the bottom card from the deck in the input hopper, the feed mechanism dragged the card past the read heads, and the stacker dropped it neatly in the output hopper. A very large fraction of a second after your program issued the **READ**, it moved on to the instruction following, full secure in the knowledge that the data from the card was copied into the designated buffer in memory.

Even in those unhurried times, programmers lamented the milliseconds wasted while bits of matter were coaxed into motion by various peripheral devices. So computer designers developed the *input/output channel,* a moderately stupid processor that knew just enough to supervise the transfer of data to or from a peripheral device. The central processing unit, or CPU, issued its **READ** request to the I/O channel, then went on about its business. When a transfer was complete, the I/O channel jerked the chain of the CPU by sending an *interrupt.* Your program could then note, in some fashion, that the transfer was complete and liberate the buffer for other uses.

At that point, the systems programmers made a mistake. They assumed that the control of overlapped I/O should be given into the hands of every

127

applications programmer. Suddenly, us FORTRAN programmers had to deal with new I/O options of frightening power. We had to specify event flags, to be set on successful completion of a transfer. We had to specify handlers to be entered on transfer error, on end-of-file, possibly even on successful completion. Most important, we had to learn to keep our cotton-picking hands off the I/O buffer until each transfer was complete.

If we didn't take on all this baggage, we suffered the stigma of Using the Computer Inefficiently (a social faux pas roughly equivalent to turning down a date with Brooke Shields). If we did, we were forced through a programmed-learning course in how to synchronize (nominally) cooperating sequential processes — with our application program providing the only courseware, and with no textbook for the course.

Eventually, the systems programmers took pity on us. They provided *spoolers* that used overlapped I/O to read ahead on card readers and write behind on printers and punches. Us wimps went back to writing programs that waited for each transfer to complete before proceeding, secure in the knowledge that most transfers involved simply a memory-to-memory buffer copy. Computer utilization was up and we were socially in a state of grace. Only the macho types persisted in coding overlapped I/O.

Just as that flap was settling down, another one emerged. Computers were being equipped with multiple terminals. Several people could sit and simultaneously negotiate with separate programs, all running on the same machine. Conversational time-sharing was invented, as a way of keeping everybody seated waiting for better response time instead of milling about the ready room waiting for spooled printer output. To make all this happen, systems programmers developed operating systems that could juggle multiple processes, or separate threads of control. (You can think of a process as a program that thinks it has a whole machine to itself, only the machine is a virtual machine that is just a subset of the real underlying hardware.)

At that point, the systems programmers made another mistake. They assumed that the ability to run multiple processes should be given into the hands of every applications programmer. Suddenly, us PL/I programmers had to deal with tasking options of frightening power. We had to specify event flags, to be set on successful completion of a subtask. We had to specify handlers to be entered on tasking errors. Most important, we had to learn to keep our cotton-picking hands off any storage used by another task until its usage was assuredly complete.

There was never quite the stigma associated with not using tasking that clung to not using overlapped I/O. What was worse was that it *looked* easy to use. Nowhere in the PL/I manual was there the least hint that tasks were hard to specify safely, or expensive to start up, or next to impossible to debug. Once again, the tuition we paid did not entitle us to a textbook.

Eventually, the systems programmers again took pity on us. They provided command interpreters that start and administer multiple processes on our behalf. They gave us processes that run on separate virtual machines and communicate only through the operating system. They invented pipelines and FIFO files for sequential data passing. They invented record locking for shared access to files. By eliminating most of our freedoms, they set us free. Only the macho types persist in writing unstructured multi-thread programs.

I have just described what is generally regarded as the first three generations of computers. (The distinction between generations has since dissolved in an acid sea of marketing hype.) These are:

first generation — a single thread of control in a private memory

second generation — overlapped I/O, used to improve the performance of a single thread of control in a private memory

third generation — multi-processing, used to support largely independent processes, each a single thread of control in a private memory

The point I am belaboring is that overlapping multiple operations that work toward a common goal is a great way to improve the performance of a computer system, but it is very hard to control. Synchronizing logic is the hardest code in the world to design, debug, and tune. Once you get it right, you stuff it in a black box, hold it at arm's length, and treat it as just another peripheral connected to your first-generation virtual machine. Nearly all the code you write should be written for a single-thread environment. Otherwise, you'll pay a stiff premium on everything you write.

This is why I call writing synchronizing code hard-to-easy design. If you have to do it, do it first, before the problem gets cluttered up with more mundane details. Identify where cooperating sequential processes absolutely must share information in order to cooperate, and keep that interface to a bare minimum. Then encapsulate that interface, both data and synchronizing functions, and document clearly the rules for using it. Finally, debug the synchronization code alone, as best you can, before you go on.

This may seem to you to be an unseemly fear of synchronization code. All I can say is that, of all the designing and debugging I have ever done, none has come close to presenting the same level of difficulty. You develop a feel, with a complex program, about how much you can perturb it with changes before it gets out of control. I have found that an operating system kernel the same size as a language translator can safely tolerate only about a fifth as many changes, before it breaks, as the translator. And when an operating system breaks on you, it quickly turns into an uncooperative lump that is inert at best, insanely malicious at worst.

If you are now sufficiently frightened, let's look at what it takes to synchronize multiple activities. Once again, I will recapitulate (more or less) the evolution of multi-thread systems from the simplest to the most ambitious. Say you need to design a microprocessor-based system that gathers data from a number of sources. The easiest way to do it is to provide a simple hardware interface, for each of these sources, that holds onto the most recent datum until the computer can do something with it.

From time to time, your program examines a status bit in the control registers for each of the hardware interfaces. If the bit is set, your program knows that a datum is present. It reads the datum in and clears the control bit, to inform the hardware interface that the datum has been delivered. This matters only if your program fails to collect a datum before the next one comes along. At that point, the hardware interface suffers a *data overrun*, which it should report to your program, via yet another status bit. Your program is obliged to do something sensible in the presence of data overruns. The control code looks something like:

```
FOREVER
    IF (data ready)
        item := <input data>
        <clear data ready>
        process(item)
    IF (data overrun)
        <evince concern>
        <clear overrun>
```

This is a popular method for interfacing to computers, particularly microprocessor-based systems where cost and complexity must be kept to a minimum. It requires a style of programming called *polling*. The design centers around an infinite loop that polls each device in turn, looking for more work to do. Synchronization is simple, because the control program gathers data only when it is ready for it, then disposes of it completely before taking on the next task.

Provided that system performance is high enough to keep data overruns to a minimum, and provided that such data overruns are not cataclysmic, the solution has admirable simplicity. Notice how much it resembles a first-generation computer performing non-overlapped reads and writes.

Polling breaks down, however, when data from one or more sources is bursty. There may be enough system capacity to handle all data presented in any given five-second interval, say, but a single device may sometimes need attention fifty times per second to avoid data overruns. You can extend the capacity of polling systems to handle such cases in two ways.

- You can build hardware that queues up data from bursty sources, to tide the interface over until the control program can service it.

- You can rewrite the control program as two (or more) control loops, servicing bursty devices in a fast loop and performing longer computations in a slower loop.

The first approach raises hardware costs, the second raises software complexity. Both can help you delay the day when you must take on even more hardware costs and software complexity, however.

A more robust solution to the problem of bursty data is to let its hardware interface generate an interrupt whenever it needs attention. When an interrupt occurs, the computer saves whatever information is needed to restore the state of the current activity, then transfers control to a piece of software called an *interrupt handler*. A properly designed handler services the attention request from the hardware interface, to the point where the interface no longer feels motivated to generate an interrupt, then terminates by restoring the state of the current activity. Whatever process was running is oblivious to its interruption.

What an interrupt does, in effect, is move the synchronization point for a device further inboard from its hardware interface. You can bring the full power of the CPU to bear on buffering data to be transferred, and reduce the need for special-purpose hardware in the interface. What an interrupt costs you is an added demand on the processing power of the CPU, and added software complexity in dealing with the necessary synchronization. Say you are using an interrupt handler to buffer data into the array **in_data**, of size **N**. You maintain a circular buffer with an index and a count:

```
IF (N <= in_count)
    <data overrun>
ELSE
    i := in_next + in_count
    IF (N <= i)
        i := i - N
    in_data[i] := <input>
    in_count := in_count + 1
```

To process this data, you need a background loop something like:

```
FOREVER
    WHILE (in_count = 0)
        <wait>
    item := in_data[in_next]
    in_next := in_next + 1
    IF (N <= in_next)
        in_next := 0
    in_count := in_count - 1
    <process item>
```

For output devices, you write very similar code. The difference is that the background loop must wait when the output buffer is full, and the interrupt occurs when more data can be output. (It is slightly more complex to restart an idle output device, but I will gloss over that for now.)

But there is a nasty problem with the loop shown above. Whenever an interrupt is serviced, the handler assumes that certain relationships obtain among the control variables for the buffer:

- There are **in_count** items unconsumed in the buffer. **in_count** may be zero, but it never exceeds **N**.
- The next item to process, if present, is at **in_data[in_next]**. **in_next** may be zero, but it never equals or exceeds **N**.

$\mathscr{S}$ince interrupts may generally occur between any consecutive instructions (or even in the middle of a complex instruction on some machines), the interrupt handler may be entered at any point in the background loop that is processing the input data. The handler may even be entered part way through one of the statements, since high-level language statements frequently translate to several machine instructions. You can identify any number of places where the necessary relationships do not hold among the control variables. Mucking with them at these places leads to numerous flavors of mayhem.

The relationships do obtain at the beginning of the loop body. When execution gets to the end of the loop body the relationships are restored. The problem is that, in between, the operations needed to update the state of the buffer are not *atomic*. Such a sequence of code is called a *critical region*.

In a critical region, shared data is in an inconsistent state. Because the data is shared by agents that are proceeding asynchronously, it is never safe for more than one of the agents to be in a critical region, for a given collection of data, at the same time. There is a similar region of code within the interrupt handler, but it will always be executed atomically (unless there is a higher-priority interrupt that mucks with the same variables and can pre-empt execution).

What you must do with a critical region is find a way to make it atomic. There are two fundamental approaches:

- You must ensure somehow that no other concerned agents can execute while your program is executing a critical region.
- You must add additional control variables, that can be updated atomically, to inform other agents when the critical region is busy. These agents must then elect to stay out of the critical region while it is busy.

Here, the other agent is the interrupt handler. You must dismiss the second approach out of hand, in this case, because an interrupt handler has very little latitude. It must dispose of its latest input and return control with a minimum of fuss, for two reasons:

- The more an interrupt handler fusses around, the more likely it will cause a data overrun while it is preoccupied.
- Any constructive fussing it might do will just involve additional synchronization problems somewhere else.

So what you do to keep interrupt handlers from interrupting critical regions is to keep them from executing. Computers can generally *disable* or *inhibit* interrupts until a more opportune time, at which point the interrupts are *enabled* or *permitted*. The need to interrupt is not forgotten, its servicing is merely postponed. The background loop must be rewritten as:

```
FOREVER
    WHILE (in_count = 0)
        wait
    <disable interrupt>
    item := in_data[in_next]
    in_next := in_next + 1
    IF (N <= in_next)
        in_next := 0
    in_count := in_count - 1
    <enable interrupt>
    <process item>
```

This code still assumes that **in_count** can be compared against zero with an operation that either is atomic or fails safe. If you have any doubt about that, then you must make the protected region even larger. Naturally, it is important to keep to a minimum the time interrupts are disabled, just as it is important to keep to a minimum the time interrupt handlers are active. Poor design or coding here can increase data overruns dramatically.

You should notice once more, by the way, how much this program resembles a first-generation computer performing non-overlapped reads and writes. Most of the loop body, in the example above, is just our old friend the **READ** statement in a new disguise.

Those of you who know something about the technology of synchronization may have noticed something odd. I have made it this far without discussing gates, semaphores, queues, monitors, or any of the other higher-level concepts that fill many of the books and papers written about synchronization. There are several reasons for this:

- I wanted to pound home the historical lesson that first-generation computing, isolated from synchronization issues, is the safest model for most program logic.
- I wanted to illustrate the nuts-and-bolts issues that even the simplest computer interface must address.
- Most of the literature on synchronization deals with cooperating sequential processes that have more or less identical stature, whereas interrupts and background loops are intrinsically asymmetric.

There's lots more to talk about on this thorny topic. What happens when you have multiple interrupts to contend with, for instance? The best code for handling this case is not always a simple generalization of the single-interrupt case illustrated here. Nor are your worries over once you have protected all your critical regions and made all your accesses to shared data atomic. That just gets you in the game. You then have to make sure that the sequences of synchronized operations you specify make sense, and never lead to deadlock. Let's consider a few more complex cases.

The situation gets far more interesting once you introduce two or more data streams. Each may have separate needs for buffering, whether aided by interrupts or simply driven by polling. The heart of the problem lies in that innocent looking **wait** that must occur in any background loop, for when the program must wait for further interrupt activity before it can proceed. It may be that no progress can be made on processing this particular stream, but what about the others?

You can extend the background loop to handle more than one data stream. Indeed, that is simply the polling program I introduced earlier. Should the background processing for one data stream reach a point where it must wait for more interrupt activity, the background loop does not wait. Instead, it looks for some other activity on which it can make progress. Each data stream has an associated set of data that memorizes the state of processing for that stream. The polling loop must continually put down one set of data, for a data stream on which no more progress can currently be made, and pick up another set of data, for a data stream that can make additional progress.

If the processing of data for one stream generates data for another, however, you can get into some messy situations. The sets of data that characterize the state of each process get intermixed. Or you may need to insure that there is input available from two sources before a computation can proceed. Now you have to hand craft logic that inspects two or more sets of data to determine the state of another set of data. Sure, you can code your way out of it, but at considerable cost in complexity. It is even harder to code your way out of a situation where higher-priority data pre-empts normal processing. Try that in a simple polling loop and see what you get.

What you find yourself doing in these cases is simulating multiple processors on a single processor, by writing a growing pile of ad hoc code. What you find yourself wishing for in these cases is a budget that lets you dedicate a separate microcomputer CPU to camp on each data stream. Each of these CPUs is easy to code — its background control loop is just like the example above for synchronizing with a single interrupt.

CPUs responsible for input from the outside world buffer the input as need be, process it as far as possible, then write out the results. Other CPUs wait for data written by these CPUs, until they have enough data to do something, process their data as far as possible, then in turn write out their results. Still other CPUs responsible for real-world output read these results as they become available and buffer the output as need be for physical devices.

The ideal result, from the standpoint of logical simplicity at least, is thus a network of CPUs, connected in a way that resembles as closely as possible the data flow being modeled. Each data transformer has its own dedicated CPU, executing a program modeled after the structure of the data that it must transform. If this sounds remarkably like what I have been preaching in earlier essays, that is hardly an accident. (See **Essay 2: Writing Predicates**, **Essay 10: Divorcing Data Structures**, and **Essay 11: Who's the Boss?**) The only ingredient I have added here is the need to have multiple CPUs, each camping on data streams that must be synchronized.

Once you arrive at this viewpoint, you are well on your way to being a successful designer of multi-process systems. You see, most designers are pretty good at identifying the data flow and synchronization points between data transforms. Those drawings that you make on the backs of napkins or on conference-room blackboards are often excellent representations of the system to be modeled. What you must learn to do is postpone implementation decisions until *after* you have partitioned the logical data flow into separate processes. Whether you assign each process to a separate CPU, or assign all processes to one CPU, or perform some division in between is a packaging issue. Packaging is done best when it follows logical design, rather than being intertwined with that phase.

You must keep firmly in mind, during the logical partitioning phase, that the purpose of each process (CPU) is to advance the cause of one data stream. It must synchronize with other agents at its inputs and outputs, but behave like a first-generation computer in between. If any CPU can block on a `wait` statement while there is progress to be made in a different part of its processing, replace it with two CPUs. If any CPU has no `wait` statements, you should merge its code with one of its neighbors and eliminate it. There may be other compelling reasons for keeping the code as a separate process, but synchronization is not one of those reasons.

Now for the packaging choices. You can implement each CPU in one of two general ways:

- as a separate process under control of a multi-processing executive or operating system
- as a separate CPU

It was not so long ago that the second alternative was too expensive even to consider. Now, the cost barrier is often not the extra CPUs and supporting chips, but the extra complexity in synchronizing data among multiple processors operating in parallel. You must have shared memory, or a sufficiently high bandwidth channel, to communicate the data. You must also have a carefully designed signaling protocol between the processors to synchronize the communication. The payoff for this extra complexity generally occurs in one of three areas:

increased performance — because multiple processors can be acting in parallel

easier growth — because you can tack on additional processors to get increased parallelism

increased reliability — because critical processors can keep operating when others die

If you can't make a case that you will get at least one of these benefits, you should rethink your desire to introduce multiple processors into your design.

As a general rule, in fact, the first alternative is preferred whenever the host processor has enough performance to do the job. The processes in a multi-processing system can be connected in myriad ways, and the connections can be changed on a whim. That's far less true of a system of CPUs wired together in some ad hoc fashion to do a given job. At work here is the Principle of Latest Binding: The longer you can defer binding decisions into a program, the more flexible it will be and the cheaper it will be to modify and to maintain.

So let's say that you want to simulate having two or more CPUs by multiplexing just one. What are your choices? In the simplest case, all but one of the processes (CPUs) is kicked into activity by the occurrence of a hardware interrupt. This is the situation I discussed earlier in this essay. All you have to do is make proper use of the interrupt-vectoring capabilities of your host CPU. The interrupt-driven processes become interrupt handlers, and the remaining process executes in the background, when no interrupts are active. The only hard part is writing the functions that enqueue and dequeue data between interrupt handlers and the background process, as I discussed earlier in this essay. There is no need for any fancier software.

It is within the capabilities of many programmers to write adequate enqueue and dequeue functions for a given host CPU. The risks of writing and debugging your own synchronizing code are probably well repaid by the reassurance that you know every byte of code that goes into the product. A program like this that has no support software is called *freestanding*. From microwave ovens to traffic lights, the world is rapidly filling up with embedded microcomputers executing freestanding programs.

The world is also filling up with more ambitious applications involving embedded computers. As soon as your application involves two or more processes that run on an equal footing, not driven by interrupts, then you need software that manages multiple logical processes.

That software must be integrated with the enqueue and dequeue functions that you need to pass data between processes. The proper behavior when a process attempts to take data from an empty queue is for that process to block (on the **wait** statement within the dequeue function) and for another process that can make progress to resume operation. And the proper behavior when a process adds data to an empty queue is to unblock at least one process that was waiting for data from that queue. Synchronization of data transfer between processes is intimately entwined with scheduling those processes.

It is not easy to write good software to manage multiple processes. Aside from the problems of getting it right and robust, about which I have harangued at length, there is the problem of getting adequate performance. The simplest approach to writing a process scheduler is to manage a set of process queues. One queue contains all of the processes that have not blocked waiting for something. Another queue contains all of the processes waiting for a time interval to expire. Still other queues contain all of the processes waiting for a data queue to become non-empty (or non-full). The simplest way to manage these queues is to scan them from beginning to end every time you need to locate, insert, or delete a process on the queue.

If you perform all queue operations with linear scans, then your enqueue and dequeue functions can take time proportional to the number of processes in your runtime system. Once you get above about a dozen processes, you will probably observe unacceptably long delays in clearing interrupts, because the interrupts may have to be active (and blind) or disabled (and blinded by a single event) while you're scanning all those queues. When I discussed searching in an earlier essay, I pointed out that there are numerous tradeoffs between insert, delete, and lookup times for collections of data. (See **Essay 13: Chaos Out of Order**.) The better performance you insist on, however, the greater sophistication you must invest in how you organize your data.

So whether or not you think it is within your capabilities to write a set of functions that cooperate to manage multiple processes, you should resist the temptation to do so. If you need multi-processing capability, then for heaven's sake buy it. There are oodles of packages available off the shelf these days that can provide the services you need correctly, with decent performance, and without too much extra baggage that you'd rather not have. The best known are the *real time executives* such as VRTX, pSOS, and MTOS, to name just a few. If you can find it in your heart, and budget, to build your embedded application upon a commercial executive, then you will be ahead of the game when it comes to writing, debugging, and maintaining your application-specific code.

I have talked glibly so far about the use of queues for passing data between logical processes. Indeed, this is an adequate mechanism that does the job. There are variations on the data queue, however, that are often better adapted to specific uses. Some of these are:

gates — one-bit messages used to provide mutual exclusion, so that only one of a set of processes enters a critical region at a given time

semaphores — queues of one-bit messages used to provide finite but multiple accesses to a limited resource

signals — one-bit messages that simply report the occurrence of some situation

events — one-bit messages that are often grouped to make it easy to test for various logical groups of events, such as `event1 AND event2` or `event1 OR event2`.

messages — multi-byte data, often kept in a shared data area, whose ownership is passed by sending a fixed-size token

monitors — sets of related functions whose activations are synchronized so that only one function is active at a given time.

rendezvous — statements within cooperating processes that provide for a synchronized function call, with argument passing, within one process from another

Before you start writing letters, I acknowledge that each of these terms has a variety of meanings. I have intentionally made only an arm-waving characterization of each. The only point I wish to make here is that there are any number of different mechanisms that have been implemented to provide synchronization between processes. In my experience, no single one of them has the proper balance between sophistication and performance to serve all needs. A nontrivial real-time application may make good use of gates, events, queues, and messages. So long as all of the different mechanisms play together, you should not hesitate to make use of any mix that seems appropriate for your needs.

When you pick your commercial executive, you should make sure that you have all of the features you need, and no more. Perhaps the worst trend in this rapidly growing marketplace is the beefing up of the more successful little executives to take on ever more sophisticated applications. Once you saddle a set of process-control primitives with hardware memory management, general device I/O, structured file I/O, dynamic loading of new processes, and/or interactive background processing, the compelling simplicity of the original product rapidly begins to fade.

When you find yourself needing any of these bolt-on services, that is the time for you to reconsider your support needs in terms of the more full-fledged operating systems. You are generally better off working with a well designed host system that has been scaled down for ROM-based (or small disk-based) operation. The UNIX computational model has now been captured as the vendor-independent IEEE standard called POSIX. A small but growing number of commercial offerings can now give you POSIX conformance with the real-time performance and services that you need for embedded applications.

*a*nd now for the bad news. No matter how clever you are at writing synchronization code, or no matter how judicious you are at picking commercial products, you still have synchronization problems to look out for. Three that spring to mind, in order of increasing seriousness, are load balancing, response prediction, and deadlock prevention.

Once you have partitioned your application into separate processes, and packaged your processes for one or more CPUs, you want to believe that the load will be distributed pretty much as you planned it. Unfortunately, it is well known that programmers are lousy at predicting where their programs will consume most of their execution time. If you guess wrong enough, you may have some serious repackaging to do before you get the performance you need.

What aggravates the problem of balancing loads among processes is:

- It can be difficult to get meaningful performance data in a multi-processing environment.
- It can be difficult to outsmart a complex scheduler once you know the behavior you want.

Both of these points argue for keeping the simplest possible process model, and scheduler, you can get away with.

Predicting response is a similar problem. Your system may be well balanced, and it may have all the performance capacity it needs, yet certain operations may not be happening fast enough. Event-driven schedulers, such as are commonly used in the simple real-time executives, seldom give the kind of response that human beings like when they interact. These schedulers give real-time processes highest priority, as well they should. They treat all other background processes equally, whether they are interactive or compute bound. You need a scheduler designed to juggle priorities in favor of interactive processes to fix this performance problem.

Some schedulers provide for assured response to high-priority events to the extreme that they permit indefinite overtaking of lower-priority operations. As soon as you introduce any place in your multi-process design where one process may unconditionally overtake another, you open the possibility that the overtaken process may be indefinitely starved for attention. The only fix is to juggle priorities by hand until you get the behavior you like.

Indeed, the worst aspect of response prediction is the prediction part. You may observe that you get desirable behavior every time you look, but your customer may demand assurances that the worst-case response has some fixed upper bound. If your application is too complex, you may be able to make such assurances only by deoptimizing the entire system.

The extreme in bad response is when your system never gets around to servicing a request. Usually, this is caused by some form of deadlock, where two or more processes have each tied up resources that another one needs to make progress, and none are willing to release the resources they currently hold. If you think of writing good synchronizing functions as getting the syntax of synchronization correct, then deadlock prevention amounts to getting the semantics correct.

𝕳ere is a concrete example. The Idris operating system, like many a UNIX system, manages disk I/O with a pool of memory-resident buffers, each capable of holding a fixed-size block of disk storage. If your program reads a file, the Idris resident code running on behalf of your process obtains exclusive rights to a buffer, gets the appropriate device handler to read the contents of the file a block at a time into that buffer, and copies the relevant buffer contents to the place specified by your program.

So long as each process requests just one buffer, and so long as no process will block while that buffer is tied up, the system can never be starved for buffers. If all buffers are tied up, eventually some process will progress to the point where the buffer is released, and the waiting process can grab the released buffer.

Unfortunately, there are situations where the Idris resident would love to tie up a buffer on behalf of a process even while it is blocked. There are other situations where the resident simply must have two buffers handy to perform an operation. (There used to be situations where more than two buffers were required, but these were carefully recoded to need only two.) What to do?

The solution lay in maintaining a count of *buffer futures*. Each process that sees a need to tie up more than one buffer requests the right to do so, before asking for even the first buffer of the pair. The buffer futures count is maintained as a semaphore — if too many processes reserve the right to ask for a second buffer, subsequent petitioners block while requesting this right until an adequate supply of excess buffers is available. With this machinery, the Idris resident will not deadlock on insufficient buffers even if there are only two available to the entire system. (And that's a ridiculously small number, given the memory available on computers today).

The point of the example is that having safe primitives for reserving and freeing buffers did not guarantee that the system would never hang up. Running the system with lots of buffers may lower the odds, but still does not guarantee that the system would never hang up. It took careful semantic analysis of the problem, and equally careful coding, to make the Idris resident reliable in this important area.

Lots more can be said on the subject of synchronization than I have covered in this essay. Whole books have been written on the subject. Even so, my personal experience is that this area of design is easily the least understood, and the least structured, of all the areas I have covered so far. Of all that can be said, I feel the simple pragmatic advice I have given here will meet most of your needs. □

fterword: This is another two-part essay combined into one. Even so, I only touched on all the things that I wanted to cover about synchronization. In the end, I opted as usual to focus on the basic concepts and pragmatic advice. Too many books plunge into the intricacies of synchronization logic without ever telling you to keep it small and encapsulated. What the world needs, I believe, is a simple real-time operating system presented as part of an extensive tutorial text. Even then, buying makes better sense than building, just as with sort packages.

15 Which Tool is Last?

When I learned how to ski, many years ago, I did it the hard way. A friend of mine gave me a few lessons, then I went off on my own. I didn't bother to take additional lessons. I didn't go near professional ski schools. All I did was read an assortment of books on skiing, watch other people who skied well, and try to look like them.

I knew how you were supposed to look when you skied properly. Your skis moved in graceful arcs, or in short businesslike hops. You could turn on a dime and stop at a whim. Most important of all, your skis stayed together at all times.

My skis, on the other hand, hopped gracelessly through arcs and made a bad business of hops. I could only stop when I wanted to turn, or turn when I wanted to stop. And my skis, left to their own devices, stabilized at a spacing of about 50 centimeters.

What I concluded, after a season or two of struggle, was that my problems would disappear as soon as I got those skis together. After all, that's how the experts looked. So for the next two seasons, I settled doggedly on a peculiar style of skiing. Every time I made it through a turn and steadied on a new traverse I would look down. If my skis were not together (and they never were), I would drag them together by main force and hold them there. For a few glorious seconds, as I traversed across the slope, I looked good. Or so I thought.

There was a flaw in this approach. My skis were apart because I was (incorrectly) keeping considerable weight on my uphill ski. To drag that ski downslope against my weight, and in defiance of panic signals from my inner ear, took both muscular exertion and a silly kind of courage. Believe me, the muscles you use for pulling your legs together are not among your stronger ones. The result was that by early afternoon my legs were quivering from exhaustion and my adrenals were drained from skiing perpetually on the edge of disaster.

All this just to look good for a few seconds at a time.

Eventually, I despaired of this approach. I focused on skiing in control and on having fun. My skis drifted apart and stayed there. I did not look good. On the other hand, I was skiing all day and getting better. I even signed up for a few ski lessons along the way.

One day, as I was swooping down a slope that was only moderately challenging, I heard a clattering noise. I looked down and saw an amazing sight. My uphill ski, relieved of all weight because I was skiing properly, had slid downhill until it rested against my other ski. I was skiing with my skis together. I looked good.

In that instant, I experienced the thrill of epiphany. It was only a lower-case insight, unaccompanied by angels or complete enlightenment. Nevertheless, it was a blast. The mini Zen lesson that came home to me on that ski slope has spilled over into many areas of my life.

The lesson is: You can know how you're supposed to look when you do it right, and still not know how to do it right. If you try to make yourself just look right, and still not do it right, you will waste a lot of energy. You won't look good, no matter how you feel that you look. If, on the other hand, you do it right, you don't have to worry about how you look. You will look good.

This essay is nominally about computer programming, not skiing. How does the mini Zen lesson apply? As you might guess, the lesson warns us to be careful of software design rules that deal more with appearance than substance. How a program appears in the end is an important indication of whether it was designed properly. But knowing how a program should look does not necessarily guide you through the design process. And focusing on appearance too early in the design process can lead you to waste a lot of effort to no good effect.

Here is a classic example. One of the earliest observations, during the development of modern structured programming, was that large modules are hard to read. If you contemplate a subroutine that sprawls over several pages of listing, you have to work hard to understand it. To see all the places where a local variable is referenced, you may have to flip back and forth through several pages. To locate the target of a GOTO is that much harder. Even if you write perfectly structured code that is always properly indented, you can lose track of the level of indentation whenever you cross a page boundary.

One of the earliest responses to the problem of reading large modules was simply to outlaw them. More than one shop decreed that each function or subroutine must be displayed on a single printed page. If the module exceeded this limit by so much as a line, coding rules demanded that it be recast as two or more modules each of which must fit on a single printed page.

The results were varied:

- Some programmers obeyed both the spirit and the letter of the single-page limitation. With numerous small modules, their programs sometimes suffered a performance penalty from all the extra function calls and returns, but their source code was arguably more readable.

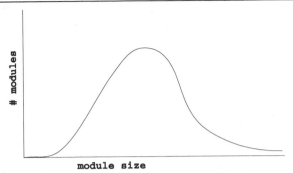

Figure 15.1 *Distribution of module sizes with no size constraints.*

- Some programmers obeyed only the letter of the law. If a module came out too large, they would chop it up arbitrarily into multiple modules, then paste the pieces together with masses of shared data. These projects lost more in readability from bad modularization than they gained from having single page modules.

- Some programmers simply ignored the limitation. They also ignored all of the other rules in the shop guide. There was seldom much rationale for any of the rules to begin with, there was little or no history of success in using them, and there was no indication as to which rules were important and which were not. Besides, nobody got rewarded for enforcing the rules. On the contrary, most programmers knew they would lose big if they focused on following coding rules at the expense of churning out lines of code.

You can usually identify which of these approaches a shop has followed. Just plot a histogram of module sizes for a complete project. If there is no preoccupation with module size, you will get the usual bell-shaped curve that shows a random scatter around some characteristic mean value. Figure 15.1 shows a typical histogram when module size is not an issue.

A religious application of a module-size limit gives a result something like Figure 15.2. Note the hard cutoff at the enforced limit. The total number

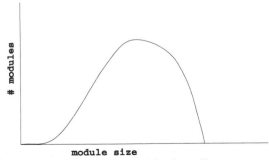

Figure 15.2 *Distribution of module sizes with hard cutoff.*

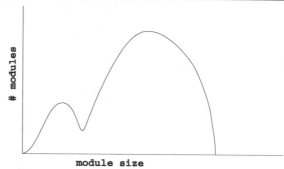

Figure 15.3 *Distribution of module sizes showing chopped-up modules.*

of modules (the area under the curve) is often larger than in Figure 15.1, because extra modules must be introduced from time to time to stay under the enforced size limit.

Figure 15.3 reveals some of the pernicious effect of chopping up modules at arbitrary places. The double peak, one at small module sizes and one close to the hard-cutoff size, warns you that you will not enjoy reading (or maintaining) many of the resulting modules.

Finally, Figure 15.4 shows the effect of an utter contempt for rules about module size. All the good reasons for limiting module size are ignored along with the arbitrary limits. You can be sure that most other rules of good design and coding are also ignored. Lest you think that I have simply created a caricature to illustrate a point, I can testify to having seen projects where the average module size was 5,000 lines of FORTRAN. I have heard of projects where module size ranged up to *one million lines* of code.

There are good reasons for keeping modules small. There are also good reasons why some modules get large. A multi-way **SWITCH** statement, for instance, or a long chain of **ELSE-IF** statements may have to choose one operation to perform from among dozens or even hundreds of alternatives. This is an effective way to encode a classic transaction center. (See **Essay 12: By Any Other Name**.) If each of the operations can be succinctly expressed

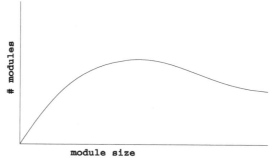

Figure 15.4 *Distribution of module sizes with no size discipline at all.*

within the **SWITCH** statement, it is foolish to incur additional overhead in execution time, code size, and source size by packaging the operations as separate modules. Readability is little compromised by spreading the **SWITCH** module over multiple pages.

Rigid rules about module size do not help you design or code better software. Guidelines about module size can tell you something about how to write modules, but not what modules to write. Evaluation criteria based on the distribution of module sizes, however, can help tell you whether you've done the job right in the end.

Many design rules developed over the last two decades are like the rule about module size. They tell you how a program should probably look if it is done right, but they don't necessarily guide you to the right program. If you apply these rules too early in the design process, at best you are wasting time. It's like painting the boards before you drive in the nails. At worst you are raising obstacles to finding the best solution, or you are homing in on a suboptimal solution.

Don't get me wrong, many of these rules are important. Before you finish any program, you should evaluate it from several different standpoints. You need to judge whether the program is sufficiently simple and robust that you (and others) can convince yourself that it is correct. You need to judge whether the program is sufficiently readable that you (and others) can debug it or enhance it years from now, long after you've forgotten why you did things the way you did. You need to judge whether the program looks enough like successful programs that it is likely also to be successful.

The key phrase here is, "before you finish." Much of my preaching in these essays has been about doing things in the right order. A popular vulgarism among software designers is Attila the Hun's maxim: If you're going to rape, pillage, and burn, be sure to do things in that order. For most of a complex project, you don't even have to know how to get to the end. You just have to know what to do next. (See **Essay 7: Which Tool is Next?**) Rules that talk about the final appearance of a program are generally best downplayed until near the end of a project. They tell you what to do *last*.

When you draw a structure chart, for instance, you can get all sorts of advice about what good structure charts look like:

- A good structure chart is balanced, because the topmost module usually derives from one of the transforms near the center of the data-flow diagram. (See **Essay 11: Who's the Boss?**)

- A good structure chart has no module that calls more than about seven subordinate modules (unless it is a transaction center).

- A good structure chart is narrow at the top, wide in the middle, and narrow again at the bottom, like an Arabic mosque. (See **Essay 1: Which Tool is Best?**)

You can also get silly advice, like:

- Every module should either call no submodules or it should call exactly three submodules (input, process, and output).
- No module should have a single subordinate.
- No module should be called by more than one superordinate module.

I've discussed why I dislike these rules in the earlier essays cited above. Whatever advice you choose to follow, please notice whether it helps you formulate a new design or evaluate an existing one. Save evaluation rules for last.

You can, of course, get some early guidance out of rules that help you evaluate designs. Larry Constantine, the guy who pioneered structured design, laid down some excellent rules that get you on the right track from the start, then help you evaluate your result at the end (**Y&C89**). The two groups of rules that I have found most useful over the years cover what Constantine calls *coupling* and *cohesion*.

Coupling is a qualitative measure of the degree to which two modules interact. The higher the coupling between two modules, the more you have to keep the innards of one in mind when you work on the other. To control complexity by the strategy of divide and conquer, you must keep coupling to a minimum.

One extreme of coupling is the traditional monolithic COBOL program. You declare all your data in one place, the **DATA DIVISION**, so every module can access every piece of data. When you call a module, you have no way to document, much less enforce, just what data the module should access or modify. You have no way to associate temporary variables with just those modules that use them. As a result, the amount of source text that you must inspect before you can make a seemingly local change can be arbitrarily large. COBOL programs have about the highest coupling you can imagine.

Other languages support unstructured sharing of data between modules, even when argument passing and local variables are also provided. Unreconstructed programmers of the old school still tend to use such machinery, rather than work out an economical passing of data on a need-to-know basis. Constantine dubbed accesses to globally shared data *pathological connections,* which is about as negative a term as you can use in polite company. There are times, of course, when you need unstructured sharing. Modules may need to conspire to provide a useful package of services. You trade higher coupling within the package for lower coupling between the package and its customers.

You can avoid pathological connections and still indulge in higher coupling than necessary. How often have you passed an entire record to a function that just accesses one or two fields of the record? Had you written the function to accept just the fields of interest as arguments, you would not have to worry about whether the function inadvertently accesses fields that should be of no concern to it. You could write the function with no knowledge of the record structure, so it is more likely to be reusable in other contexts.

Constantine dubbed accesses to excessive data *stamp coupling*, a term with a curious etymology. Evidently, some early software projects began by making up a rubber stamp that listed all of the variables used in the program. To design a module, you stamped out a copy of the full set of variables, then ticked off the ones you planned to use in this particular module. I suppose you could look on the stamp as a poor man's data dictionary, but as a productivity aid the effort was certainly misplaced. Worst of all, making up a stamp encouraged the practice of gathering unrelated data into a single structure to make what is affectionately known as a "garbage vector."

The subtlest way to raise coupling is by implicit assumption. How often have you written a function that was intended to handle only, say, positive arguments? When some innocent maintainer later calls it with a negative argument, you can disavow responsibility. But the extra maintenance cost in discovering this limitation is still chargeable back to your inadequate design. You can lower coupling by implicit assumption in several ways:

- Eliminate the need for the assumption by writing the function to work properly for all possible inputs, even if it doesn't (yet) need to.
- Enforce the assumption by checking argument values before the function gets in trouble. Better a surprise diagnostic than erratic behavior.
- At the very least, document the function prominently so that future users are less likely to go astray.

If you want to learn more about coupling, read Yourdon and Constantine's *Structured Design* (**Y&C79, Y&C89**). For a different perspective on the same issue, read the classic paper on information hiding by Dave Parnas (**Par72**).

Cohesion is another invaluable concept, both for elaborating designs and evaluating them when you're finished. Cohesion is a qualitative measure of the degree to which a module stays intact as a program evolves through debugging, maintenance, and enhancement. The lower the cohesion of a module, the more likely you will find the need to break it up into multiple modules at a later date. To get the maximum benefit from a modular design, you must keep the cohesiveness of each module as high as possible.

You can get a feel for cohesion by watching groups of people whom you don't know. Stand near an elevator at lunch time, for instance, and note what happens to each collection of people disgorged when the doors open.

Try to guess which people are staying together and which are going their separate ways.

When the doors first open, you might have trouble. The people are packed closely together just by the accident of having gotten on the same elevator at the same time. As the crowd moves outward, however, a natural evolution takes place. People with different destinations move off in different directions. Couples, families, luncheon parties, and the occasional posse stay together. They may disperse a bit and mingle in different combinations (particularly families with energetic children), but you can see the effect of the powerful social forces that keep them bound together.

Similar forces are at work within every computer program. You may be tempted, when writing a program, to make a module out of a pattern of five statements you see occurring in several places within your program. When space is at a premium, it can be hard to resist optimizations of this sort. If this pattern recurs purely by happenstance, however, the module has only *coincidental cohesion*. A change needed to correct the behavior of the module for one use will probably not be suitable for the other uses. You can support the change sensibly only by replicating the module and changing one version. If the module was used in just two or three places, you may soon find you have as many versions as calls. The justification for making a separate module evaporates.

Highly optimizing compilers, by the way, will sometimes create modules with coincidental cohesion. Common-subexpression elimination tries very hard to do just that. You needn't worry about additional maintenance cost, however. The compiler reconsiders what modules to create every time you alter the source text. It doesn't leave dead wood lying about the way us humans do.

At the other extreme of the cohesiveness scale lies the ultimate goal, *functional cohesion*. When you can describe what a module does in a simple, active sentence, then you probably have a highly cohesive module that will stay around. Descriptions such as, "clear update record," or, "compute alternative minimum tax," indicate functional cohesiveness. Descriptions such as, "initialize everything," or, "output update record and clear it," are wanting. Any changes you make to calls on the module should be to make more appropriate use of the function. Any changes you make within the module should be to better implement the functional specification, which should benefit all callers.

Constantine describes several levels of cohesiveness between coincidental and functional. The distinctions are useful in revealing just what forces will eventually dismember the module. They can also educate you about some of the ways you can delude yourself into thinking a module is functional when it is not. Otherwise, the distinctions are unimportant, because you should not settle for less than functional cohesiveness in every module you write. I say this as a person who has often written modules that implement two successive data transforms. Constantine calls this *sequential cohesiveness*, and predicts with frightening accuracy that sooner or later you will be moved to break the module into its two separate functional parts. He's right.

There are other tools in your programmer's tool kit that you should save for last. Among the more important of these are the tools you use for evaluating, and tuning, the performance of your final program. Unlike many programmers, I do not believe that performance should rank first and foremost when you write a computer program. I believe that it should rank last and foremost. Brian Kernighan and I have discussed this topic at length in several other books. (**K&P76, K&P78, K&P81**) □

Afterword: I would write this essay just a little differently were I to do it over today. The current intense interest in object-oriented technologies begs at least some mention here. I chose not to add any such words, however, since they would be mostly negative in this context. Object-oriented design, like all methods, is at its best when it tells you what to do next. And, like all methods, it is at its worst when it merely tells you what you have done wrong. I fear that much of what is currently taught as object-oriented design falls in the second category.

16 A Designer's Bibliography

$\mathcal{A}$ bibliography can serve many purposes. In degenerate form, it is merely a list of references cited explicitly by the author in the running text of a presentation. Various intermediate forms offer you a sampling of other works in the field that you might find of interest, assuming that you still care about the field after having stumbled through the current offering. At its best, a bibliography leads you on a guided tour of a field that you know little about, pointing out the tourist attractions and stimulating interests you barely suspected that you harbored.

You can often tell more about the motivation behind a paper or book from reading the references at the back than the author ever wanted you to discover. As an author, you tend to let your guard down near the end of a project, and the bibliography (or at least its presentation) is usually the last tiresome installment in a saga that took longer than you ever imagined. So like it or not, you leak out subliminal messages, such as:

- "Look, this is really original work. Whatever has gone before is for the historians to document. I have taken a new departure." Accompanied by either no references, or citations only to the author's earlier works.

- "Okay, I've done my homework. I know there are other people out there working in this field, and I've included the standard references so that you know I'm not completely out of touch." Accompanied by about six references, such as the original Ritchie and Thompson article on UNIX in the *Bell System Technical Journal*.

- "You're not going to catch me with an indefensible idea. I've got citations for every sentence not in the passive voice. Let's see if my orals committee can find anything to challenge." Accompanied by 50 to 100 references, mostly obscure. About a third are private communications.

- "All right, my adviser made me spend four months in the library before I could start any real work. I've skimmed every book in the library that has the words *finite* or *automaton* in its title. I may as well get a paper out of all of this busy work." Accompanied by yards of references that look like the output you get from **grep** with a poor search pattern.

- "Isn't archaeology fun? I'll bet nobody knew that Thales of Miletus wrote several offhand remarks that could be construed as observations on the future problems of data processing. My literature searches go farther back than yours ever will." Accompanied by amusing, if useless, references tracing the evolution of an idea through two millennia.

Some bibliographies really help, of course. My favorites are the ones where the author unbends enough to give you a hint about the nature of each reference, and where it fits into the overall scheme of things. My absolute favorites are the ones where the author tells the unvarnished truth about each source, so you know whether to waste your time digging it up and reading it.

What I'd really like, and have yet to see at the back of a paper or book, is an annotated bibliography that crosses over the line into the more subjective world of book reviews. Wouldn't you love to know, for instance, the five most informative books about Markov chains? And what is good and bad about each? Even if the reviewer is opinionated (and all reviewers are, if they're worth anything), and even if you don't always agree with the reviewer (which you should not, if *you* are worth anything), such a guide to a specialized area of technical literature would be invaluable.

A variation of this approach is somewhat more anecdotal. Can you list the ten (or twenty, or thirty) papers and books that really made an impression on you, that you feel taught you something new? What books do you reach for when you need an algorithm, a memory refresher, or an inspiration? Wouldn't it be fun to compare your private list with someone else's, so that you could trade a few gems? Bibliographies could certainly be a lot more interesting, and probably more useful, if the author intentionally revealed some personal background along with the dry facts.

With all that in mind, I present my long-promised bibliography for designers and coders of computer programs. By now you can probably guess that it is idiosyncratic. These are some of the books that made a difference to me when I read them (or in some cases when I helped write them), and that I think might make a difference to you. I accompany each with a few pithy remarks designed to give you a sense of how it can help you in learning more about your craft.

I make no attempt to be historically complete. We all know, for instance, that Bohm and Jacopini wrote an important paper about flow of control (**B&J66**). What they demonstrated lies at the heart of structured programming, because they showed that a small set of control-flow structures is sufficient in an important sense. They weren't exactly talking about structured programming, however. And you don't have to read their paper to practice that important discipline. So I do not suggest that you read their paper simply because it was an important milestone.

I do believe, however, that you should go back and read Dijkstra's original letter to *Communications of the ACM* titled, "Go To Statement Considered Harmful" (**Dij68**). Why? Because it's short and to the point, and because it doesn't say what most people who haven't read it think it says. Two decades after this letter there are still periodic eruptions of the tiresome debate over **GOTO**s, in the Letters section of *CACM*. That's a classic example of people doomed to repeat history when they don't study it.

Dijkstra's paper is included in a superb collection, by the way, that Ed Yourdon put together some time ago (**You79**). Bohm and Jacopini are there too, if you want to ignore my advice and read that paper. The collection includes a number of essays by Dijkstra, and other fun reading from all sorts of people (including me).

Without further ado, here's my reading list. I begin with books on design and analysis.

E. Yourdon and L. Constantine, *Structured Design*, Prentice-Hall, 1989 (**Y&C79, Y&C89**) — This is the original book on structured design. (I think Glenford Myers beat them to press with his *Composite/Structured Design* (**Mye78**). But Constantine deserves recognition for having developed many of the seminal ideas in this field.)

Ed Yourdon and Larry Constantine were classmates at M.I.T. Yourdon went on to found Yourdon inc., part of a subindustry that promoted training in productivity-improvement techniques for programmers. Constantine has practiced family therapy, industrial counseling, and writing the odd symphony. It was Yourdon's drive to bring enlightenment to the masses of programmers that forced Constantine's hoary notes into book form and into the light of day.

Some of the ideas expressed in the original book are a bit dated now. You might want to stick with the later revision. Nevertheless, even in the original version you will find a high density of good ideas and just plain common sense. This is not so much a single-minded approach to writing all programs as it is a collection of observations on what works and what doesn't. It's a good starting point, particularly if you're new to the field.

J. Warnier, *Logical Construction of Programs*, Van Nostrand Reinhold, 1978 (**War74, War78**) — This is one of the pioneering works on the data-structured approach to designing computer programs. Here you will find a clear presentation of the rules for composing data into simple structures, for modeling program structure after data structure, and for marrying multiple input-data structures.

In more recent years, Ken Orr has worked hard to popularize many of Warnier's ideas (**Orr77**), just as Yourdon has preached the gospel according to Constantine. And like Yourdon, Orr has met the commercial programming marketplace more than halfway (as you must, if you want to win the hearts, minds, and money of perennially overworked EDP personnel).

Warnier's book is dry reading, by comparison. His emphasis is more on logical exposition than on motivation. Perhaps it was more exciting in the original French, but somehow I don't think so. You should read this book if you have a mathematical bent, or if you're really sold on the data-structured approach and want to understand Warnier's very logical approach uncluttered by later interpretations.

M. Jackson, *Principles of Program Design*, Academic Press, London, 1975 (**Jac75**) — Michael Jackson is a British counterpart to Yourdon and/or Orr. He, too, has packaged his approach to program design for commercial consumption, and he has won over many adherents in the process. (He's not afraid to relate his theories to the world of COBOL programming, for instance.)

Like Warnier and Orr, he focuses heavily on the data-structured approach to program design. But he goes beyond data structure to both higher and lower levels of abstraction. His descriptions of "structure clashes" and restructuring by "program inversion" are quite readable. This book is a good starting point if you want to better appreciate Jackson's later presentations.

G. Gane and T. Sarson, *Structured Systems Analysis: Tools and Techniques*, Improved Systems Technologies Inc., 1977 (**G&S77**) — Chris Gane and Trish Sarson were two of the handful of employees at Yourdon inc. when I joined the staff in 1975. Both were determined to bring the same discipline to the analysis process that Yourdon and Constantine had brought to program design. (Structured design was, of course, inspired in large part by the early successes of structured programming.) I am continually amazed at how much they got right on the first try with this book.

There is nothing highfalutin or theoretical about the presentation. Written by two experienced systems analysts, it speaks straight to an analyst's daily needs. I would almost accuse the authors of writing mere common sense, if that were ever "mere" or "common." If you're aspiring to be an analyst after getting your feet wet in commercial programming, here is a good introduction to the craft.

T. DeMarco, *Structured Analysis and System Specification*, Yourdon inc., New York, 1979 (**deM78, deM79**) — Tom DeMarco was one of my luckier finds when recruiting and auditioning instructors to teach Yourdon inc. courses. And I was privileged to work with some of the best people in the business in those days. When he put together his version of a structured-analysis book, somewhat after Gane and Sarson had done theirs, I was pleased to see a companion work emerge instead of a competitor.

DeMarco goes into considerable detail about how to use data-flow diagrams to capture the result of analysis and to represent the overall design as it evolves. He even touches on how to use data structuring to build the innards of each code module, but he stops shy of wandering out of the analysts domain. I should also point out that the author has a polished delivery and a sunny sense of humor that shines through at the most pleasant of moments.

Now for some books on coding and style.

B. Kernighan and P. Plauger, *The Elements of Programming Style*, McGraw-Hill, 1974 (**K&P74, K&P78**) — Brian Kernighan and I ended up with adjacent offices, at Bell Labs in Murray Hill, almost by accident. (Our management chains converged only with the V.P. of Research and Development.)

We began by commiserating over the sad state of computer programming and ended up in the authoring business, both for the first time, by writing this little book over a period of about four months. As far as I know, it marks the first time that "programming style" was identified in print as a legitimate topic of discussion by adults.

The book is terribly dated now, of course. All the examples are in FORTRAN and PL/I. Our gimmick was to find flawed examples in current programming texts, which was not hard to do in those days, and savage them in the guise of teaching lessons on good style. Occasionally we lost control and went into a sort of feeding frenzy, but mostly the book keeps a light tone. It's still worth reading for the pithy style rules (inspired by the classic on writing English prose by W. Strunk and E.B. White, *The Elements of Style*, MacMillan, 1972).

J. Nevison, *The Little Book of BASIC Style*, Addison-Wesley, 1978 (**Nev78**) — I first met Jack Nevison in 1975, while he was still at Dartmouth. Later he came to be, and remains, my neighbor in Concord, Massachusetts. None of that has anything to do with his having written this marvelous little book.

Little it is, and about BASIC to be sure. What he shows, however, is that even a language as intractable as BASIC can be made readable. And even a subject as pious as programming style can be presented with warmth and humor.

You will find no feeding frenzies here.

T. Plum, *C Programming Standards and Guidelines*, Plum Hall, Cardiff, New Jersey, 1981 (**Plu81**) — I have known Tom Plum, and his wife Joan Hall, since we worked together at Yourdon inc. many years ago. We are the best of friends.

Plum is also one of the best educators plying the commercial EDP trade that I know. Even before he began devoting a large fraction of his life to producing the ANSI standard for C, he was writing books like this on good C style.

This is the style book you should be using today. It happens to preach what I consider a good style for writing readable and maintainable C code. It also deigns to show alternatives and give some rationale for the choices it makes. I consider it a must for a programming shop of any size that uses the programming language C.

B. Kernighan and P. Plauger, *Software Tools*, Addison-Wesley, 1976 **(K&P76)**. Also, *Software Tools in Pascal*, Addison-Wesley, 1981 **(K&P81)** — Yes, me again. Brian and I wrote *Software Tools* over a ten-month period, during which I relocated from Bell Labs to Yourdon inc. It still ranks as one of the hardest jobs I've ever undertaken. (It was definitely harder than my Ph.D. thesis and comparable to writing a C compiler.)

Our goal was to show an unsuspecting world that the then little known operating system called UNIX was something new under the sun, and that not all of the good ideas that came with it were necessarily tied irrevocably to the UNIX kernel. We succeeded well enough at making software tools a topic of interest that we were encouraged to address the Pascal boom with *Software Tools in Pascal* a few years later.

Both of these books teach program design and style by example. The examples are a number of relatively small programs inspired by the more heavily used utilities of UNIX. Much of what we preached has become a standard part of the culture now. Between the widespread use of UNIX, and its influence on nearly all other systems, the lessons have been taught in many other ways. You still might find some useful insights in these books, however.

E. Dijkstra, *A Discipline of Programming*, Prentice-Hall, 1973 **(Dij73)** — Dijkstra, in case you don't know, is a theoretical physicist who turned himself into a theoretical programmer. He has brought a rigor and professionalism to the trade of writing code that was sorely lacking. (Many will say that rigor and professionalism are still sorely lacking in our trade.) He has the uncompromising hauteur of the European Herr Professor, the theoretician's natural love for mathematical rigor, and a distressing habit of being right.

This is a tough book to read. It is easy to bog down in notation or to get bowled over by Dijkstra's juggernaut presentation. I find two things to recommend in it, however. First, the book presents a way of expressing algorithms with what Dijkstra calls *guarded commands*. Seeing a few simple algorithms presented this way can shake you loose from years of procedural thinking that obscure intent with method. Second, the book is scrupulously honest. Dijkstra tells us about all the false trails he pursued and the mistakes he made in arriving at each solution. He presents a much more realistic treatment of stepwise refinement than any other book I have read on the subject. If you can survive the notation, it's worth the effort.

Well, those are my leading contenders for books you should read, and/or keep handy, in the areas of analysis, design, coding, and style. I have more books, in other categories, on my list of favorites, so I will provide more bibliography in the next essay. (See **Essay 17: A Designer's Reference Shelf**.) □

𝕬fterword: I got a lot of positive feedback on this essay. Seems everybody has a favorite book or two and is eager to share it with others. Mostly, I incorporated those suggestions in a series of columns for Embedded Systems Programming, *a sister publication to* Computer Language *published by Miller Freeman. The bibliography at the end of this collection is not annotated, despite what I said in the preamble to this essay. Mostly, that was to avoid redundancy with this essay and the next.*

Sadly, I must report that Joan Hall died a few years ago. (I included her obituary in my essay "State of the Art: Soft Stuff," Embedded Systems Programming, *October 1989.) She was a special person who is still sorely missed by many of us. Tom Plum eventually remarried. His wife Lana and my wife Tana are twin sisters. Thus, Tom and I are even closer friends than before.*

17 A Designer's Reference Shelf

In the previous essay, I presented a bibliography of a number of books from the fields of software design and programming. (See **Essay 16: A Designer's Bibliography**.) Perhaps it would be more precise to characterize that essay as a concatenation of more or less related book reviews, since I indulged my usual habit of tendering advice along with the raw information. I figure that a bibliography is a lot more useful if you have some notion, however opinionated, of the position and worth of each entry.

As promised, I continue in this essay with my stroll down the fifteen-odd feet of shelving that passes for my reference library. Having hit the high spots with my favorite design and coding books, I pass on to texts of a more general nature.

A reference book, to me, is one that I'm not likely to reread from cover to cover. Ever. But a good reference book is one that I find myself pawing through from time to time to find a useful bit of information that I vaguely recall having seen there when I first digested the book. The following list gives the books that I have found to be useful references over the years.

A. Aho, J. Hopcroft, and J. Ullman, *The Design and Analysis of Computer Algorithms*, Addison-Wesley, 1974 (**AHU74**) — If you've ever taken a serious course on compiler design, you probably recognize these guys as the authors of the famous "Dragon Books." (The name comes from the moderately outrageous cover pioneered with the first of the books, showing a knight slaying a dragon.) Of all the books they have written, in various combinations of authors, this is my favorite.

First, it is a good source of algorithms. If you ever have to write hairy code for climbing over trees, or manipulating matrices, or performing polynomial arithmetic, or matching patterns of text, then this is a good place to start looking. You will either find just the algorithm you need, or learn enough about the issues in the problem area of interest to know what you have to do to make your own algorithm.

Second, the book tells you a lot about the time and/or space complexity of the algorithms it presents. It does you no good to find an algorithm that needs only 1 kilobyte of memory if it runs for two weeks on a PC/AT. Nor can an algorithm help you that runs in 3 seconds, given 100 megabytes of memory. You need to know what the tradeoffs are before you can make them. This book raises your consciousness in that area better than any other that I know.

Finally, Aho, Hopcroft, and Ullman are masters at presentation. They lay the groundwork, touch all the bases, and keep a consistent level of detail from beginning to end. You need to be comfortable with mathematics to keep these authors from intimidating you, but they never indulge in unnecessary notation.

𝕯. Knuth, *The Art of Computer Programming, Volume 1: Fundamental Algorithms, Second Edition,* Addison-Wesley, 1973 (**Knu73b**). Also *Volume 2: Seminumerical Algorithms, Second Edition,* Addison-Wesley, 1981 (**Knu81**). Also *Volume 3: Sorting and searching,* Addison-Wesley, 1973 (**Knu73a**) — Donald Knuth, in case you didn't know, is a Turing Award winner and one of the more energetic contributors to the discipline of computer science.

Two decades ago, he embarked upon an extremely ambitious project. He put out the first volume of what was designed to be a seven-volume series (yes!) covering essentially all aspects of computer science. Volume 1 was titled "Fundamental Algorithms." It covered basic concepts and information structures. Volume 2 was titled "Seminumerical Algorithms," and covered random numbers and arithmetic. Volume 3 was titled "Sorting and Searching." And so on.

Over the years, he has emitted the first few books of this series. He has also gone back and generated revised editions of the earliest volumes. Whether the world will ever see all seven volumes I don't know. But what Knuth has produced to date is nothing short of phenomenal. This is the nearest thing to an encyclopedia of computer algorithms that you can buy. (When I want to learn the basic algorithms in a field, I first go to Aho, Hopcroft, and Ullman. When I need seven variations on a theme, I browse through Knuth.)

The saddest thing about this impressive opus is that Knuth chose to present his algorithms in a contrived machine language (called MIX). It is unfortunate that he began just on the threshold of the widespread acceptance of high-level languages. Had he presented an equivalent amount of code in Algol 60, Pascal, or C, he could have significantly lowered the barriers to understanding for thousands of students.

These make great coffee table books. They are the kind of references that your supervisor keeps on his or her shelf years after the last technical project, just to remind you and the other minions that even managers know how to program, at least sometimes.

𝕻. Sterbenz, *Floating-Point Computation,* Prentice-Hall, 1974 (**Ste74**) — I first mentioned this book when I discussed floating-point arithmetic. (See my essay "Programming on Purpose: Floating-Point Arithmetic," *Computer Language,* March 1988.) I cheerfully repeat here the quote from R.W. Hamming that ended that essay, "Nobody should ever have to know that much about floating-point arithmetic. But I'm afraid sometimes you might." Coming from a man who has little patience for anything that is not first rate, that is high praise.

I first encountered the minefield that surrounds floating-point arithmetic a decade before this book appeared. I'm sure those ten years would have been much better spent had I known half as much about floating point as I learned on first reading Sterbenz. (Sterbenz is, I believe, the guy who convinced IBM to retrofit a guard digit on System/360 double-precision arithmetic after any number of units had been shipped. I'm sure he has thus kept more than one missile from going astray since then.)

This book is getting a little old, obviously. But until someone can turn out a readable text explaining why IEEE 754 has all those strange features in it, this may well be your best introduction to floating-point arithmetic.

J. Hart, et al., *Computer Approximations*, Robert E. Krieger Publishing Company, 1978 (**Har68**, **Har78**) — I mentioned this book a couple of times when discussing how to approximate functions. (See my essay "Programming on Purpose: Do-It-Yourself Math Functions," *Computer Language*, June 1988.)

To the practicing numerical programmer, it is invaluable. The first half is a rather nice discussion of general methods for computing functions numerically on a computer. It is very succinct, but it touches all the bases. The second half is an assortment of tables of coefficients. You pick your popular math function, you pick the precision you need, and you look up the most economical approximation in the back of this book. Chances are, you'll find just what you need.

The book I used for years, before I discovered Hart, et al., was the lordly *Handbook of Mathematical Functions*, edited by Milton Abramowitz and Irene A. Stegun (**A&S65**) and later corrected editions). It has more than you can ever imagine wanting to know about an astonishing assortment of math functions. I still reach for it first when I want to explore new territory. But I have quicker results with Hart, et al. when I just want to bash out a good approximation to a widely used math function.

If your budget permits, and you do serious amounts of numeric programming, I'd recommend having both on hand.

E. Tufte, *The Visual Display of Quantitative Information*, Graphics Press, 1983 (**Tuf83**) — This book is a rare delight. It contains some of the most insightful, inspired, and prettiest graphs you have ever seen.

Accompanying the graphs is a narrative guided tour of the typography, psychology, and even physiology of visual displays. If "user friendly" is more than just a buzz phrase to you, and if you are seriously concerned with presenting displays that inform effectively, then you should read this book from cover to cover (once, anyway).

What Tufte has given us is the pictorial version of an older classic by Darrell Huff called *How to Lie with Statistics* (**Huf54**). Both books tell you all the tricks of the trade, and how they can be used to misdirect or deceive the reader. Both books, however, come from honesty. They assume that you as a presentor should learn to avoid such trickery, and that you as reader should learn to spot it when it is being perpetrated.

This really is a coffee-table book. You can lay it alongside your *Pictorial Guide to the Hummingbirds*, with every confidence that you will wow your visitors. Just watch your techie guests. They may want to steal it.

The following books touch on various aspects of computer program design sometimes only peripherally. Nevertheless, I have found each one to be an important source of philosophical inspiration about some aspect of our chosen trade.

F. Brooks, *The Mythical Man-Month*, Addison-Wesley, 1975 (**Bro75**) — Fred Brooks was the lucky guy chosen to head up the development of OS/360. As someone who presided over one of the most impressive cost and time overruns in modern program-development history, Brooks is perforce an expert on dealing with many of the problems of large software products.

This is a book you can read in an evening. It is worth buying just for the clever pictures and quotes that start each essay. I consider it must reading for anyone who hopes to head up a software-development project for the first time. It is also must reading for anyone who feels ready to tackle a project somewhat larger than the last one. Brooks rubs your nose in just how huge a factor "somewhat" can become.

Again, some of the material is dated. The hope that Brooks extends with chief-programmer teams has not panned out since those early optimistic reports (that were fresher when he wrote this book). If you read his essays on "planning to throw one away" and "the second-system effect" in quick succession, you will quickly figure out that you should plan to throw *two* designs away.

But hindsight comes easy. Brooks showed us many things about our trade for the first time, and in a way that stuck. Brooks' Law has become a platitude. We all know that you don't dare add programmers to a late project, lest you make it even later. Here is the first clear statement of that and several other important principles of software engineering.

G. Weinberg, *The Psychology of Computer Programming*, Van Nostrand Reinhold, 1971 (**Wei71**) — Gerry Weinberg has written a number of books, over the years, on various aspects of data processing. Anything he writes is a fun read, and worth the bother. My favorite, however, still remains this, the first of his books that I read.

Weinberg found his way into data processing from the psychology department. He quickly turned the magnifying glass on that new breed, the computer jock. What he has to say, while less novel than when it first appeared, still provides valuable insights to those of us who need to understand the techies around us. Or ourselves.

I have always suspected that Weinberg talks psychology around computer types and computers around psychologists. That way, he leaves each group thinking that his real expertise lies in the other realm. If he is running a scam, then he is pulling it off. His Technical Leadership Conferences alone have convinced many that he knows how to bridge between the two realms.

What I like most about this book (and all the others that Weinberg has written) is the anecdotal style of presentation. He can wrap a parable in a cute little story, tag it with an unforgettable name, and it sticks in your memory for years to come. I'm sure that my own penchant for doing similar things was aggravated by frequent contact with Weinberg's books. He does it much better than I do, however.

R. Pirsig, *Zen and the Art of Motorcycle Maintenance*, Bantam Books, 1975 (**Pir75**) — I have yet to find a good book on debugging computer programs. Until one comes along, you should read this one, which has next to nothing to do with computers. It is, just as its title says, about Zen and maintaining motorcycles. If you happen not to enjoy reading essays, or if you don't get caught up in inner quests by introspective people who happen to be good writers, then you may find this book heavy going. If you find that to be the case, please don't put the book down unfinished. At the very least, skip to the chapter on debugging motorcycles. You will learn more about the process of debugging software there than anywhere else I can point you.

Don't put the book down until you understand what Pirsig means by "gumption traps," or until you accept the fact that a 59-cent bolt can be worth far more than the contents of your wallet. Particularly if you strip its threads alongside the road, 50 miles from civilization in either direction.

If you finish the book, you will also get a first-rate sermon on Quality (with a capital Q, by all means). After all that has been written in recent years about how the Japanese are beating us on quality this and quality that, Pirsig can put you back in touch with Quality.

C. Alexander, *Notes on the Synthesis of Form*, Harvard University Press, 1964 (**Ale64**) — Christopher Alexander is a loud presence in architectural circles. What he has written here speaks directly to those of us who would dare to invent complex systems from the ground up. He comes at it from the standpoint of architectural evolution and tradition, but what he has to say can bring an important note of humility to an overly ambitious design project.

In this rather dry essay, Alexander discusses the social forces behind tradition in architecture. Why do the locals persist in putting that rococo little cupola up there? Or why must the straw be thatched just so? For answer, Alexander explores the sheer complexity involved in designing all aspects of a dwelling. Given that no single person is likely to be inventive enough to arrive at a consistent solution with all of those variables, the safest answer seems to be not to let things vary. What was good enough for our parents is good enough for us. Probably better.

If you've ever been in a house designed in a very nontraditional style, you understand quickly. There are annoying drafts, unexpected dead spaces, worrisome cracks in the walls. Maybe three releases later, your grandchildren will get a version that they can enjoy, but meanwhile you have to debug and/or adapt to all of the oversights.

Applying the same reasoning to the design of computer systems shows us why we have made so many drafty habitats. We just don't know enough yet to master all of the complexity. In time perhaps we will, but only after we develop an architectural sense, and a humility, that will keep us in check. Read Alexander if you want to develop that architectural sense.

I end this essay with something even farther out of the ordinary. I would like to list the handful of authors whose books I buy without first looking at the titles. Not that these are infallible people, or literary giants. I would not embarrass them with such silly flattery. Rather, each of them always seems to have something interesting to say, about a topic that I care about.

Edsger W. Dijkstra is certainly on the list. He persists in taking an original view of everything he tackles. I mentioned a couple of his works last in the previous essay. (See **Essay 16: A Designer's Bibliography**.) He has a number of other essays that are well worth reading. Sometimes my lips move when I read his stuff, and I often have to trace the same line over five times with my finger, but I usually find the effort rewarded.

Tom Plum is another. (I already confessed in the previous essay that Tom is a close friend. That he is also a good writer I consider a pleasant coincidence.) Tom has written several books, alone and with Jim Brodie, on various aspects of programming. His primary focus to date has been the C language. He also writes frequent articles in the trade press. When Plum reviews products, he brings an honesty and compassion to the job that other reviewers could well emulate. When he explains a technical topic, he persists until the cobwebs are swept away.

Finally (for now, at least) I list Gerry Weinberg. I gave you most of the reasons why I like him earlier in this essay. Anyone who can be consistently both entertaining and insightful in the same (written) breath has to be considered a safe bet. □

𝕬fterword: It was fun writing this essay. I look on it as a sort of distillation of Computing Reviews, *the ACM periodical that endeavors to review all books and articles of interest to the computing profession. Much as I like* Computing Reviews, *I despair at having to scan it every month for the stuff I care about. (It is one of about 20-30 publications I read regularly.) I'd love to have someone learn my profile of interests well enough to pick out just those books I care about that earn good marks. I figured others would appreciate the same service.*

18 A Preoccupation with Time

My association with the magazine *Embedded Systems Programming* has forced me to think once more about design methods. It has also forced me to read quite a lot, since I do a monthly review column for *ESP* called "State of the Art." As a consequence, I have become sensitized to the use of certain buzzwords that are now widely bandied about. In particular, the terms "embedded" and "real-time" strongly attract my eye.

I keep hoping I will read something that is fundamentally special about programming embedded systems. I keep getting disappointed. At Software Development '89, I expressed this disappointment in a talk titled "Designing Embedded Systems." That talk was not enough to get the issue unstuck from my craw, however. So I find myself chewing over the same theme once again.

It seems abundantly clear to all sorts of people that embedded systems differ in fundamental ways from other kinds. Miller Freeman went so far as to start another magazine to address the topic, rather than divert *Computer Language* more in that important direction. (It is a truism in publishing that if you aim for the union of two diverse markets, you get only their intersection.) I figured that if the difference is so fundamental, then it is worth articulating. That's why I asked for, and got, the privilege of writing the introductory essay in the premiere issue of *ESP*.

It was fun writing that essay. It even helped clarify in my mind some of the things that are special about programming embedded systems. But it also forced me to realize that there are no clear boundaries between the different flavors of computer systems that we work on. For every touchstone I could contrive, I could find examples of both embedded and non-embedded systems that satisfied the touchstone.

But you have to start somewhere. So let's begin by spelling out a few definitions. An *embedded system* is one that is dedicated to a particular task. By contrast, a general-purpose system is one that you can fairly easily switch among diverse tasks. The chip running your microwave oven is inarguably an embedded application. You can't run a spreadsheet on it, or play Adventure. The PC or workstation that dominates your day at work is a general-purpose system. You can aim it in almost as many directions as your management endeavors to aim you.

A *real-time system* is one that must respond to its inputs soon enough to make a difference. For some systems, soon enough is measured in microseconds. For others, an answer in half a day is arguably a real-time response. While many embedded systems are also real-time systems, you can find examples of each flavor that are not also of the other flavor.

An *interactive system* is a real-time system that must respond to human interaction. I know that is not the common definition, but I think it is the most revealing. Human beings impose a very demanding load in some ways. They get impatient when operations they find trivial take a long time. They go mildly crazy when they see a large variation in response time. They have a high error rate for which the computer must be prepared to compensate. At the same time, humans impose a lighter load than other real-time tasks. They take many milliseconds to perform most actions, and many seconds to compose requests. And they can correct for naive program behavior that can drive other computer systems bonkers. It is easy to see why most people view interactive systems as qualitatively different than real-time systems.

Finally, a *batch system* is one that is atomic in its response to its inputs. It offers no serious opportunity for any sort of interactive give and take between the reading of its first input and the writing of its last output. Again, this is not a conventional definition of batch systems, but I think it provides the irreducible minimum that happens to be true.

Now that we have several distinct categories, let's start blurring the lines. As I have often pointed out, there are embedded systems that you *can* play Adventure on. AT&T began many years ago to use UNIX systems to oversee its extensive network of telephone trunks. You could log on to those systems, compile replacement code, and yes, even play games while the system sniffed at trunks and made pretty displays. Nevertheless, such a UNIX system is embedded because it is just a (small but reasonably important) component in a dedicated system.

Similarly, there are embedded systems involving some of the biggest and fastest IBM 30XX machines, enough to fill a Big Ten college gymnasium. Systems like these run the big airline reservation systems that keep people moving through airports. They are embedded because they are fanatically dedicated to a single, economically very important application.

At the other extreme, I have developed serious quantities of commercial software on computer systems so small that no self-respecting brat would now accept any of them as an embedded video-game engine. I do not exaggerate when I say that some traffic lights today have more MIPS and megabytes than those early development systems of mine. You tell me where to draw the line between general purpose and embedded, at least when it comes to flexibility and size.

The other touchstone you can apply to identify embedded systems is that they have peculiar devices attached to them. In a sense this is true. Your PC has no need for switch-closure detectors (except the keys in your keyboard) or position sensors (unless you have a joy-stick attached). I stretch the truth a bit to make a point, since the set of conventional gadgets is finite. It is not stretching the truth, however, to point out that conventional gadgets are often just as idiosyncratic to *program* as the peculiar devices you find in embedded systems. Try writing an MS-DOS or UNIX device driver sometime. For any device. You will find that *all* devices are peculiar, if you have to program them in detail.

Then there is the myth of real-time. Show me a program of any flavor with no real-time constraints, and I will show you a program that is not worth running. Even a monthly batch payroll program must be deemed inadequate if it takes two months to run, or if it can only deliver results three months after the day paychecks must be handed out. And there are batch programs with performance requirements tighter than some embedded systems. All you can talk about is the *degree* of real-time response required, not the presence or absence of such a requirement.

A related issue is the need for synchronization. We know that embedded systems tend to have special requirements for coordinating the actions of one or more processors with one or more real-world processes. What we tend to overlook is that even programs run in batch mode can have synchronization problems. Consider, for example, a data-base server operating on a multi-user system. Try writing a reliable server without record locking or some other safe synchronizing primitives. Whenever you have cooperating sequential processes, which is often, you have synchronization problems.

After going through this little exercise in iconoclasm, I looked around to see if anyone else had better luck. You can find lots of books out there with "real-time" in their titles. Surely one or more of them had found a way to distinguish clearly between real-time and more conventional systems. And maybe that would help us all to better distinguish between embedded and more conventional systems, since real-time is so often identified with embedded. It is clear that there is a qualitative difference. It would be nice to make it quantitative as well.

I even devoted two consecutive episodes of "State of the Art" to reviewing books on real-time design. (See "State of the Art: Designing Real-Time Systems," *Embedded Systems Programming*, February 1989, and its continuation, March 1989.) In the process, I turned up two books that are widely acclaimed as good references for those who would design real-time systems. One is by Paul T. Ward and Stephen J. Mellor, *Structured Development for Real-Time Systems, Volumes 1-3* (**Y&M85**). The other is Derek J. Hatley and Imtiaz A. Pirbhai, *Strategies for Real-Time System Specification* (**H&P87**).

Both are good books. Both start with data-flow analysis, one of the more popular organizing approaches popularized by structured analysis. Both add various bits of notation to document the flow-of-control information atop the more conventional data-flow diagrams. That seems to make real-time designers happy, since they are often preoccupied with control issues. But neither book really discusses real-time.

Another of my favorite publishing truisms comes from the world of science fiction. It helps you test whether a story is genuine science fiction or just an interloper from some other genre. Try substituting "horse" for "space ship," "six gun" for "laser cannon," and "ranch" for "moon base." If it reads like a Western, then that's what it is. Only the nouns have been changed.

I found you could do the same with Ward/Mellor, or Hatley/Pirbhai, or any of the other books on real-time design. Reword the putative examples of embedded, real-time systems and either of these books could serve as a design guide for on-line banking or payroll systems. Don't get me wrong. These two are still good books, and they seem to be useful to designers of real-time systems. But I believe that is because real-time systems share so many problems in common with all other systems. It is not because the authors have learned to identify and address peculiar requirements of real-time systems.

It should be reassuring, in fact, that computer systems have so many common design issues. We have struggled for decades, and continue to struggle, to develop a collection of methods that we can bring to bear on the software-design process. I am happy to see these authors successfully transfer many of the techniques that have worked for years in the commercial arena to the realm of real-time and embedded systems. It is encouraging to think that the machinery they have added can be carried back to the commercial arena and used to deal with such problems as shared access to common data.

But where does that leave real-time design? Is it a separate discipline or not? Personally, I have learned to be comfortable with the notion that many of the categories we humans make up are only qualitative. The engineer, the scientist, and the mathematician often look in vain for the quantitative touchstone that can simplify the sorting of things into categories. That's a noble endeavor, but one that is often neither necessary nor sufficient to the working designer. The designer still brings the same tools to bear. Some design problems just use a given tool more than others.

To me, what is peculiar about real-time design is right there in its name. What we characterize as real-time systems have an unusually strong preoccupation with time. An acceptable solution must respond *soon enough*, as always. For a real-time system, soon enough may push the limits of the chosen hardware, or software, or even the state of the art. So great is a preoccupation with adequate performance in real-time systems that this branch of our business has been one of the last hold outs in the use of high-level languages and other productivity aids. No responsible designer wants to risk delivering a system that fails to meet performance specifications. Fortunately, improved compilers and a growing collection of success stories have encouraged more and more real-time and embedded implementations to use up-to-date technology.

The preoccupation with time takes other forms as well. A solution that is fast enough on average may still be unacceptable. Every real-time system usually has one or more situations where a worst-case response time must be guaranteed. As an extreme example, running a 747 jumbo jet on a LISP-based system has a lot of appeal, provided it doesn't decide to indulge in five minutes' worth of garbage collection on a final approach to LAX. It can be far more important to the designer to be able to *predict* the worst-case response of a solution than to get the fastest possible. Predictable solutions are the stuff of engineering. Wing-and-a-prayer landings are the stuff of drama. Engineers dislike drama in their working lives, and rightly so.

When I started writing these essays, I focused primarily on presenting a series of design methods. These were methods that I had found useful over many years of writing programs for a living. I tried to identify and codify all the different methods that I or my coworkers brought to bear in solving design problems. I even made up (sometimes cutesy) names to help people remember the different methods and when to apply them.

Of all those methods, only one dealt with time. (See **Essay 14: Synchronization**.) It focused on the fundamental importance of getting synchronization right and demonstrably safe in any system that involves cooperating sequential processes. I called the method hard-to-easy design because it is always hard to debug synchronization logic. Despite years of papers by a variety of smart people, nobody has invented a language that delivers foolproof synchronization. You do the hard part first, before synchronization issues get cluttered up with other details. Then you add the details that do not involve synchronizing code.

I still believe that this is an important aspect of real-time design. And it is a separate issue from getting adequate performance. Another stock truism is, "Make it right before you make it faster." You put in semaphores, record locks, etc. to make sure the code always behaves properly. Only after that is debugged do you put serious effort into measuring performance and tweaking code to make it faster. (Of course, you must pick algorithms with sensible time complexity from the outset. Otherwise you may not have a prayer at souping up underachieving code. But in the early stages of design and coding, you must not embellish those algorithms in the hope of picking up speed that you may or may not get or need.)

So the design methods I outlined focused most heavily on one aspect of time, getting parallel processes to cooperate properly. I paid the conventional lip service to tuning systems only at the appropriate stage of development. (See **Essay 15: Which Tool is Last?**) And, I now see in hindsight, I overlooked an important aspect of designing with a preoccupation for time. A system must also be stable over time.

If you've ever worked at one terminal on a multi-user time-sharing system, you know some of the issues. All time-sharing systems bog down, naturally, under a heavy enough load. Some systems are more gracious than others when they bog. The worst offenders are the ones that seem to fall over a cliff when they pass some undocumented limit. Response goes to hell, and any attempt to sniff out the extent of the disaster sends the system to deeper reaches of hell. I have even been on systems that brood for a spell after the excess load is removed. They sit there licking their wounds and pouting until various secret internal parameters become convinced that the world has returned to normal.

Networks exhibit all sorts of pathological behavior in the time domain. You can get some of the simpler ones to "ring." Just like a microphone that howls when you turn the sound system up too loud, simpler networks can start packets endlessly circulating and regenerating. Messages still get through, but the capacity to transmit information is diminished.

If you read the SIGSOFT newsletter (from the ACM Special Interest Group on Software Engineering), you will see a steady stream of reports on complex systems that bog, oscillate, or even collapse under unusual loads. Sometimes those loads are caused by happenstance, the data processing equivalent of Mothers' Day for the phone company. Sometimes those loads are the result of malice, or at least carelessness. I need not recite yet again details of the well publicized worm that crawled into several thousand Berkeley UNIX systems. As a cautionary tale, it has certainly been effective.

But how do we display our caution? It is clear, to me at least, that designing for stability in the time domain is just as important as designing for correct synchronization and designing for adequate performance. It is also clear that this is the least understood of the various disciplines for dealing with our preoccupation with time in real-time systems. I can only offer a weak analogy and a general observation.

The analogy is to electrical engineering. The time-dependent behavior of currents in electrical circuits has been thoroughly studied for decades. Most real-world components can be represented by just a few parameters. Most circuits can be modeled as a sequence of transforms. Modern circuit theory can often predict quite accurately the behavior of a circuit to a given stimulus, such as a sine-wave voltage applied across two points in a circuit. In fact, you can often plot out the behavior of the circuit for sine waves of a broad range of frequencies.

Now here is the really interesting part. If you know the response of a circuit as a function of frequency for a broad range of frequencies, you can tell a priori whether that circuit is stable. You can predict whether it will ring or cook components, with rather good accuracy. And once you know the instabilities in a circuit, you have a good guide to making it stable. The general principle is to sacrifice some of the amplification in a circuit through negative feedback. Gain goes down but stability goes up. It's a classic tradeoff.

The analogy to computer design is weak, of course, because we don't understand complex systems nearly as well as simple electrical circuits. We can only guess, measure, or test many properties of the systems we build. Nevertheless, I believe that we as designers have an obligation to pay more attention up front to the time stability of the systems we contrive. Knowing that complex systems are not automatically stable, we must devote a certain amount of our time to anticipating, looking for, and correcting problems in this area. As usual, if we do not, then our customers will do it for us in the field, at a premium price, before an audience of eager competitors.

The general observation is that enhancing stability will probably cost you performance. That is just a specific application of Robert Heinlein's favorite truism, "There ain't no such thing as a free lunch." Adding extra checks or redundant transmissions is going to cost you cycles and bytes. So you'd better be prepared to up your measure of what constitutes adequate performance. Make sure you have some performance left over to spend on this important aspect of the design.

In the end, there's nothing wrong with being preoccupied with time. That's the hallmark of real-time design. It is also an aspect of conventional design that has probably not received adequate attention to date. Just make sure that your preoccupation has a payoff. Spend your time worrying about time wisely. □

Afterword: I still have fights with people over this approach to defining real-time systems. It's like art — nobody can define it, but they know what they like. For want of a quantitative measure, this is the best qualitative way I know to identify what is special about real-time design and programming.

19 Structuring Time

The previous essay was on one of my favorite topics — how to design software systems in an orderly fashion. (See **Essay 18: A Preoccupation with Time**.) My thesis in that essay was that the time behavior of computer systems has not received the attention it deserves, particularly in designing embedded and real-time systems. I discussed three aspects of a program's time behavior that you must address: adequate performance, safe synchronization, and stable response.

Thinking about time led me to wondering why more people haven't addressed this important area in greater detail. Sure, there are lots of academic books on semaphores, monitors, and other synchronization mechanisms. But there are still very few operating systems, languages, or subroutine libraries that make synchronization substantially safer in the programs you have to write.

There are also lots of books, both academic and trade, that purport to address the needs of the real-time designer and/or programmer. Nevertheless, these almost always devote the bulk of their attention to conventional design issues. The examples are from the problem domain of real-time systems, but the shapes of the examples are remarkably universal. Little attention is devoted, in any of these books, to the peculiar problems of dealing with time.

You'd think, with the emphasis placed on time in the very phrase "real-time" that designers would be encouraged to begin with time considerations and work their way down to the relatively trivial (or at least mundane) coding details. Yet this is not how most of us were taught in real life. It is seldom how newcomers to the field are being taught today. There is little prospect that kids entering college next fall will be taught much differently. How come, I asked myself, we pay so much lip service to dealing with the most important design issues first, yet we persist in starting with other aspects of a design in practice?

Then it hit me. Discovery is usually a bottom-up process. The first things we learn about a subject are the basic abstractions. Over time, we learn higher-level abstractions, built on the basics, that provide the really important unifying principles. The basics appear relatively unimportant in hindsight. Nevertheless, they had to come first.

Certainly this is true in the discipline that passes for computer science. We had to learn the importance of using assemblers (rather than code by

177

hand in octal) long before we could begin to appreciate a higher-level language such as FORTRAN. We needed a decade or more of experience with rough-and-ready languages such as FORTRAN and COBOL before we could appreciate the need for the refinements of C and Pascal. Only now are languages catching on that demand even greater levels of abstraction.

None of these newer languages completely displace their forebears. You can still find serious programmers who swear they need the control you get by writing in assembly language. FORTRAN is nowhere near dead, despite many an obituary tossed off by an enthusiast for later technology. I venture to predict that C will cheerfully endure the onslaught of C++, Ada, Eiffel, and whatever else appears between now and the end of the century. Not everyone wants to inhabit the current topmost layer of the pyramid. And only the hardiest of pioneers enjoy hauling rocks all day to build the pyramid higher.

What this means in the world of design methods is that we discover the lowest-level methods first. These are the ones we learn earliest. These are the ones we get the most experience with and grow most comfortable using. These are the ones we therefore turn to first when we need to do *something* and we're not quite sure what to do next. Under stress, people almost invariably revert to an earlier pattern of behavior that made them feel in control, whether or not it is relevant to the current situation. And those early patterns of behavior are often more relevant than you might expect.

It's been over twenty years since Dijkstra first told us to structure the control flow in our code more carefully (**Dij68**). In the cosmological scheme of things, we now know that minimizing the number of **GOTO**s in your code is treating a symptom instead of the disease. Indeed that is the purport of Dijkstra's letter, a fact generally overlooked or curdled in the **GOTO** debate that has continued even to the present day.

Something that addresses the disease more directly is to look at the structure of the data that your program is manipulating. Structure the data, some say, then reflect that structure in the code that manipulates it and everything will turn out fine. Few methods for imposing structure on data encourage you to write **GOTO**s, it turns out. Those that do tend to use **GOTO**s in a sufficiently disciplined manner that you needn't worry about code readability or maintainability.

Worrying about data-structure alone is still designing in the small. You can have the prettiest data structure diagrams in town and still get swamped by a project that requires 100,000 lines of code. It is clear that imposing structure on the organization of your code into modules is much more important. Structure the hierarchy, some say, and the data will reflect the structure of the clean interfaces between modules. Few interfaces can achieve the laudable goals of yielding high cohesion within modules and low coupling between modules without also yielding well structured data. And well structured data, as we saw before, leads to well structured code.

But the best structured hierarchy is worthless if performance is not adequate, or if the program is subject to lockups and race conditions, or if the overall system is unstable over time. Hence we must address timing demands before we do anything else. You can seldom retrofit adequate performance if the basic algorithm has unacceptable time complexity. You cannot retrofit correctness in a system written without proper concern for safe synchronization. You can stabilize a system only if you have designed in excess performance and adequate feedback to exploit it.

In short, our highest goal should be to structure time. Then we can safely partition a system and structure its hierarchy. Then we can identify the information flow within the hierarchy and structure that data. And finally, we can write structured code. Now *that* is top-down design.

When was the last time you designed a system by performing those design steps rigorously in that order? My guess is that you never have. I know that I haven't. Then again, maybe we all have more than we think. People who preach software design as a disciplined activity spend considerable energy making us all feel guilty. We can never be structured enough or object-oriented enough to achieve nirvana in this lifetime. We all truck around a kind of original sin from having learned BASIC at an impressionable age. But my bet is that most of us are better designers than the purists will ever acknowledge.

The usual excuse we give is that developing a product involves several trips up and down between levels of abstraction. We do a little mental top-down design to get a feel for the low-level stuff that may be difficult to implement. Then we suspend the orderly process of stepwise refinement long enough to do some good old fashioned bottom-up implementation of a few critical pieces. Reassured that we're not completely out to lunch, we go back to the top-down approach, at least long enough to spot the next potential hang-up. With sufficient luck, skill, and patience, we eventually converge to a complete design and implementation.

Another view is that we must make several trips around a spiral. We design the system at a very abstract level, often over beers, after work, on the back of a napkin. The process is allegedly top-down, but the only documentation is soggy and tears easily. Then we go through the process at a greater level of detail, more on the lookout for those low-level gotchas I just mentioned. This is the round that looks most like an orderly process, one that leaves your boss with the mistaken impression that he or she is really in control. Then we do it again and again, as often as necessary to fill in the details. After enough rounds, each at a greater level of refinement, the process nominally converges to a deliverable system.

Or perhaps you use the Michaelangelo Approach, where you keep chipping away pieces of marble that do not look like a statue of David. Or the Columbus Method, where you discover a problem and land on it. Or the Woody Allen Approach — "If it moves, fondle it." Or you can use Drunkard's Walk, or Outlive the Testers, which I believe are self explanatory. The only technique I don't approve of is the one first attributed to Jiminy Cricket — "Wishing will make it so."

The point is, those of us who develop software for a living have learned to direct our efforts with some degree of efficacy over the life of a project. We often cannot articulate why we do what we do when we do it. That's why we hide behind self-deprecating humor so often when we describe our jobs to civilians. But most of the time we're doing something that needs to get done and that seems to be in the way at the moment. (See **Essay 7: Which Tool is Next?**)

What we fail to credit is that each of the many design methods has more than one thing to say. Some aspects of a method tell you what to do to launch a brand-new design. Others guide you through the difficult shoals of converting an abstract design to a very concrete and specific implementation. Still others tell you what to look for once the project is fully afloat, lest it sink from a hundred leaks. A few even help you steer a course toward future enhancements.

To put it another way, every design method has to provide different services at different stages of the development process. First of all, a method must help you predict the future. It promises you that a problem of a given shape can benefit from a solution of a corresponding shape. It tells you what details you must focus on to capture the design and where the interesting coding problems will lie. It should even give you good hints about how to test and debug the almost final code, and how to measure and tune the really final code. And, of course, a method must tell you what documents you need to produce to capture the critical design decisions.

As I have preached for years, you have to apply numerous design methods to complete any nontrivial programming project. Even the purists who think they use just one method really use several. And even if you think you are applying methods one at a time, you can't help but overlap them throughout a project.

With all those methods nattering at you throughout the software-development process, it's no wonder you can't articulate why you're doing any particular job at any particular time. If you have an urge to see structure in everything, you will see reciprocating motion, or a spiral climb, or a waterfall. You will probably not see 20 or 30 interlaced checklists being filled out from left to right. Not unless you are more organized than the average bear. Nevertheless, I maintain that that is what most professionals end up doing.

Ignorance can, of course, get you in trouble. Often large unsolved design problems remain at a stage where everyone is pretending to be in final systems integration. One or two checklists just got lost in the shuffle. Or they got bent and twisted to fit into the pretty spiral. Even more often, the planners gloss over a few hundred microsteps in the checklists to satisfy the needs of Back-to-Front Scheduling — "I need it in seven and a half months, when can I have it?" More often than we all care to admit, weekly progress meetings are run by disciples of Jiminy Cricket.

Still, my basic message is to be more kind to yourself as a designer. You tend to forget about all the successes that got you where you are in your career. (You can at least afford to buy this book, *nicht wahr?*) Just try to be more aware of how many fronts you are fighting on. You'll get the troops to the critical battles more often.

I have discussed about a dozen methods in this collection of essays. Some of them are admittedly low level, using the rating scheme I outlined above. Others are very high level. Some of them are most useful in the earliest stages of design. Others are weak on prediction but strong in the final stages. If you are indeed going to juggle multiple applications of these methods, it helps to be aware of where each makes its best contributions. Let's look at them.

Starting at the lowest level, three of the methods deal primarily with just structuring code:

Inside-out design is preoccupied with writing good predicates, those control expressions you write in **IF** and **WHILE** statements to get flow of control right. When you have a lot of decisions to make, it can provide important structure through the use of decision tables and encoded Karnaugh maps. Otherwise, its contribution is mostly in the middle stages of coding.

Bottom-up design is mostly about building finite-state machines. When you have a problem that requires hidden state memory it can't be beat. (Two obvious examples are a handler for some peripheral device and the guts of an object in object-oriented design.) So this method is long on prediction, but at a fairly low level of abstraction.

Easy-to-hard design deals with handling exceptions. It tells you to code for the "normal" case, so the code reflects the commonest situations, then deal with the less common exceptions with special handlers out of line. Thus the method guides you early on in partitioning the control logic. In the final stages of testing, it also gives you a neat checklist for verifying that all errors are properly handled.

Three more methods address various aspects of data-structured design. These are:

Right-to-left design encourages you to describe the data your program generates in terms of sequences, alternations, and repetitions of simpler structures. A program that reflects the data it generates is perforce structured in the classical sense. It offers most guidance at the design and coding stages, somewhat less during testing and tuning.

Left-to-right design is about recognizing structure in input data, or parsing if you will. It is very important during early design because the form and flexibility of input languages have a profound effect on program usability. A well designed grammar also is important, however, in designing for good test coverage.

Chaos-to-order design focuses on exploiting any order that has been imposed on a data base. It can help you speed up data insertions, deletions, replacements, or accesses. Or it can simply help you preserve the integrity of a data base by limiting the number of agents that manipulate its internal structure. This method captures many of the virtues currently advertised for object-oriented programming. As such, it is an important organizing principle in the early stages of design, even if it addresses a relatively low level of abstraction.

Three more methods address how you structure a hierarchy of modules. These are:

Outside-in design helps you break up modules that are too complex to design by simpler data-structuring methods. It deals with marrying data structures that are compatible and divorcing those that are incompatible. It is mostly of importance while designing and coding, but it can warn of testing problems in modules that must retain static memory.

Chaos-to-order design has a simple message. It tells you to treat any need for reordering data as a sort, then isolate the sorting in a separate module. (It also encourages you to use commercial sort packages rather than reinvent your own.) It applies almost exclusively in the earliest design phases.

Top-down design provides an orderly method for converting data-flow diagrams to structure charts. It guides you in picking a top module that is likely to lead to relatively low coupling and minimal complexity within modules. As such, it deals almost exclusively with early design issues, and only moderately with coding issues.

Finally, there are three methods for structuring time (only one of which I have so far graced with a name):

Hard-to-easy design tells you to get your synchronization problems out of the way as early as possible. They are too hard to get right to risk postponing until you have accumulated any added complexity. Since languages and systems still let you get into arbitrary amounts of trouble in this arena, you must nevertheless keep alert to synchronization issues through all phases of design, coding, testing, and tuning.

Stable-to-fast design is an obvious term for the well worn dictum, "Make it right before you make it faster." It encourages you to focus in the early design stages purely on the time complexity of algorithms. It discourages you in the middle stages of coding and debugging from adding *any* complexity for the sole purpose of improving performance. It guides you in the testing phases to successful techniques for locating performance bugs. Finally, it suggests the kind of tuning you can safely do in the end to improve performance without a major sacrifice in maintainability.

Fast-to-stable design is an equally obvious term for the concerns I addressed in the previous essay. (See **Essay 18: A Preoccupation with Time**.) You must not consider a design complete until you have reason to believe that the time-dependent behavior of the delivered system is sufficiently stable. Since there are only a few very general design principles you can apply in the early stages to ensure stability, this method kicks in most strongly at the end. It tells you to look for instabilities and to sacrifice performance as needed to eliminate them in the final product.

So there you have it. A dozen different methods, at four levels of abstraction, each providing varying degrees of guidance at different stages of the program-development process. It may not be tidy, but I bet it covers a lot of what you do when you do what you call computer programming. And mostly it works. □

Afterword: This was my attempt to better unify all the different essays presented earlier in this collection. I suspect some of the regularity is specious — why are there exactly three methods for each of the four levels of abstraction, and why does "X-to-Y" design always have a companion "Y-to-X" design method? We human beings can find patterns where we want them, regardless of the actual supporting evidence in the real world. Nevertheless, I do believe that this collection of approaches subsumes many of the design methods we actually use. And I believe that this way of presenting them is as good as any. At the least, it's mnemonic.

20 Abstract It

*E*verybody knows that abstraction is a Good Thing. Computers spend all of their microseconds walloping bits around. They are profoundly concrete. We programmers, on the other hand, try to impose some higher-order meaning to those flying bits. We must at least pretend that the bits stand for something more abstract than ones and zeros.

Programmers are continually distracted away from the problem domain and into the world of machine representations. The customer complains that credits over $200 million suddenly turn into debits. The programmer explains that 32-bit signed numbers do that when they overflow. The customer is unimpressed with this lame excuse and demands a working program. The programmer is annoyed that customers don't appreciate the "natural" limitations of the computer. The two are living at different levels of abstraction.

I can always spot a programmer who has only worked on one architecture. He or she looks on the basic data types of that machine as God given. The same goes for how the system names files, how it represents lines of text, and dozens of other arbitrary design choices. There is a level of abstract thinking that comes only from writing code intended to be portable across architectures.

Years ago, I concocted a seminar titled "Structured Programming in Assembly Language" and taught it several times. All the classes took the control-flow primitives in stride. Most were even willing to entrust the choice of tests and branches to a package of macros that generate the primitives for you. Where I hit a brick wall, however, was when I tried to teach assembly-language programmers that data has structure. Data was bits and bytes to them, not subranges and records. Nary a one was willing to refrain from peering at the underlying representation.

I wrote that experience off as one of the dangers of pioneering. Not everyone was ready to be structured, and assembly-language programmers were likely to be the most ardent holdouts. That explanation sat comfortably in the attic of my brain until just the other day. I saw a description of some new system calls in MS-DOS 4.0. Each of the data items was characterized as having 1, 2, or 4 bytes. Period. No internal structure, no range limitations, no additional semantics. People coding all those hot new PC applications still pretend all too often that data has no structure beyond its overt representation.

What finally pushed me over the edge was the spate of seminars I recently attended in my capacity as reviewer for *Embedded Systems Programming*. Religious converts to object-oriented programming often act as if they invented abstract thinking. The typical before-and-after examples stack up crassly short-sighted functions against well-crafted objects. Now, some of us old timers think we know a thing or two about data abstraction. It is annoying to see straw men set up as examples of our breed.

On the other hand, there are still a lot of assembly language programmers in the world. The number of programmers writing MS-DOS system calls may well rival the ranks of the older bit twiddlers. Can it be that the OOPs-a-daisies are at least half right? Do most programmers avoid abstract thinking unless it is forced upon them? Maybe I've been hanging around good programmers for so long that I've lost touch with common practice.

Or maybe the picture isn't all that bleak. Using abstraction to good effect is a skill that everyone has to learn. Like many aspects of computer programming, it doesn't come naturally. I can't recall ever reading a simple, straightforward set of guidelines for how to do it. Not in a textbook, not in a famous paper. Perhaps our educations are merely spotty in this area, not the subject of a national scandal.

I decided to write down the obvious. Probably you know all this stuff already, if only at a subconscious level. Maybe you've never bothered to articulate it. Conceivably some of it is news to you. Whatever, here are the simplest guidelines that came to me on the subject of abstraction.

First, you need to keep in mind your reasons for introducing abstractions when you program. You don't do so lightly, because you always pay a price. With each benefit comes a drawback:

- **insulation** — You want to protect your program from excessive dependence on the underlying implementation. Protect it too much, however, and you introduce inefficiencies in size and speed.

- **documentation** — You want to convey extra information that is not obvious from the choice of implementation. Convey misleading information, and you have a debugging and maintenance nightmare.

- **completeness** — You want to ensure that you've thought through all the states your data can assume and all the ways that states can change. Go overboard with completeness and you saddle your development with unnecessary extra work.

Keep these three goals in mind as we examine a few guidelines.

The first guideline is: **Give all your numbers names**. It is an old mathematical truism that there are only three good numbers — none, one, and all. The programming equivalent is that you should be suspicious of any constant in your code other than 0 or 1. (I have learned to be suspicious of most of those, as well.) All those **80**s peppering your code are not constants of nature. They represent some value that has a story attached. The story is more likely to stay unchanged over the years than the value.

So you summarize the story behind each number in a memorable name. Assemblers have **EQU** directives, Pascal and its ilk use **CONST**, C has **#define**. Whatever the mechanism (and it is a rare language that lacks one), you use it to bind each funny number to its name. And keep an abbreviated version of the story with the definition in the form of a comment. You or your successor will need the reminder some day.

Sound obvious? Then how come a large fraction of the code I see published still contains funny numbers? It's bad enough when code is peppered with **80**s, but it's worse when some are masquerading as **79**s, **81**s, and **40**s. Even **grep**, that most stalwart of software tools for software maintainers, doesn't help you much the day **80** becomes **120**.

Don't tell me that the **80** will never change. I once consulted for a company that owned three mines. Every program they owned was peppered with **3**s (and the odd **2** or **4** that also counted mines). You should have seen the sheepish programmers the day top management ordered one of the mines closed. If a giant hole in the ground can go away, a card can grow 40 columns.

The only thing worse than failing to name a number is numbering a name. I have seen programs that define **FOUR** as **4**, or **K1024** as **1024**. Lest you think this is merely a waste of time, I must tell you that later versions of those programs changed the definition of **FOUR** to **5**, and **K1024** to **4096**. Stupidity transmutes easily to perversity.

Another guideline says: **Give all your data distinct types**. You are already increasing entropy when you decide which computational types to use for your data. You can at least document that the long integers you use for counting apples differ from the long integers that count oranges. One day, you may want to change just one of them.

Language designers have tried many ways to help you better tailor your data declarations. Declaring a subrange captures more information than just choosing the smallest adequate integer representation. Declaring an enumeration lets you give names to values (see above) and frees you of the temptation to pick clever values. Declaring a powerset makes clear that you intend to twiddle individual bits. All these mechanisms are very helpful.

The only problem is, I'm always wanting to mix them up. A classic example is the Standard C function **getchar**. It returns a value that is either in the subrange representable as an **unsigned char**, or the distinct code **EOF** (for end-of-file). That's useful behavior which C programmers indulge in all the time. I've just never seen a language where you can declare such usage. So I pick an adequate representation and list the semantic restrictions in the type definition.

One reason for picking a given computational type is, of course, the computations that the language supports for that type. You pick integers for counting whole apples and floating point for weighing apple sauce. The language may let you add apples and oranges. It probably won't implicitly convert apples to applesauce by the standard rule of thumb. Don't count on a language to replace your own documentation and discipline, no matter what the proponents promise.

You can also declare types for your data that inherit almost none of this baggage. Make a new type and you get to spell out just those operations you wish to define for it. (Even in C, which treats most type definitions as synonyms for existing types, every structure is a new and distinct type.) You then have the chore of spelling out all those operations, either as macros, functions, or overloaded operators.

In my experience, the division is a natural one. A datum that you can represent as a scalar computational type generally wants most if not all of the operations that go with it. (It makes sense to add and subtract apples, but only to multiply apples by dimensionless types.) I prefer functional notation for the operations I must supply. The last thing a maintainer needs is to have operators redefined for scalar operands.

On the other hand, a datum that requires two or more components begs a new set of functions to manipulate it. (For a screen window, you can imagine wanting to open, close, read, write, and position it, at the very least.) And the functions can look like functions, for all I care. I can tolerate overloading the plus operator to add two complex numbers, but I don't want it to paste two windows together. That's cute, but hardly a boon to code reading or debugging.

Combining these two guidelines yields a third: **Give each named number a type**. I didn't mention this up front because it can be hard enough to get some programmers to name their numbers at all. The fact remains, however, that each number you name belongs only in certain places. You can store it only in data objects of the proper type and you can legitimately perform only certain operations on it. Pretend otherwise and you're back in the **K1024** school.

Pascal has enumeration constants that carry both an unspecified value and a specified type. It also has **CONST** declarations that carry a specified value and an implicitly specified type. It would be nice to be able to specify both. C has only weakly typed enumeration constants and **#define**s that are even weaker. Fortunately, you can also write a type cast before any constant to get all the type checking you can. (Detractors will say that still is not enough type checking.)

I am all for having your programming language enforce the restrictions you want to impose. It irks me when you get more restrictions than you'd like. That leads to twisty code, to evade the checks, or inefficient code. I don't mind too much, however, when the language fails to help in this area. I figure that you'd better be imposing a strong discipline on your code no matter what. Don't abrogate your responsibility to the compiler.

In this case, that means you'd better know what type each of your named constants has even if the compiler doesn't care. Document it and check it by hand. There's no such thing as a typeless number.

Another guideline is: **Give each datum a complete set of states**. Not every combination of bits in the representation is likely to have meaning for the abstract data that you are modeling. The opposite must, however, be true. Every sensible state in the abstract must have a concrete representation. You should be able to write a predicate that determines every sensible state with a reasonable amount of computation.

Even the simplest computational type can often overflow or be in an undefined state. Set aside discrete values, if at all possible, to represent these special cases. Or make sure that you handle errors so well that nonsense values don't propagate far. If your code has to be really robust, check for special cases before you bull ahead with a silly computation.

For more complex, structured types, the opportunities for inconsistent states abound. Like Topsy, the typical ornate data structure "just growed." Even if there was a concerted effort at design in the early days, an accretion of enhancements has long blurred its outlines. And if you've never viewed a complex data structure as a finite-state machine, chances are it began in trouble. For an eye-opening experience, go take a look at the largest data structure in a large program you've worked on recently. Try describing all the valid states of that data structure and you will see what I mean.

Some languages encourage you to provide a *tag* field for each union (variant record). The value stored in the tag determines which variant is active in the union. That's a step in the direction of state completeness, but only a small one. Some languages encourage you to specify an initial value for each data object that you create. That too is a help, provided you can easily specify a sane state when you write an initial value.

Here is a situation where state-transition diagrams can really help. (See **Essay 4: Finite-State Machines**.) Drawing the diagram forces you to think about where you start, where you can go, and how you can get there. Just don't quit until you are sure that you have considered every possible transition from every possible state.

A companion guideline is: **Give each datum a complete set of operations**. It's one thing to know all the possible state transitions, it's quite another to provide them. The temptation is always strong to leave out the ones you don't need right now. They are always the ones you are going to need next week. What I am talking about here is an explicit investment in the future. I realize that is a hard thing to sell to management in these days of quick return on investment. You have to be convinced yourself that there is a payoff in the present, if only in debugging with greater confidence.

The winning argument these days is code reusability. If you can make a case that doing the whole job now means not doing it over next month, you'll more likely get a hearing. One of the big selling points of object-oriented programming is that it encourages writing reusable code. It does so to the extent that it forces you to think about *everything* you want to do to a data object. Whether you're crafting data objects or just building conventional sets of functions and data declarations, however, it pays you to be complete about it.

Go back to the state-transition diagram you made to design the data structure. Is there a function that creates data objects in a consistent initial state? Are there separate function calls for making all the state transitions? When a data object dies do you need a function to tidy up properly before its storage goes away? If you are performing any of these operations with inline code, make sure that it will survive likely changes in data representations.

That's enough guidelines for a fairly simple subject. The important thing is to keep in mind the underlying reasons I listed above for introducing abstractions. Then abstract whenever you serve one of those reasons, and never abstract when you don't.

I end with a few touchstones for checking your work:

- It ain't abstract if you have to look at the underlying implementation to understand what's going on.
- It ain't portable if the underlying representation cannot change.
- It ain't reusable if it is not complete. □

Afterword: I wrote this essay and the two that follow because of the surge of popularity of object-oriented design and programming. Having seen several "revolutions" go by over the past few decades, I know how religious zeal can distort perspectives, if only for awhile. Thus the emphasis on how we have used abstraction in the past, and the price we pay for using it more in the future.

21 Encapsulate It

In the previous essay, I discussed the basic principles of data abstraction. It's a simple topic, involving lore basic to the programming trade. (See **Essay 20: Abstract It**.) Nevertheless, I find that too many practicing programmers don't know when to introduce abstractions. Some don't even seem to know how to. At the risk of insulting half my putative audience, I reviewed the obvious. I continue in this essay with a related topic, encapsulation. It too is simple. And it too contains lore that is not as widely known as I once thought. So the review continues.

Abstraction and encapsulation are not synonymous. You can introduce abstractions and spread them throughout your code. You can encapsulate code that makes no use of abstraction. In either case, you are ahead of the game. You have done something to make your program easier to maintain.

The two often go hand in hand, however. Stuff all the code that is likely to change in a module and hide its innards. Then introduce whatever types and named constants you need to define the interface. The abstractions aid the encapsulation, and conversely.

You can't encapsulate everything, of course. Nor should you. Imagine a program where every executable statement is a function call. You have a great mound of primitive functions off to one side, each containing one executable statement. Or imagine that every term in an expression is a function call. You have another great mound of primitive functions, each returning the value of a constant or data object. Everything that can possibly change is carefully encapsulated.

Such antics dramatically increase program size and execution time, but they add nothing to program maintainability or readability. In fact, they are sure to make matters worse. It is clear that encapsulation per se is not the road to perfect programs. In the previous essay, I cited three goals for introducing abstraction. You have the same three goals when you encapsulate. The tactical emphasis is different, but the danger is the same. Accompanying every benefit is a drawback:

- **insulation** — You want to protect your program from changes that are likely to happen. Build too many walls and you lose performance.
- **documentation** — You want to emphasize what parts of your program interact strongly and what parts interact only weakly. Pack the wrong things together and you increase coupling between modules and mislead maintainers.

- **completeness** — You want to keep all related code and data together so that you can easily check for missing states or functionality. Pile the wrong things together and you get overwhelmed in combinatorial complexity.

With those goals in mind, we can now look at a few guidelines.

The first guideline is: **If it's likely to change, make sure there's exactly one right place to make the change**. That sentence contains a number of critical phrases. Let's look at them in turn.

The first critical phrase is "likely to change." You don't want to take out insurance against changes that are not likely to happen. Insurance costs money. You needn't redefine the keywords in C, as in:

```
#define IF_KEYWORD if
```

I can assure you that committee X3J11 is much too tired to consider changing the keywords of C for the next five years or so.

You certainly want to introduce a **#define** for each "constant" in your program. We all know how often those critters change. You may want certain parameters to be alterable at program startup. A program to be used across Europe may adjust its prompts to match the language of the executing locale. You may even want to make some supposed constants into data objects whose values can vary when the program runs.

Your job as a programmer is to determine the most flexible point to bind a value to the name the program uses for it. The well known Principle of Latest Binding encourages you to defer binding as long as possible. That gives your program maximum flexibility. I would further encourage you to defer it no longer than the latest sensible point you can imagine. Beyond that point, you sacrifice more performance and readability than you gain in flexibility. I freely admit that determining when to bind values is one of the toughest skills for a programmer to acquire. (I have heard it said that a programmer is someone who can decide on insufficient information when to bind values.) As a beginner, you should err in favor of later binding. When you get to the hotshot stage, start binding sooner than your enthusiasm encourages you to. As an expert, trust your instincts.

The next critical phrase to address from the guideline is "exactly one." If there is more than one place to change, you will probably miss at least one of them. (The next maintainer will miss one even if you don't.) If there is no place to change, then your program is suspiciously insensitive to a change in its environment. Or worse, the changes are too diffuse to identify.

Here, of course, is where abstraction and encapsulation work hand in glove. The act of giving a name to a number confines the changeable number to one place in your code. You can foolishly replicate definitions across all your separately compiled modules. Fortunately, that takes even more work than doing it right.

The final critical phrase is "right place." It does you no good to know that a change is localized if you cannot locate the right spot. You want your intuition, or a sensible reading of the program text, to lead you to the spot where the change *must* occur. Then you want the change to be unequivocally hidden from the rest of the code. That way, you don't have to scan acres of code (either by eye or by `grep`) to check the implications of the change. Encapsulation does little good if the walls of the box are transparent instead of black.

Another guideline is: **Limit access to information until it just begins to hurt**. It's really wonderful when you can make a change with no fear of affecting other parts of the program. It's less wonderful when those other parts need information and have to jump through hoops to get it. As in all things, you have to strike a balance.

The basic principle at work here is, of course, information hiding. David Parnas was one of the first to preach the benefits of partitioning to limit the scope of each design decision (**Par72**). You want to avoid combinatoric explosion by having each decision interact with as few others as possible.

Naturally, there must be some way to access each design decision. If the behavior of the program is not affected by a given choice, you have dead wood on your hands. What you want, ideally, is *one right way* to sniff out each decision. In C or C++ you pack definitions and declarations into a header file. In more structured languages you include the visible part of a package declaration. At best, you get the information at translation time directly from the declarations. At worst, you have to call a function at run time to find out what you need to know.

This is not a matter of deferred binding to improve the flexibility of a program. Rather, it is an unfortunate side effect of building effective fire walls between clumps of information. You can put up with a little inefficiency in the interest of improved maintainability. If the performance price gets too high, however, you have to compromise the principle of information hiding.

Information hiding is not the same as secrecy. The idea is not to prevent outsiders from knowing what you are doing inside a module. Rather, it is to encourage them not to depend on that knowledge. That leads to a kind of secondary coupling which is more pernicious than obvious dependencies because it is less visible. You should encapsulate information to keep it *private*, not secret. (What you do in the bathroom is no secret, but it is private.)

So assuming that your modules have no important secrets, there are various ways you can trade privacy for performance. Rewrite functions as macros that peer directly inside private data structures. That eliminates function-call overhead at the cost of potentially larger code size. (If the whole purpose of the function call is to access a single field, you can win on code size as well.) You can also collapse several layers of function calls into a single call, at the cost of greater shared knowledge between different data types.

To use the older language of structured design, you want to keep coupling as low as possible. Coupling cannot be nonexistent, for the obvious reason I cited above. Some forms of coupling, however, are definitely lower than others. Passing the value of a data object as an argument to a function is very low coupling. Broadcasting the name of a static data object to all modules is very high coupling. In fact, Larry Constantine stigmatized this practice for all time by dubbing it *pathological coupling*. Nevertheless, you may choose to indulge in pathological coupling to share widely used parameters with reasonable efficiency.

In the more stylish language of object-oriented programming, you want to keep the innards of each object private. Access those innards only by "sending a message to a method" associated with the object. In other words, you must call one of the functions defined for the object to peek inside. Only such a function has the savvy to do the job. (A smart translator may expand simple methods to in-line code, of course.)

An object-oriented programmer will be quick to tell you that a little pain is good for you. If you aren't forced to think through the design of each object before you use it, you aren't doing it right. If it's too easy to get at information, you aren't doing it right. An old-school programmer will be equally quick to tell you that too much pain is bad for you. If it costs too much performance to do it right, you aren't doing it right.

Still another guideline is: **Chop your code into modules, but only along the seams**. We all know that modularity is a Good Thing. The only area where we differ is in how we go about making modules.

In the early days, some shops tried to enforce modularity by fiat. Programmers accustomed to writing monoliths responded in their customary passive-aggressive style. They applied what is now known as the Chinese Duck algorithm. (Where the cleaver falls is where the pieces separate. Never mind the bones.) They would write their usual monolithic program, then chop it every 500 lines and paste the pieces back together with branches. (See **Essay 15: Which Tool is Last?**)

Later programmers honestly tried to honor the spirit of modularity. They just didn't have many guidelines about how to locate reasonable seams. A module might be 5 lines or 5,000. Worse, the larger modules might prove to be more maintainable than the smaller ones. What's a mother to do?

Then along came structured design and modularity came into its own. Constantine gave us the concept of *cohesion* as a measure of the goodness of a module. You want to keep cohesion high by keeping related things together and unrelated things apart. Minimizing coupling is important, to be sure, but maximizing cohesion is vital. Whether your functions are chunks of assembly language or methods defined in a class, you must keep cohesion high.

Making better functions did wonders for modularity, but soon even that was not enough. As programs got larger, we found ourselves awash in a sea of function names. On large projects, programmer A had a good chance of making up names that clashed with those generated by programmer B. The project manager either created a central clearing house for external names or handed out funny prefixes to each of the subprojects. Neither solution scales at all well.

One obvious solution is to nest functions. Put inside each function all of its subfunctions (and so on, recursively). That way, the normal block scoping of the language partitions your name space quite nicely. Pascal uses this approach, as does PL/I.

The obvious solution has one obvious failing. If you draw a structure chart of a typical large program, you seldom get a pure tree. Near the top you find that each module has one or more subordinates that it uses exclusively. But farther down the tree, you invariably find increased sharing of modules. More and more functions make use of a handful of low-level primitives to carry out their jobs. (See **Essay 1: Which Tool is Best?**)

In a good design, in fact, fan-in dominates at the bottom of the structure chart. That indicates a clean interface to a lower level of abstraction, as preached by Edsger Dijkstra (**DDJ72**). It manifests itself in a structure chart shaped like an Arabic mosque, as preached by Constantine (**Y&C89**).

An alternate way to group functions is by the abstractions they enforce. Good C programmers know to put highly related functions in one source file, along with any static data they must share. If you minimize the number of names you make external, you can hide a considerable amount of complexity in separately compiled modules. You publish in an **#include** file only what others need to know to use a given module.

Object-oriented programming offers an even better way to encapsulate related functions. A *class* is essentially just a data-object type with a bunch of associated functions attached. (Purists insist on calling these functions *methods*, to confuse the uninitiated.) The type presumably is one of interest to all the functions in the class. (Otherwise, the class has low cohesion.)

Now here's where the fun comes in. To call one of these functions, you have to name its class as well as the function name within the class, as in **window.open**. Or you can name a data object of that class to qualify the function name, as in **prompt_win.close**. You have a hierarchy of names, just as with Pascal-style nesting. Only now the clumping matches the fan-in of the structure chart. You are encapsulating groups of functions in a way that matches the shape of the problem. By now you should know that that is a Good Thing.

Object-oriented languages offer other niceties as well. A function call of the form **prompt_win.close** essentially passes the name of the data object as a secret argument zero. You have nice ways to talk about this special data object. You are encouraged to write *constructors* and *destructors* that help data objects of that class stay consistent from cradle to grave. You can sometimes even overload the standard operators of the language by defining what function to call when operands of that class appear in expressions.

All that frippery can easily obscure the simple importance of encapsulation. That service alone can dramatically improve your ability to maintain a program of a given size. If you have a large system that manipulates several low-level abstractions, the payoff is obvious. That's why, I believe, object-oriented programming came to the forefront about the same time that graphics and windowing software began to burgeon. It is a marriage made in heaven.

Two caveats are in order, however. When I described the typical structure chart of a large program, I noted that the fan-in occurs near the bottom. That fan-in is a loud signal that you should introduce objects for each cluster of related functions. Equally, the absence of fan-in higher up the structure chart should serve as a warning. If you try to stuff *all* of your modules into objects, you won't get nearly the same return on investment. The code that uses an object, even the code inside that implements all the methods, may not itself be a good candidate for this organizational paradigm. Use objects where they work, but don't feel you have to use them exclusively.

The second caveat is that structured design still matters. People new to object-oriented programming are often at a loss about what to include in each class. If you consider coupling and cohesion in terms of the whole class, not just individual functions, you will find the guidance you need. You can make truly ugly classes that are hard to maintain and unlikely to be reused. Or you can make gems that you'll use unchanged for years. I assure you that the gems will have low coupling to other objects and high internal cohesion.

My final guideline is: **Don't finish a module until it's complete**. There's lots of blather about how reusable code is in object-oriented languages. That's true only for modules with good coupling and cohesion, of course. It's also true only for modules that come with a complete set of operations (methods). Cut corners here and you're wasting much of your extra investment in designing for the future.

Some people think you can always toss in the missing code later, when the need arises. My experience is that you always have to change part of the existing code when you do. You can argue that the functionality remains unchanged when you alter the guts, but try explaining that to a project manager who's sharing the code for a delivered product. I've yet to see a competent manager allow a baseline change without extensive retesting. Making changes later can be more expensive than you think.

You don't have to code in C++ or Eiffel to write reusable code, by the way. Some of us old hands feel like we've been doing that for some time now. What we called subroutine libraries are now packaged with fancier names. Granted, the language assist is nice. But the rules for writing reusable code haven't changed. □

Afterword: This is the second of a series of three essays on the underlying principles of object-oriented programming. I wrote it to demystify some aspects of the business of choosing objects. Many authors and lecturers were making a great thing out of this new trade. The strong implication was that designing in terms of objects was a) a new skill that existing programmers would find hard to learn, and b) a skill that would soon be essential to your professional survival. Both implications contain a grain of truth, but are typically overstated. Thus, I present object formation as a natural outgrowth of our 20 years' experience in encapsulating portions of a design.

22 Inherit It

This is the third and last essay in a series. I began with a series of simple guidelines for how and when to introduce abstractions in your code. (See **Essay 20: Abstract It**.) I continued with more guidelines for how and when to encapsulate portions of each program you write. (See **Essay 21: Encapsulate It**.) I conclude this series with some observations on how you can use inheritance to improve your programs.

All three of these terms — abstraction, encapsulation, and inheritance — have become buzzwords. To be *au courant* as a software designer, you must pay regular homage to these three techniques for controlling the complexity of computer programs. While I basically agree with that stylish position, I hasten to point out that the words alone do not a design guide make. You must have some notion of when each technique helps, when it does not, and how to apply it when it does help. That is why I have focused on the "when and how" of using each technique.

The proponents of object-oriented programming generally agree that a language is truly object-oriented only if it supports all three techniques in the construction of objects. I also agree with that position. What I don't buy is the false contrapositive that many such proponents arrive at through some twisty little maze of conjectures. They conclude that unless you are writing in a proper object-oriented language, you can't possibly be using abstraction, encapsulation, or inheritance properly.

Baloney. Some of us have been doing all that stuff for most of our professional programming careers. A good language helps you use the techniques better. (A good language does not, however, *guarantee* that you will use them better.) But all of the techniques go back many years.

I gave a number of examples of how you use abstraction and encapsulation in the previous two essays. Inheritance is, in many ways, even more widely used in common practice. It also has a rather precise meaning in the world of object-oriented programming. The double meaning for the term only adds to the confusion.

In the general sense, you make use of inheritance every time you declare a scalar data object. Procedural languages since the days of FORTRAN provide an assortment of arithmetic types — Booleans, integers, and floating-point representations — in a variety of sizes. Later languages even let you manipulate storage addresses (pointers) to some degree. Each scalar type supports a variety of operations, such as equality comparison and addition. There are built-in rules for converting between types and for mixing certain types across an operator within an expression.

So as soon as you write **int x** in your code, you inherit a slew of properties and methods. Your newborn **x** has a birthright that helps it quickly become a productive citizen. You don't have to write a pageant to describe its future life and times in excruciating detail. The language designer gives you, and your newly conceived data object, a bouquet of useful stuff.

You probably get more than you bargained for, in fact. It is a rare **x** that really should assume all of the values representable by an **int**. You may have to add code to certain assignments to ensure that only the sensible subset of values actually gets stored. (Some languages let you define a subrange of values, which is helpful. But not all subsets are subranges, as I have pointed out in the past.) Similarly, your **x** may hold values that should not be added to the values stored in **y**, or divided by 17. Nevertheless, you inherit permission to write such nonsense along with all the properties you want from **int**.

Another traditional way to inherit useful stuff is to call on the services of a support library. When you include the standard header **<stdio.h>** in a C program, you get (among many other things) a type definition called **FILE**. Call the function **fopen** with a valid filename and you get back a pointer to a **FILE** data object. You can pass this pointer to a wide assortment of functions that manipulate the contents of the opened file in all sorts of wondrous ways. The services you buy with that one **#include** directive would cost you pages of declarations and kilobytes of code to replicate.

Of course, **FILE** provides even more overkill than **int**. What you want to do to a given file is typically but a shadow of what the Standard C library is prepared to do on your behalf. You probably wouldn't provide all that machinery if you were defining your own object for manipulating a sequential file of names and addresses. Some of the code you write will certainly be geared toward holding that inherited power in check.

The obvious point I am trying to make is that we use inheritance all the time. There is nothing profound about the concept and there is nothing particularly difficult about the practice. The more subtle point is that we also *derive* new types from inherited types much of the time. Your code says, "I want **x** to behave mostly like an **int** except in the following ways." Or, "This is just like a **FILE** but with the following severe constraints." The objects that come with a general-purpose programming language are almost always too general purpose to be used without being circumscribed.

The central theme of object-oriented programming is to make your own objects. One promised payoff is code reusability. You reuse code when you can recycle an object that does mostly what you want. If it does exactly what you want, you're home free. But we all know how often that happens in real life. So you are happy when the language lets you inherit all the properties of an almost-right object, then derive the right one by amending those properties.

This is the more precise meaning of inheritance that I alluded to earlier. It is really the same thing we have always done, but more stylized and more centralized. (The stylization is a form of abstraction and the centralization is a form of encapsulation.) To the extent that it makes you think explicitly about how you want to edit what you inherit, object-oriented programming is a Good Thing. To the extent that it obscures a simple practice, and introduces inefficiencies in the bargain, it is not.

Where do the inefficiencies come from? They arise when you try to do something simple in a language that is prepared to handle complex cases as well. If the translator cannot determine that what you really want to do is simple, it must bring to bear the full power of general-purpose machinery just to be safe. That invariably costs you some performance.

In the case of object-oriented programming, one of the worst sources of inefficiency lurks in the machinery for matching up methods with objects. To explain what that means, and why it can be a problem, I have to back up a bit.

In the previous essay, I described how you can group functions to minimize clutter in the space of external names. The principles of coupling and cohesion apply just as much to these groups as to individual functions, so you want the functions in a group to be highly related. Typically, all the functions manipulate a specific data structure. (And no other functions need to know the innards of the data structure.)

A language that supports encapsulation well will let you declare the functions along with the data structure in a *class*. The function names occupy a private space, just like the names of the data structure members. You identify which function to call by naming the class, as in **window.open()**. Or you name an instance of the data structure, as in **new_window.close()**. That way, any number of classes can have functions with simple and meaningful names like **open** and **close** with no fear of collision or reader confusion.

You can encapsulate groups of functions this way even in Standard C. Put all the functions in a separate file and declare them **static**. All that you make external is the name of a structure containing the addresses of the functions you want to make visible, as in:

```
struct Win {
    Window *(*open)(void);
    (*close)(Window *);
    ..... );
extern struct Win Win = {
    &open, &close, ..... };
```

Once you include a header that contains these declarations (without the initializer, of course), you can call the functions by writing expressions like **Win.open()**. (Standard C lets you write this simpler form as well as the older **(*Win.open)()**.)

As a matter of fact, object-oriented languages like C++ actually do this sort of thing under the hood. Each object has an accompanying transfer vector much like the C structure in the example above. Why? That's where inheritance comes in.

When you derive a new object from an existing one, you inherit all of its functions. But you can override some of the functions you inherit with a new version for the new object. And you can add functions that do not appear in the original object. The transfer vector for the new object starts out looking like the old one. The address of each replacement function displaces the corresponding address from the old object. The addresses of new functions get added on the end.

What this machinery gives you is dynamic binding of methods. You can write an expression that invokes a method where it is not clear whether the actual operand is an object of the older or the newer type. In that case, an instance of each type contains an additional field that designates which transfer vector to use. To call a method, the translator generates code that uses this field to determine the transfer vector. The code then uses the appropriate member of the vector to determine which function to call.

The unmitigated C code for such an expression is:

```
(*object->vector.func_ptr)()
```

Such a call clearly takes longer than calling a function whose address is known directly to the translator. It doesn't take much longer, to be sure. But C++ is rife with function calls, both explicit and implicit. Given enough secret calls on constructors and destructors, an elegantly ambiguous object reference can cause considerable churning beneath the surface. (I hesitate to say, "below C level.")

Now, C++ is pretty good about this sort of thing most of the time. When the translator can determine exactly which method to call, it calls it directly. Only when you indulge in clever overloading of method references do you pay the price. The price can be higher than you expect, but it is one you can avoid paying with a bit of training.

Other object-oriented languages are less flexible. Smalltalk, for example, is essentially untyped at translation time. You can send a message to an object designating any method you choose to name. That means the run-time system must be prepared to look up a method name in an open-ended list of methods for each object. No fixed offset into a transfer vector here. It also means that the object may have no instance of the method. The runtime can only panic in that case.

The up side of Smalltalk is that you can incrementally enhance objects by adding methods a bit at a time. The down side is that you never know when a production program is going to cough on an unexpected method reference. And, of course, the performance is substantially worse than for simpler procedural languages.

Inheritance is very sexy. Proponents of object-oriented programming are convinced that any cost in performance is well worth the improvement you get in code reusability. They give wonderful examples of whole trees of objects derived in stages from a well crafted root. (The entire Smalltalk system is itself rather a good example of the possibilities of inheritance.)

I remain dubious. The real world examples where I see inheritance pay off are fairly specialized cases. Most involve not so much trees of objects as two-dimensional arrays of data types versus methods.

You have circles, squares, and triangles. You want to draw, move, and rotate them. The classic solution is to make a parent object, called **shape** for instance. A shape has a location, so it is easy to provide a generic **move** method that all objects can inherit. Any other methods must be fleshed out in the derived objects. (They are *virtual* methods.) **rotate** is trivial for a circle, not so easy for the others. They may or may not share a full blown **rotate** method by having a common ancestor.

The point is, you use the tree nature of inheritance mostly to factor out common methods. That saves replicating some code, but it doesn't reflect the shape of the problem. What the problem begs is a two-dimensional array of functions, some of which happen to be identical.

And even when you see the array of functions, you can still build the wrong objects. A standard straw man set up by proponents of object-oriented programming is the poorly factored program. Write functions called **draw, move**, and **rotate** then see what happens when you add a new shape. Each function has to handle a new case, so all must change. The good guys just derive a new object and redefine the methods that have to change. That makes them the clear winners.

But you can rig the game the other way. What happens if you have to add a new method such as **reflect**? Maybe you're lucky and can get away with adding it in the root object. Probably you'll have to modify every object, if only to get a consistent level of optimization. You can also plan for this by making your objects **drawing, movement**, and **rotation**. The three methods become **circlify, squarify**, and **trianglify**. But just try to get an object-oriented programmer to swallow "circlifying a drawing."

The simple fact is, you can plan for change even without indulging in object-oriented programming. If you've ever passed the address of a function as a parameter, or indexed into a table of function pointers, you've deferred binding of a method. With any foreknowledge of what is likely to change, you can use such machinery to isolate the change to your heart's content. Write another function, add a pointer to a table, and you're done.

I freely admit that a good object-oriented language can help the readability of some programs. It's nice to have all those pointers being dereferenced under the hood. Just make sure you're happy with where your horsepower is being consumed.

𝕴 conclude this ranging overview of abstraction, encapsulation, and inheritance with my own revisionist viewpoint. The end result is that I support object-oriented programming, but not for the usual reasons.

One of the big problems you must solve in organizing a large program is imposing some structure on all the functions you have to write. The early practitioners of structured design told us to draw a structure chart. You draw a box for the main function at the top. Below that you draw boxes for all the functions called directly from the main function, with arrows to document the calls. Below each of these boxes you draw still more boxes for the next immediate subordinates, with still more arrows — and so on until you've written a box for every function in the program. (See **Essay 1: Which Tool is Best?**)

That's fine for a language like FORTRAN or COBOL, with no recursion. Recursion turns your neat tree into a directed graph. All sorts of interesting arrows loop from deep in the hierarchy to functions closer to the root of the tree. Structure charts with as few as a score of boxes suddenly become marginally readable.

Even without recursion, you still have the problem of documenting fan-in. That's where more than one higher-level module sees fit to call upon one lower-level module. With enough fan-in, a structure chart that spreads out at the top begins to close in again toward the bottom. This makes the familiar Arabic mosque shape beloved of structured designers.

Fan-in is not only likely in a nontrivial design, it borders on being *de rigeur*. The mosque shape indicates that you have properly interfaced your program to the next lower level of abstraction. Whether it's a data-base management system, a file system, or a multi-processing operating system underneath, you want to interact with it through just a few portals. You pass through those portals by calling upon half a dozen or more functions. The boxes for those functions lie at the bottom of your structure chart.

For upwards of three dozen functions, you can draw a useful structure chart. The fan-in at the bottom may call for a few crossed arrows, but the document is still fairly revealing and easy to read. Beyond that number, however, structure charts begin to lose their usefulness.

Documenting all the calls on system interface functions is, in many ways, as silly as documenting all the **print** statements. It may be nice to know which modules actually perform I/O, but capturing that information in the structure chart just causes clutter. And if you're going to show all the modules with **print** statements, then why not show the ones with **switch** statements as well? They may well make secret calls to runtime support functions. Then you have to argue whether you want to show **if** and **while** usage as well.

For most of us, it's clear where to draw the line. Statements are somehow part of the language in which we code. We don't document the plumbing. The functions we write are our value added. That's the part we want to describe.

What you have to realize, however, is that we make up mini-languages as we go along. A program that consists of a hundred or more functions almost certainly uses them in clumps. One clump may implement a simple data-base management system. Another may impose an indexed-sequential organization on an underlying set of files. Still a third may simply interface to the process scheduling primitives of the host operating system.

Try to draw a structure chart subsuming the top-level control plus all these clumps and you have a useless rats nest. With fan-in going to three different clumps, plus additional structure within the clumps, you'll never see the boxes for the arrows.

Instead, you should characterize each of the clumps in terms of the half dozen or dozen functions it presents to the outside world. (This is abstraction at work.) Draw a separate structure chart for each of the clumps. (This is encapsulation.) Then draw a structure chart of the top-level control, leaving out all the calls to the functions in the clumps.

As far as that structure chart is concerned, such calls are just additional statements in the underlying programming language. Those statements may often be implemented as a handful of interface functions that make use of an existing library or set of system services. (This is inheritance.)

If an object-oriented language lets you express a large program more readably, then by all means use it. Don't be deluded into thinking that you are no longer programming procedurally, however. All those functions are still there. They still must be organized into hierarchies. You just found a better technique for managing them in clumps. □

*A*fterword: *I don't pretend that the approach outlined here is a complete substitute for object-oriented design as conventionally taught. Sometimes, building a hierarchy of classes is so central to the design that you simply must do it first. Rather, I put forth this approach for the many cases where objects are important but peripheral to other design considerations. In such cases, "mining" a design arrived at by other means gives better guidance in how to form objects.*

The simple fact is, choosing the best set of objects is indeed more of an art than a science. **drawing.circlify()** *can make sense in an application where the shapes are stable but the operations are subject to change. People skilled in object-oriented design know a good solution when they see one. Often, that is enough to guide them to a good solution from a standing start. Less skilled people (in this area) need more guidance at the outset, however. Any method that leads you to a good solution deserves a place in your kit of tools.*

23 Heresies of Software Design

esigning software is a field that has a checkered record of successes. I have been a student of such methods for nearly three decades. Often, I have tried to exercise the latest methods in practical programming situations. Occasionally, I have even tried to serve as teacher. I cannot honestly report that any method will guarantee success. The good ones will improve your odds, but even the best can leave you in the lurch.

If dogma doesn't work reliably, you have an obligation to look at other approaches. The opposite of dogma is heresy (at least along some axes). I believe that it is worthwhile to examine a number of heretical design principles, even though heresies generally deserve their bad reputation. At the very least, such an examination can open your mind to new approaches. At worst, it can reinforce your conviction that there is no reliable way to design computer software.

One of the seminars I gave at Miller Freeman's Software Development '90 conference was on various heresies of software design. It was sufficiently well received that I was asked to repeat the talk at Software Development '90 East. Not one to abandon good material before it is worked to death, I decided to recycle the topic for this essay.

Of course, there is a certain shock value in using a term as emotionally charged as "heresies." I am not above a bit of showmanship, as some of you may know. But I do like to educate as well as entertain. It's one thing to lure people in the door with the promise of an interesting topic. It's another to get them to leave with the sense that their time was not ill used.

The seminar took an open-minded look at software design principles both in and out of vogue. The goal was to formulate an approach to design that works, for whatever reason. It was not to prove that the establishment is doing everything wrong. Nor was it to replace one set of dogma with another.

A heresy is a belief that opposes the common view. Some people gravitate to heresies simply because they like to oppose. They (erroneously) assume that opposition is the mark of the independent thinker. I have certainly enjoyed playing the opposer more than once in the past. There is a certain comfort in knowing that you are not making the same mistakes as the majority. There is also a certain chill in being alone when you make your own brand of errors.

Others gravitate to heresies because they have lost faith in the common view. They (erroneously) assume that a heretical view must be right because it differs from a view that is wrong. It's sometimes comforting to think that we live in a world of binary choices. But the chill reality is that life is never so simple, at least for the responsible.

The common view generally becomes common because it is mostly right. Heresies are worth examining only when the common view has a poor track record. In that situation, even erroneous heresies serve a useful purpose. They force you to think. I believe it is fair to say that software design can use a bit more thinking. So let's trot out a few heresies.

𝕳 eresy: **If you know exactly how to do it, it's not worth doing.** Writing computer software is all about controlling complexity. We need to control complexity because our minds, wonderful as they are in certain ways, are easily overwhelmed by it. That's the attraction of computers, that they let us extend the powers of our minds in useful ways. Programming is unique in that you need never do exactly the same job twice.

Yes, I know that it doesn't feel this way. It seems as if we spend half our professional careers writing the same handful of programs over and over again. Somehow, the last payroll program — or screen generator, or matrix inverter — is never quite appropriate for the next application.

We focus on the repetition and don't see the novelty. Often the reason that the old version doesn't work is that we have more sophisticated requirements for other parts of the program. We need better input checking, or more reliable code, or fancier displays. Even then, we recycle successful algorithms unconsciously. That saves us the mental cost of mastering yet another chunk of complexity.

For all that we complain about redoing software too often, we have accreted quite a bit of power over the years. Look at the size of the library that you get with a typical compiler these days. Compare that with what you got ten years ago. Look at the operating-system services of a Macintosh, or UNIX, or even MS-DOS 3.x. Then throw in the libraries you can buy off the shelf. Add the powerful applications programs you can drop into an application with a minimum of configuring. We've come a long way, baby.

If you are faced with a task that you understand thoroughly, you should therefore be suspicious. What's the glory (or sense, or profit) in it? Surely that particular chunk of complexity has been mastered before.

You need to put your energy into adding significant new value to whatever you do. If you are merely recycling an old design to reimplement old code, you're being left behind. Someone else out there is building on code that is good enough, to do something wonderfully new. You can't afford to play it completely safe.

eresy: **If you've never done it before, you don't know how to do it.** This is the flip side of the previous statement. You can put it positively and say that each new job is a challenge. Or you can put it negatively and say that each new job is a risk.

What makes programming unique, again, is that we have trouble judging the depth of complexity that we cannot fully grasp all at once. That makes it particularly difficult to estimate how long it will take to write a new program. The more new things lurking in the program specification, the more out of control you are as a programmer.

What gets us every time is the linear extrapolation. We estimate, perhaps honestly, that a new task will take twice as many lines as one we've done in the past. We then assume erroneously that the effort will also simply double. That makes no allowance for dealing with any unknowns. It also fails to account for the exponential increase in potential interactions between different parts of the code.

There is one fairly safe situation. That is when a large project is the sum of several small projects that you have done before. You can scale the effort linearly because there are few unknowns. You can also suspect that the job is not worth doing, since it violates the previous heresy.

Fred Brooks has given us one trick for writing new programs. One chapter of his wonderful book *The Mythical Man-Month* (**Bro75**) is titled, "Plan to throw one away." To figure out how to write a program, says Brooks, write a draft of it. Since that draft will be marred by misperceptions and false starts, don't plan on keeping it. Instead, allow sufficient time to write a draft and then spec out the actual writing of the code.

Interestingly, Brooks also includes in his book a chapter titled, "The Second System Effect." There he gives a different warning. Writing a second version of a program tempts you to add all the whistles and bells you left out the first time. If you can't discipline yourself to avoid this tendency (and it is hard to avoid), you must be even more conservative. Plan to throw *two* away.

It takes one try to figure out how to write a program and a second to figure out how to write it elegantly. After writing a program three times, you should have it good enough that you need never rewrite it again.

eresy: **Trust your customer or systems analyst to tell you how to do it wrong.** We all pay lip service to listening to the customer. We bemoan the lack of emphasis on proper systems analysis before committing to design. Nevertheless, you must guard against giving too much weight to input from either of these worthy sources.

The problem stems from a lack of abstraction. People tend not to think in terms of what they want. Rather, they focus on *one way to get it*. Customers know how they have run their enterprise for years. They implicitly assume that every piece of paper, every file, every communications channel is necessary. They will expect to see those concrete relics captured in various parts of a computer system. Not knowing the ways of computers, they will inadvertently close off your options as a designer.

Even analysts, who are nominally trained to elicit abstract specifications, often fall prey to the same tendency. In some ways, they are worse. Many analysts come up through the ranks of programming and software design. Knowing how to do a job at least one way colors their thinking. Some want to control the design and coding. Others try to do so without thinking. Either way, they overstep boundaries and tromp on your turf.

As a consequence, any specification you get for a software project will almost certainly be tainted. The taint comes from a deep presumption that the final product should be implemented in a certain way. Your customer will envision the existing paper system reconstituted electronically. Each form will have a corresponding screen or printer form. And every human being currently in the loop will still have a hand in processing the electronic paper.

For a program to be really useful, however, it must streamline more than just the flow of paper. You as a designer must take a hard look at the information flow, and how data is stored. By the time you streamline processing, ensure robustness, and provide adequate backup systems, you may have to radically alter the current architecture.

A systems analyst is supposed to do this for you, of course. The only way to get an untainted specification can be tough, however. You have to apply another Rule of Three. This rule is similar to the one derived from Brooks's precepts, but it comes from a different angle.

Require the analyst to outline two quite distinct implementations that meet the stated specifications. That will force the analyst to let go of a particular mind set and start thinking more abstractly. It's hard to bias toward one implementation if another is on the table as well. If you really want to be tough, then, ask for three.

I found that writing portable software was next to impossible for programmers who worked on a single computer architecture. Require them to prove in the code on two quite different machines and you eliminate many portability bugs. Require them to do it for three and you have won just about all the portability you ever need. After that, only exotic architectures cause many problems.

Analysis and coding are remarkably similar in this regard. If you want to eliminate dependencies, you have to invest the extra effort up front.

𝕳eresy: **Prototype a system to find out what *not* to do.** Prototyping is one of those practices that seem impervious to criticism. The worst I have heard is that some customers are willing to settle for the prototype. If you have your heart set on doing the whole project as originally envisioned, that can of course be disastrous. Nevertheless, most modern designers appreciate the beneficial feedback you can get only from customer experience with a prototype.

What you have to keep in mind, however, is that the useful feedback is mostly negative. Customers are quick to discover what they don't like about a system from mucking with a prototype. They tend to be complacent, or even oblivious, about the parts that work as expected. Listen carefully for any criticism and give it more weight even than the customers. That will tell you where to spend your energy most wisely.

The other thing you learn from prototyping is what parts of the system to postpone indefinitely. Your preoccupation as a designer will be with the challenges. You will automatically focus on the bits of complexity that will be hardest to tame. With rare exception, however, the customer won't share your concerns. You will find that the hardest parts of a program to implement are generally the ones least desired by the customer.

A past master of focused prototyping is Brian Kernighan. (See my essay "Programming on Purpose: The Seven Warning Signs," *Computer Language*, October 1989.) He has designed any number of languages and applications by getting early customers to tell him what not to implement. Those of us who love solving complex problems are still untangling complexity long after Brian has cheerfully moved on to his next success.

The lesson is simple — never put off until tomorrow what you can put off indefinitely.

*H*eresy: **If you don't understand how to apply a design method, it's probably not your fault.** Practically everyone who preaches organized methods of software design try to make designers feel lazy or stupid. Just put enough energy into designing the system right (for a change), and you are bound to increase your productivity dramatically. You can guess that the "right" way is the way they happen to be teaching this year.

You must not lose sight of two factors. One is that you are probably smarter than they give you credit. Otherwise you couldn't afford to pay for their books and seminars, now could you? The other is that they are probably not as smart about writing software as they think. Otherwise they would be making millions writing the best software instead of books and seminars, now wouldn't they?

All those methods being taught have something of value. Your job is to figure out what the value is and where you can best apply it. If you can't apply a given method in a given situation, it probably doesn't apply very well. Try something else. If that fails, try *anything* else.

Eventually, you will succeed.

Heresy: **Don't tune a system if you can get away without tuning it.** This is not the usual truism about tuning systems only after they are debugged. It's not about measuring to find the hot spots because you invariably guess wrong. It's not even about picking good algorithms up front. It's about avoiding unnecessary work.

The simple fact is, most programs that you write work fast enough. Tuning them to go even faster may seem like a socially responsible thing to do, but it's not. And that's because everything you are likely to do to make a program smaller or faster is going to cost you something. That something is invariably readability, maintainability, extendibility, or all of the above. Those virtues are far more important than saving CPU cycles that no one is currently missing. Don't sacrifice them lightly.

A corollary to this is, stop tuning as soon as you can. It's seductive to keep tweaking a program once you start. A part of you wants to produce the "best" program by some arbitrary performance metric. Know well, however, that the tweaks you perform after the first round are even more costly of those virtues listed above. Cut it out.

Heresy: **Don't jump to projects or jobs that are too far from your level of expertise.** Programmers evolve through various stages of professionalism. At the lowest, you can contrive a small program and get it mostly correct on your own. Then you learn to design with greater discipline, work with others, document properly, estimate more accurately, test more thoroughly, and so on. You need to learn the levels of professionalism in software development. And you need to know where you stand, as accurately as possible.

The Software Engineering Institute has begun the process of defining the evolutionary scale for programmers and programming shops (**Hum89**). What they have published to date can only be described as preliminary, but it is a start. As a science, it is still descriptive and a long way from prescriptive. They are at least formulating guidelines for us to assess our abilities and levels of sophistication.

The main thing you need to know is that you can't skip steps. You don't climb out of the primordial ooze of hackerdom one day and work on million-line projects the next. If you see an opportunity to join a new project, first ask yourself where it lies on the evolutionary scale. If it's one notch up from you and you're ready to be stretched, go for it. Two notches up is out of reach. Your chances of failure are too great.

Likewise, you can't go back. Once you get accustomed to working to budget and to deadline, with detailed specifications and a testing organization ready to support you, anything less smacks of anarchy. It may have felt like the headiest of freedom to you five years ago, but no longer.

This is not a rationale for a class structure in programming, by the way. I simply observe that it is important for you to know your place. You must also know that you can improve your place, if you go about it properly. How far you go is up to you. □

fterword: This essay has a companion on software management. (See "Pro-gramming on Purpose: Heresies of Software Management," Computer Language, *March 1991.) Both were written only 0.2 in jest. I have observed far too often that technical training in software-design methods is wasted. A sensible designer must have some awareness of the context in which he or she works, lest people issues sabotage the technical ones. I could try to build such awareness by discussing management and politics directly. (I have done so, in a separate collection of essays.) Here, however, I chose to focus on how politics perverts and inverts truisms. The resultant rules are cast as heresies, but I believe in them religiously.*

24 Remedial Software Engineering

$\mathbb{I}$ recently spent a year teaching software engineering at the University of New South Wales in Sydney, Australia. It was my first foray back into academic life since I earned my doctorate over two decades ago. I took the post mostly as an excuse to spend a year in Australia. I happily returned to my life as an unemployed writer. But I must say that I enjoyed my year on campus.

For one thing, it's nice to see young people eager to learn. No, the current generation is no more dedicated than you and I were. They still drink beer, doze through lectures, and botch assignments miserably all too often. But every once in awhile, I got to witness that brief *Aha!* that repays so much frustration. At my age, a few of those go a long way.

For another thing, teaching people is a great way to learn what you don't know. I showed up on campus with hundreds of pages of essays accumulated over decades of preaching. I soon learned which presentations scored and which flew wide of the mark. I left with hundreds of pages of edited notes. Back, as they say, to the drawing board.

The first term, I was one of three lecturers teaching a senior course in software engineering. We had over 170 students, for many of whom English is a second language. (Australian schools have become very popular among Asians, both immigrant and overseas visitors.) That queered many of my puns from the outset. On the other hand, it forced me to express ideas with added clarity and simplicity.

I was nominally responsible for presenting conventional structured-analysis techniques. The (preselected) text was Tom DeMarco's excellent *Structured Analysis and System Specification* (**deM78**). Naturally, I deviated freely and often from DeMarco's presentation. I have been known to express my own ideas on that topic in the past.

I got only limited feedback from a class of that size. The students had to perform a term-long analysis project in teams of three. I saw how they applied data-flow and related analysis techniques on the preliminary report and on the final submission. I wrote and graded a few questions on their homework and their final examination. I answered a lot of questions from individual students.

The main thing I learned (or was reminded of) was that drawing data-flow diagrams is an inexact craft. Sixty groups can contrive almost as many distinct diagrams for a nontrivial problem. Most may be correct, but only a few are sufficiently elegant. Teaching elegance is at least as important as teaching the mechanics, I now realize.

The other thing I learned is that students seldom know what they think they know. Many were exposed in earlier courses to Karnaugh maps, decision tables, and state-transition diagrams. Few had suffered enough experience to *really* know how to apply them. But most were secure enough in their knowledge to be bored by a review. Just enough exposure to form antibodies, I suppose.

I hope some of what I tried to teach rubbed off on that large mob. I felt the old twinges of conscience from past teaching experience. Probably, many students learned just enough from me to be dangerous. Well, at least I tried to be entertaining.

The second term was lots more fun. I got a first-year graduate seminar all for my very own. I ended up with almost four dozen assorted honors and graduate students. More of them understood my puns and the rest were crafty enough to laugh along with the others. We met Monday evenings from 6:00 to 9:00 (a mixed blessing).

I anguished a lot about what to present to this crew. My colleagues assured me they needed much the same material as I had taught the first term. But this time I was responsible for the entire course content. It was up to me to give these serious computer-science students a serious dose of software engineering.

I joked for a spell that what I really wanted to teach was somewhat less lofty. I figured that even the best of those students would have one or more major lacunae in his or her prior education. The field is still sufficiently young and spotty that no two students are likely to have a large overlap of shared experience. I told my colleagues that I intended to teach Remedial Software Engineering.

After awhile, however, I realized that I was not joking. That was *exactly* what I felt these students needed. Perhaps none of them intended ever to be software engineers. They might want to be computer scientists, managers, or just good programmers. That's fine. But they should know the basic skills required of a working software engineer. Just as they major in computer science to learn the basic skills of that more academic discipline.

So I began by listing the various skills and bits of knowledge that I have found to be important. I then structured the course to at least touch on the most important of these. I soon found that I had no trouble filling up the allotted meeting time.

I chose a simple working definition of software engineering. It's that body of skills you need to tackle large software projects and deliver the goods reliably. Many people can design and write programs if they can hold all the details in their heads long enough. A software engineer has the tools for partitioning much larger problems into manageable chunks. It's like the difference between writing a one-page letter and outlining a 40-page reference manual.

*A*nother way to handle larger projects is to divide them up among a team of people. That requires a knowledge of how to divide work wisely and how to organize groups of people. It demands practical skills in working in groups, including how to survive committee meetings. Again, it's like the difference between writing a document yourself and working with co-authors.

Reliability is at least as important as the ability to handle larger projects. The larger the projects, in fact, the greater the stakes you're playing for. People who fund large projects understandably want a high level of confidence that they will succeed. The sensible ones gladly pay a premium to lower the risk of failure. That's why publishers often favor hack writers who always deliver stuff that sells over the hard-drinking genius who sometimes falls flat.

I intentionally chose analogies to writing here instead of to other branches of engineering. That's because I feel that software engineering is still underdeveloped. It is less like circuit design than it is like writing scripts for a weekly TV series. At least lore and formulas are the precursors to predictable techniques.

With this definition, it was obvious what I should lecture on. Begin with a discussion of various ways to organize large projects. Discuss the relative merits of hierarchical v. matrix management. Introduce the concept of surgical teams as a way of limiting communication overload. Discuss the tradeoffs between robustness and efficiency for projects of varying complexity.

With people issues out of the way, I could then pick a coherent analysis and design method and present it in detail. Hatley/Pirbhai (**H&P87**) or Ward/Mellor (**W&M85**) are both modern updates of the approach pioneered by DeMarco and others in the 1970s. That would lead naturally to a discussion of modern CASE tools and object-oriented design and programming techniques. I could end with a discussion of the latest ideas from the Software Engineering Institute (**Hum89**) and other places seriously concerned with making software engineering real.

I didn't do any of that stuff. Remember, this is a *remedial* course. No point in leading students to the mountain top if they haven't learned their way around the foothills adequately. My goal was to make sure they at least knew about all the low-level terrain. They could climb their own hills later, if they chose. So I split each three-hour meeting into three equal parts. For the first hour, I lectured on one particular topic. Usually, it was a technique I felt that all programmers should know. Typically, the technique was of use primarily in chopping larger problems into smaller ones. These are not the sort of techniques that a seat-of-the-pants programmer picks up without concerted effort.

For the second hour, I had the class work in groups. They had to perform an exercise that used the technique I had just lectured on. That reinforced the message before it faded completely. (It also rescued those who had daydreamed through the lecture, provided *someone* in their group managed to stay alert.)

Almost invariably, the exercise came in two parts. Halfway through the hour, I would ask the groups to alter or enhance the solution they had almost completed. That's what they will be spending the rest of their careers doing, I figure.

I also obliged each group to submit a written report on what they accomplished by the start of the next week's lecture (their only workload outside of class time). All members of the group had to sign the report, and all got the same grade. No minority reports accepted. Once again, that's often the way real life works.

The third hour was spent on book reports. Each student had to report on some book, periodical, or magazine that might be of use to a software engineer. I provided an initial list and preapproved any additions to the list. Publications ranged from ACM's *Software Engineering Notes* to Pirsig's *Zen and the Art of Motorcycle Maintenance* (**Pir75**), from the magazine *Computer Language* to Tufte's *The Visual Display of Quantitative Information* (**Tuf83**).

A student had less than ten minutes to show a copy of the publication, summarize it, and put it in proper perspective for software engineers. My goal in this case was to familiarize students with the myriad sources of information they can draw upon. Books teach techniques and perspective. Periodicals keep you current. A software engineer needs to read widely and continually to supplement whatever formal education he or she gets.

That, in outline, was the overt agenda. Gerry Weinberg and Larry Constantine have taught me to be sneakier than that, however. Often, the best way to deliver a message is to disguise it. A good part of what I taught came almost in passing.

For example, I devoted almost no lecture time to the business of working in groups. Instead, I let the class find out the hard way. On the first night, the nominal exercise was to perform two technical tasks. The first was to derive a specification for a simple binary-search function. The second was to review a C version of the binary search and locate any errors. (I salted it with half a dozen.) I broke the class up into teams of varying sizes. The smallest was one person, the largest was about 20. I then unleashed the groups on these two exercises with no additional preparation.

If you know group dynamics, you can predict the outcome. Writing a specification is essentially a solitary activity. The smallest groups got the most done, the larger groups spent their time haggling over details. The largest group got nowhere. Reviewing a specification, on the other hand, is a good use of group time. You benefit from having multiple pairs of eyes looking for flaws. (You must, of course, have a good group leader to control discussion.) Here, the groups of three to ten did well. The one-person group didn't know C — he lacked the resources to do much at all. The largest group again got nowhere.

After the first night, I mostly let people form their own groups. I didn't have to tell them that groups of three to seven people were most likely to get things done. They *knew*.

$\mathfrak{H}$ere is another example. The exercise for the second week was to interview customers. That's the origin of many proposals and the starting point of nearly all analysis. I labeled half the groups *A*, the other half *B*. First the *A* groups interviewed the *B* groups to elicit one specification. Then the *B* groups interviewed the *A* groups to elicit a different specification.

Again, this was an exercise in frustration. No groups learned much technical in half an hour. What everybody learned was that it is silly for a dozen people to sit around a table and hope to communicate much about a brand-new problem. Yet that is *exactly* what businesses persist in doing week in and week out. Those students now know to avoid such meetings as much as possible. When such meetings are unavoidable, they know to keep them small. When the meetings get large, they know to lower their expectations.

My favorite exercise was the one on brainstorming. The idea was to emphasize that any system can be implemented many different ways. A data-flow diagram is just a starting point, not a recipe for the final deliverables. So I asked the groups to come up with as many different implementations as possible for a problem. They were rewarded on quantity, not quality. The winning group had 39 solutions that arguably met specifications. I then asked the groups to come up with the most bizarre implementation possible for another problem. Here the reward was for strangeness, not sensibility. The winning solution was marvelously disgusting. I can't describe it in an essay meant for general consumption. But it met the specs.

In each case, the winning group got a case of beer. (They got to choose the brand.) The extra effort they put in to get that beer was all out of proportion to the payoff. To me at least. But then, my student beer-drinking days have faded to a hazy memory. What the class learned was that larger groups often brainstorm better than smaller ones. And public recognition of a job well done is at least as important as conventional payoffs such as salary and grades.

The lecture topics were the sort of things I have been harping about for years. Most of them, in fact, were based heavily the essays that appear in this collection. The topics included:

- scope and goals of software engineering
- capturing specifications in a data-flow diagram
- evaluating modules in terms of coupling and cohesion
- deriving structure charts from data-flow diagrams
- creative packaging alternatives
- decision tables and Karnaugh maps
- finite-state machines
- data-structure diagrams and structured programming
- resolving structure clashes
- object-oriented design and programming
- first-order testing
- deciding what to do next

None of these topics is particularly highfalutin, at least not the way I present them. But each involves a skill that can be taught and reinforced by practice. A nodding acquaintance with all these skills is, I feel, a minimum prerequisite for studying software engineering. Someone comfortable with these skills needn't blush at being called a software engineer. At least not if that person knows the relevant literature and has a few basic skills at working in groups.

At this point, I'm supposed to prove to you that I did the right thing by my students. I should cite statistics that they are 82 per cent more productive, or that they got 17 per cent higher grades, or they landed better jobs or more attractive spouses. Naturally, I can't do that. Like any wise carpetbagger, I skipped town before people learned the consequences of my actions.

I can tell you that it *felt* right while I was doing it. I speak as one who was often ready to leave town long before I finished delivering an expensive seminar. And many of my students *said* they enjoyed the experience. They even looked sincere when they said it. Only time will tell whether they truly benefited, of course.

For me, it helped clarify a vision that I have been grappling with for decades. I believe that many practicing programmers suffer the same inconsistent preparation that students often experience. Once in the work force, however, you have fewer opportunities to fill in the holes in your education.

I see a gap in the literature available to the commercial world. You can find computer-science texts on parsing theory and Petri nets. You can find pragmatic introductions to programming in C++ and SQL. Those books prepare you to be a computer scientist or a programmer. At the other extreme, you can study project organization and design methodologies. You can learn to use CASE tools. Those sources teach you how you're supposed to *behave* as a software engineer.

What's missing is the training you need to *become* a software engineer in the first place. Earning a B.S. in computer science won't do it. Nor will writing 30,000 lines of working code. That's why I think the world needs more emphasis on remedial software engineering. □

𝔄fterword: This essay summarizes everything I have tried to say in this collection. It is fitting to present it last. I finally learned why I've been unable to assemble much of this material into a traditional book on design methods. Any such presentation would be too pretentious. The people I am trying to reach are my fellow practitioners of the programming arts. Most of us are humble enough to admit that we have gaps in our education. Many of us are willing to admit when complex approaches leave us in the dust. It doesn't hurt to review the basics, from time to time. That fills in the holes and helps us better understand the complex stuff.

I can finally admit that I am more of an essayist than a textbook writer. Doling out useful information in bite-size chunks comes easy to me. I believe it better serves the needs of many busy professionals in our field. It's not a bad way to speak to students either.

This collection probably is the textbook on Remedial Software Engineering that I have hankered to write all these years. My other collections of essays provide useful supplemental reading — on people issues and on more specialized issues of programming technology. Being my own best fan, I enjoyed rereading these essays as I edited them for publication in this form. But I can still report that I found few statements that were dated, even after over half a decade. That says something about the continuing need for a source book on design methods. And it says even more about the constancy of basic principles even in the teeth of rapid technological change.

Appendix A List of Columns

The following list gives the publication date, destination, and title of each installment of "Programming on Purpose" published in *Computer Language* through December 1992. For example, the entry

| Jul 1986 | Design | 1 | Which Tool is Best? |

tells you that the essay "Programming on Purpose: Which Tool is Best?" was first published in the July 1986 edition of *Computer Language*. You can also find it as Essay 1 in the collection *Programming on Purpose: Essays on Software Design*, Prentice-Hall, 1993. The other two collections are *Essays on Software People* and *Essays on Software Technology*.

Date	Collection	#	Title
Jul 1986	Design	1	Which Tool is Best?
Aug 1986	Design	2	Writing Predicates
Sep 1986	Design	3	Generating Data
Oct 1986	Design	4	Finite-State Machines
Nov 1986	Design	5	Recognizing Input
Dec 1986	Design	5	Recognizing Input, Part 2
Jan 1987	Design	6	Handling Exceptions
Feb 1987	Design	7	Which Tool is Next?
Mar 1987	Design	8	Order Out of Chaos
Apr 1987	Technology	1	You Must Be Joking
May 1987	Design	9	Marrying Data Structures
Jun 1987	Design	10	Divorcing Data Structures
Jul 1987	Design	11	Who's the Boss?
Aug 1987	Design	12	By Any Other Name
Sep 1987	People	1	Honestly, Now
Oct 1987	Design	13	Searching
Nov 1987	Design	14	Synchronization
Dec 1987	Design	14	Synchronization, Part 2

Date	Collection	#	Title
Jan 1988	Design	15	Which Tool is Last?
Feb 1988	Technology	2	Computer Arithmetic
Mar 1988	Technology	3	Floating-Point Arithmetic
Apr 1988	Technology	4	The Central Folly
May 1988	Technology	5	Safe Math
Jun 1988	Technology	6	Do-It-Yourself Math Functions
Jul 1988	Design	16	A Designer's Bibliography
Aug 1988	Design	17	A Designer's Reference Shelf
Sep 1988	People	2	You Can't Do That
Oct 1988	Technology	7	Locking the Barn Door
Nov 1988	Technology	8	Half a Secret
Dec 1988	People	3	Protecting Intellectual Property
Jan 1989	People	4	What and How
Feb 1989	People	5	Skin and Bones
Mar 1989	Technology	9	It's (Almost) Alive
Apr 1989	Technology	10	The (Almost) Right Stuff
May 1989	People	6	Product Reviews
Jun 1989	People	7	Awaiting Reply
Jul 1989	Design	18	A Preoccupation with Time
Aug 1989	Design	19	Structuring Time
Sep 1989	People	8	Soup or Art?
Oct 1989	People	9	The Seven Warning Signs
Nov 1989	Design	20	Abstract It
Dec 1989	Design	21	Encapsulate It
Jan 1990	Design	22	Inherit It
Feb 1990	People	10	The Politics of Standards
Mar 1990	People	11	Setting the Standard
Apr 1990	Technology	11	Instant Lies
May 1990	People	12	All the Standard Reasons
Jun 1990	People	13	The Physicist as Programmer
Jul 1990	Technology	12	What Meets the Eye
Aug 1990	Technology	13	Technicolor and Cinemascope
Sep 1990	Technology	14	What Meets the Ear
Oct 1990	Technology	15	Warm Fuzzies
Nov 1990	People	14	Shelfware
Dec 1990	People	15	It's Not My Fault

Date	Collection	#	Title
Jan 1991	People	16	Customer Service
Feb 1991	Design	23	Heresies of Software Design
Mar 1991	People	17	Heresies of Software Management
Apr 1991	Technology	16	Font Follies
May 1991	Technology	17	Text Editors
Jun 1991	Technology	18	Approximating Functions
Jul 1991	Technology	19	Economizing Polynomials
Aug 1991	People	18	Watching the Watchers
Sep 1991	People	19	Washing the Watchers
Oct 1991	Technology	20	Technical Documentation
Nov 1991	Technology	21	All I Want to Do Is
Dec 1991	Technology	22	Programming for the Billions
Jan 1992	Technology	23	All Sorts of Sorts
Feb 1992	Technology	24	Transforming Strings
Mar 1992	Design	24	Remedial Software Engineering
Apr 1992	Technology	25	Books for Our Times
May 1992	People	20	Who's Always Right?
Jun 1992	People	21	The Cycle of Complexity
Jul 1992	People	22	Pity the Typist
Aug 1992	People	23	Criticism
Sep 1992	People	24	Piled Higher and Deeper
Oct 1992	Technology	26	Through the Grapevine
Nov 1992	People	25	Lawyers
Dec 1992	People	26	Bankers

Appendix B Bibliography

The references that follow are all cited in the essays in this collection. I do not include references to "Programming on Purpose" — Appendix A summarizes all of those essays.

A&S65 — M. Abramowitz and I. Stegun (editors), *Handbook of Mathematical Functions*, Dover Publications, 1965.

A&U72 — A. Aho and J. Ullman, *The Theory of Parsing, Translation, and Compiling, Volumes 1 and 2*, Prentice-Hall, 1972.

A&U77 — A. Aho and J. Ullman, *Principles of Compiler Design*, Addison-Wesley, 1977.

A&U86 — A. Aho and J. Ullman, *Compilers: Principles, Techniques, and Tools*, Addison-Wesley, 1986.

Ale64 — C. Alexander, *Notes on the Synthesis of Form*, Harvard University Press, 1964.

AHU74 — A. Aho, J. Hopcroft, and J. Ullman, *The Design and Analysis of Computer Algorithms*, Addison-Wesley, 1974.

B&J66 — C. Bohm and G. Jacopini, "Flow Diagrams, Turing Machines, and Languages with Only Two Formation Rules," *Communications of the ACM* 9:5, p. 266, May 1966.

Ben86 — J. Bentley, "Programming Pearls: Little Languages," *Communications of the ACM* 29:8, p. 711, August 1986.

Bro75) — F. Brooks, *The Mythical Man-Month*, Addison-Wesley, 1975.

DDJ72 — O. Dahl, E. Dijkstra, and C. Hoare, *Structued Programming*, Academic Press, 1972.

deM78 — T. DeMarco, *Structured Analysis*, Yourdon Press, 1978.

deM79 — T. DeMarco, *Structured Analysis*, Prentice-Hall, 1979.

Dij68 — E. Dijkstra, "Go To Statement Considered Harmful," *Communications of the ACM* 11:3, p. 147, March 1968.

Dij72 — E. Dijkstra, "The Humble Programmer," *Communications of the ACM* 15:10, p. 859, October 1972.

Dij73 — E. Dijkstra, *A Discipline of Programming*, Prentice-Hall, 1973.

G&S77 — C. Gane and T. Sarson, *Structured Systems Analysis: Tools and Techniques*, Improved Systems Technologies Inc., 1977.

H&P87 — D. Hatley and I. Pirbhai, *Strategies for Real-Time System Specification*, Dorset House, 1987.

Har68 — J. Hart, et al., *Computer Approximations*, John Wiley & Sons, 1968.

Har78 — J. Hart, et al., *Computer Approximations*, Robert E. Krieger Publishing Company, 1978.

Hoa69 — C. Hoare, "An Axiomatic Approach to Computer Programming," *Communications of the ACM* 12:10, p. 576, October 1969.

Huf54 — D.Huff, *How to Lie with Statistics*, W.W. Norton & Co., 1954.

Hum89 — W. Humphrey, *Managing the Software Process*, Addison-Wesley, 1989.

Jac75 — M. Jackson, *Principles of Program Design*, Academic Press, 1975.

Jac83 — M. Jackson, *System Development*, Prentice-Hall, 1983.

K&P74 — B. Kernighan and P. Plauger, *The Elements of Programming Style*, McGraw-Hill, 1974.

K&P76 — B. Kernighan and P. Plauger, *Software Tools*, Addison-Wesley, 1976.

K&P78 — B. Kernighan and P. Plauger, *The Elements of Programming Style*, *Second Edition*, McGraw-Hill, 1978.

K&P81 — B. Kernighan and P. Plauger, *Software Tools in Pascal*, Addison-Wesley, 1981.

Knu68 — D. Knuth, *The Art of Computer Programming, Volume 1: Fundamental Algorithms* Addison-Wesley, 1968.

Knu69 — D. Knuth, *The Art of Computer Programming, Volume 2: Seminumerical Algorithms*, Addison-Wesley, 1969.

Knu73a — D. Knuth, *The Art of Computer Programming, Volume 3: Sorting and Searching*, Addison-Wesley, 1973.

Knu73b — D. Knuth, *The Art of Computer Programming, Volume 1: Fundamental Algorithms, Second Edition* Addison-Wesley, 1968.

Knu81 — D. Knuth, *The Art of Computer Programming, Volume 2: Seminumerical Algorithms, Second Edition* Addison-Wesley, 1969.

Mye78 — G. Myers, *Composite/Structured Design*, Van Nostrand Reinhold, 1978.

Nev78 — J. Nevison, *The Little Book of BASIC Style*, Addison-Wesley, 1978.

Orr77 — K. Orr, *Structured Systems Development*, Yourdon Press, 1977.

Par72 — D. Parnas, "On the Criteria to be Used in Decomposing Systems into Modules," *Communications of the ACM* 15:12, p. 1053, December 1972.

Pir75 — R. Pirsig, *Zen and the Art of Motorcycle Maintenance*, Bantam Books, 1975.

Plu81 — T. Plum, *C Programming Standards and Guidelines*, Plum Hall, 1981.

Ste74 — P. Sterbenz, *Floating-Point Computation*, Prentice-Hall, 1974.

Tuf83 — E. Tufte, *The Visual Display of Quantitative Information*, Graphics Press, 1983.

W&M85 — P. Ward and S. Mellor, *Structured Development for Real-Time Systems, Volumes 1-3*, Yourdon Press, 1985.

War74 — J. Warnier, *Logical Construction of Programs*, H.E. Stenfert Kroese B.V., 1974.

War78 — J. Warnier, *Logical Construction of Programs*, Van Nostrand Reinhold, 1978.

Wei71 — G. Weinberg, *The Psychology of Computer Programming*, Van Nostrand Reinhold, 1971.

Wir71 — N. Wirth, "Program Development by Stepwise Refinement, *Communications of the ACM* 14:4, p. 221, April 1971.

Wir73 — N. Wirth, *Systematic Programming*, Prenice-Hall, 1973.

Y&C79 — E. Yourdon and L. Constantine, *Structured Design*, Prentice-Hall, 1979.

Y&C89 — E. Yourdon and L. Constantine, *Structured Design, Second Edition*, Prentice-Hall, 1989.

You79 — E. Yourdon, *Classics in Software Engineering*, Yourdon Press, 1979.

Index